Shakespeare and the Future of Theory

Shakespeare and the Future of Theory convenes internationally renowned Shakespeare scholars, and scholars of the early modern period, and presents, discusses, and evaluates the most recent research and information concerning the future of theory in relation to Shakespeare's corpus. Original in its aim and scope, the book argues for the critical importance of *thinking Shakespeare now*, and provides extensive reflections and profound insights into the dialogues between Shakespeare and Theory. Contributions explore Shakespeare through the lens of design theory, queer theory, psychoanalysis, Derrida and Foucault, amongst others, and offer an innovative interdisciplinary analysis of Shakespeare's work.

This book was originally published as two special issues of *English Studies*.

François-Xavier Gleyzon teaches at the University of Central Florida, Orlando, USA. He is the author of *Shakespeare's Spiral* (2010), and *David Lynch in Theory* (2011) along with a number of peer-reviewed articles on English Renaissance Literature and Visual Arts. His recent publications include two edited volumes on *Shakespeare and Theory I & II* (2013) and *Reading Milton Through Islam* (2015).

Johann Gregory is a Postdoctoral Lecturing Fellow at the University of East Anglia, Norwich, UK. He is the author of several articles on Shakespeare in relation to theatre and theory, and has also published work on John Taylor, the Water-Poet (1578–1653).

Shakespeare and the Future of Theory

Edited by
François-Xavier Gleyzon and
Johann Gregory

Routledge
Taylor & Francis Group

LONDON AND NEW YORK

First published 2016 by Routledge

2 Park Square, Milton Park, Abingdon, Oxon OX14 4RN
711 Third Avenue, New York, NY 10017, USA

Routledge is an imprint of the Taylor & Francis Group, an informa business

First issued in paperback 2017

British Library Cataloguing in Publication Data
A catalogue record for this book is available from the British Library

ISBN 13: 978-1-138-93077-3 (hbk)
ISBN 13: 978-1-138-09484-0 (pbk)

Typeset in Minion
by RefineCatch Limited, Bungay, Suffolk

Publisher's Note
The publisher accepts responsibility for any inconsistencies that may have
arisen during the conversion of this book from journal articles to book chapters,
namely the possible inclusion of journal terminology.

Disclaimer
Every effort has been made to contact copyright holders for their permission to
reprint material in this book. The publishers would be grateful to hear from any
copyright holder who is not here acknowledged and will undertake to rectify
any errors or omissions in future editions of this book.

Contents

CONTENTS

Citation Information

The following chapters were originally published in *English Studies*, volume 94, issue 3 (May 2013). When citing this material, please use the original page numbering for each article, as follows:

Chapter 1
Thinking through Shakespeare: An Introduction to Shakespeare and Theory
Johann Gregory and François-Xavier Gleyzon
English Studies, volume 94, issue 3 (May 2013) pp. 251–258

Chapter 2
Shakespeare by Design: A Flight of Concepts
Julia Reinhard Lupton and C. J. Gordon
English Studies, volume 94, issue 3 (May 2013) pp. 259–277

Chapter 3
Of Cause
Madhavi Menon
English Studies, volume 94, issue 3 (May 2013) pp. 278–290

Chapter 4
"After the Takeover": Shakespeare, Lacan, Žižek and the Interpassive Subject
Étienne Poulard
English Studies, volume 94, issue 3 (May 2013) pp. 291–312

Chapter 5
Wordplay in Shakespeare's Hamlet *and the Accusation of Derrida's "Logical Phallusies"*
Johann Gregory
English Studies, volume 94, issue 3 (May 2013) pp. 313–330

Chapter 6
Storm at Sea: The Tempest, *Cultural Materialism and the Early Modern Political Aesthetic*
Christopher Pye
English Studies, volume 94, issue 3 (May 2013) pp. 331–345

The following chapters were originally published in *English Studies*, volume 94, issue 7 (November 2013). When citing this material, please use the original page numbering for each article, as follows:

Chapter 7
Listening to the Body . . .: Transitioning to Shakespeare and Theory
François-Xavier Gleyzon and Johann Gregory
English Studies, volume 94, issue 7 (November 2013) pp. 751–756

Chapter 8
Performing Disability and Theorizing Deformity
Katherine Schaap Williams
English Studies, volume 94, issue 7 (November 2013) pp. 757–772

Chapter 9
Ship of Fools: Foucault and the Shakespeareans
Richard Wilson
English Studies, volume 94, issue 7 (November 2013) pp. 773–787

Chapter 10
"Untimely Ripp'd": On Natality, Sovereignty and Unbearable Life
Arthur Bradley
English Studies, volume 94, issue 7 (November 2013) pp. 788–798

Chapter 11
Syllogisms and Tears in Timon of Athens
Drew Daniel
English Studies, volume 94, issue 7 (November 2013) pp. 799–820

Chapter 12
Opening the Sacred Body or the Profaned Host in The Merchant of Venice
François-Xavier Gleyzon
English Studies, volume 94, issue 7 (November 2013) pp. 821–844

For any permission-related enquiries please visit:
http://www.tandfonline.com/page/help/permissions

Notes on Contributors

Arthur Bradley is Professor of Comparative Literature in the Department of English & Creative Writing at Lancaster University, UK.

Drew Daniel is Associate Professor in the Department of English at Johns Hopkins University, Baltimore, Maryland, USA.

François-Xavier Gleyzon teaches at the University of Central Florida, Orlando, USA. He is the author of *Shakespeare's Spiral* (2010), and *David Lynch in Theory* (2011) along with a number of peer-reviewed articles on English Renaissance Literature and Visual Arts. His recent publications include two edited volumes on *Shakespeare and Theory I & II* (2013) and *Reading Milton Through Islam* (2015).

C. J. Gordon is completing his doctorate at the University of California, Irvine, CA, USA. He is writing a dissertation entitled "Shakespeare's Landscape Futures: Designed Ecologies and Renaissance Conjectural Terrains".

Johann Gregory is a Postdoctoral Lecturing Fellow at the University of East Anglia, Norwich, UK. He is the author of several articles on Shakespeare in relation to theatre and theory, and has also published work on John Taylor, the Water-Poet (1578–1653).

Julia Reinhard Lupton is Professor of English and Comparative Literature at the University of California, Irvine, CA, USA. She is currently writing a book entitled *Shakespeare by Design: Objects, Affordances, and Environments in Renaissance Drama*.

Madhavi Menon is Professor of English at Ashoka University, India.

Étienne Poulard recently completed his doctorate at Cardiff University, UK.

Christopher Pye is Class of 1924 Chair of English, Williams College, Williamstown, Massachusetts, USA.

Katherine Schaap Williams is Assistant Professor of Literature at New York University Abu Dhabi, United Arab Emirates.

Richard Wilson is the Sir Peter Hall Professor of Shakespeare Studies at Kingston University, London, UK.

Thinking through Shakespeare: An Introduction to Shakespeare and Theory

Johann Gregory and François-Xavier Gleyzon

> Shakespeare continues to write us.[1]

"Shakespeare and Theory"—where to begin? "[T]here is no period so remote as the recent past", Irwin declares in Alan Bennett's play, *The History Boys*.[2] Let's start there. Why not return to the London Olympics 2012? Let's zoom in to the beginning of the opening ceremony, entitled "The Isles of Wonder". The actor Kenneth Branagh—on a green hillock of Peter Jackson's Shire—is dressed as the Industrial Revolution's engineer, Isambard Kingdom Brunel. The soundtrack: Edward Elgar's "Nimrod" variation. The text: William Shakespeare's *The Tempest*. In a play within a play, Branagh, dressed in nineteenth-century top hat and black suit, speaks to an audience of similarly dressed men triumphantly:

> Be not afeard. The isle is full of noises,
> Sounds, and sweet airs, that give delight and hurt not.
> Sometimes a thousand twangling instruments
> Will hum about mine ears, and sometimes voices
> That if I then had waked after long sleep
> Will make me sleep again; and then in dreaming
> The clouds methought would open and show riches
> Ready to drop upon me, that when I waked
> I cried to dream again. (*The Tempest*, 3.2.130–8)[3]

Branagh's sentimentalising tone was not dissimilar to *Henry V*'s "St Crispin's Day" speech in his film: a rousing speech written by the Bard of Avon, spoken by a famous British knighted actor who "brings to life", as the television commentator

---

[1] Peter Stallybass describing Marjorie Garber's work (Garber, backmatter).
[2] Bennett, 74.
[3] Shakespeare. Line numbers for the plays are taken from The *Norton Shakespeare: Based on the Oxford Edition*, and citations are given in the text.

put it, a famous British civil engineer (who had in fact commissioned his own "Shakespeare Room"[4]), and accompanied by the music of a British composer.[5] How very British. What a "delight"! The London Mayor, Boris Johnson, admitted, "I don't blub much, but there were tears from the beginning last night."[6] In the aftermath of the ceremony, viewers, journalists, bloggers and tweeters attempted to make sense of it all.

Critics who admit to taking an openly theoretical approach to Shakespeare—and many others—will attest that whenever we speak, write or act we always say, write or do more than we mean to. As Catherine Belsey writes in *Shakespeare in Theory and Practice*, "[j]ust as in daily life we commonly signify more than we intend, give ourselves away so the saying goes, so texts too may reveal more than their authors supposed."[7] This is the problem and joke of Alice's predicament at the Mad Hatter's Tea Party: she hopes that "say[ing] what you mean" is "the same thing" as "mean [ing] what you say."[8] There was a similar abundance of signification during the opening of the Olympic ceremony. One web user insisted in a comment on a blog post concerning the performance of the speech, "I think people posting on here analyse something that is not meant to be analysed so much. The Olympic ceremony was just meant to convey a potted history of Britain, with no hidden meanings or special messages intended."[9] However, the point with the ceremony was not so much what it was using Shakespeare to try to say, but what it failed, or chose *not*, to give voice to. Tellingly, the London Mayor conceded in an interview, "there wasn't much about empire but you know, hey, maybe that wouldn't have been entirely that right thing to shove in there."[10] *USA Today* reported on the Shakespeare speech:

> For Shakesepeare [sic] expert James Shapiro, an English professor at Columbia University, it was a strange choice.
> Shapiro says the lines were taken from Caliban's speech in one of Shakespeare's final plays, *The Tempest*. Caliban, a half-man, half-beast, says the words when he's about to kill a colonialist ruler who took the Isles [sic] away from Caliban.
> "Why you would choose Caliban's lines as—in a sense—a kind of anthem for the Olympics, I'm not sure," Shapiro said. "If you gave those lines some thought, especially in the light of the British Empire, it's an odd choice."
> The lines are quite beautiful, and I guess they wanted to rip them out of context and talk about how magical a place the British Isles are.[11]

---

[4]See Faberman and McEvansoneya.
[5]The "Nimrod" variation is a tribute to his German friend and music publisher Augustus Jaeger: the surname Jaeger being German for hunter. See Allen.
[6]Boris Johnson quoted in the *Evening Standard*, see Dominiczak.
[7]Belsey, 1.
[8]Carroll, 88.
[9]Comment by Danny on the blog post, see Bloomfield.
[10]*BBC News*, "London 2012."
[11]Florek.

As the *USA Today* phrases it, the selection was "strange"—Shakespeare's word for the uncanny.[12] For a literary critic, theorist or English literature student with an ounce of post-colonial theory, Branagh's Mad-Hatter performance at this moment in the ceremony will undoubtedly be seen as uncanny, recognisable yet uncomfortable, familiar and strange. Shakespeare's text goes on meaning more than intended by the ceremony organisers here especially because more openly theoretical readings of Shakespeare were apparently ignored.[13]

The Tempest has been read by critics, theatre directors, playwrights and theorists as a powerful space to think through (post-)colonial situations.[14] In *Caliban's Voice*, Bill Ashcroft writes:

> Interestingly, the possibilities for reading this play in terms of the political and cultural relationship between Caliban and Prospero date from the last century. J.S. Phillpot's introduction to the 1873 Rugby edition of Shakespeare [published just fourteen years after Brunel's death] notes that "The character may have had a special bearing on the great question of a time when we were discovering new countries, subjecting unknown savages, and founding fresh colonies."[15]

Given the possibilities of thinking *through* Shakespeare, what makes the selection "odd", as Shapiro phrases it, then, is not that Shakespeare was chosen to provide an anthem for the Olympic Games—after all, as Terence Hawkes proposes, so often, "Shakespeare doesn't mean: *we* mean *by* Shakespeare."[16] But, for the Olympics, the speech involved Caliban's voice and dream being re-appropriated to articulate a dream to do with British history and culture that systematically glossed over and repressed Britain's colonial past. Stephen Greenblatt commented in his famous reading of *The Tempest* in *Learning to Curse* that the "rich, irreducible concreteness of the verse compels us to acknowledge the independence and integrity of Caliban's construction of reality": the play does not invite us to "sentimentalize this construction … but we cannot make it vanish into silence".[17] The sentimental use of Shakespeare in the ceremony, however, seems to have unconsciously raised the spectre of the colonised Caliban even as it attempted to silence this issue.

When "the major European empires were beginning to be dismantled"[18] and O. Mannoni tried to think through the colonial situation in Madagascar in 1948, he turned to Shakespeare's characters in a book translated into English as *Prospero and Caliban: The Psychology of Colonization*. Reflecting on the Prospero "inferiority complex" and the Caliban "dependence complex", Mannoni suggested,

---

[12]On Shakespeare's uncanny strangeness, see Royle, *The Uncanny*; and Royle, *How to Read Shakespeare*.
[13]For the relationship between the institutions of theatre and the academy in readings of Shakespeare, see Bretzius.
[14]On readings of *The Tempest*, see, e.g. Graff and Phelan, eds.
[15]Ashcroft, 16, n. 1.
[16]Hawkes, 3.
[17]Greenblatt, 43.
[18]Ashcroft, 16, n. 1.

[w]hat is resented in Caliban is not really his physical appearance, his bestiality, his "evil" instincts—for after all it is a matter of pride to keep half-tamed apes or other wild animals in one's household—but that he could claim to be a person in his own right and from time to time show that he has a will of his own.[19]

Viewed in its worst light, the "multi-cultural"[20] elements of the opening Olympic ceremony showed just how much Britain—with its own inferiority complex—wanted to be seen as able to "keep half-tamed apes or other wild animals in one's household", showing how these "other" cultures could be assimilated into the nation and into the show. But, as Eric Taylor Woods has argued, what the opening ceremony ended up presenting was "a rather inward-looking and parochial image of Britain".[21] In this sense, the re-appropriation of a play that considered Caliban's voice in order to "show how magical a place the British Isles are" was profoundly ironic, or at least short-sighted. As Woods notes, "while the ceremonies made much of the impact of immigration on Britain, there was no mention of British emigration": this is an uncanny omission given that the ceremony began by quoting a play *about* emigration. Shakespeare's "beautiful" lines cause all kinds of unforeseen ripples on the waters of meaning for those around the globe.

In his reading of "What the Olympics didn't say about Britain's place in the world", Woods ends by suggesting that "[o]penness to global influences on Britain, and Britain's influence on the global, is surely better than retreating from the global altogether". If the Olympic ceremony did use Shakespeare to enact a process of "collective amnesia",[22] then, this is all the more disturbing given the fact that the London Mayor told BBC viewers that the ceremony's performative historicising "was actually the truth about this country in the last two or three hundred years told in a big, dynamic way".[23] Trying to nail Shakespeare's circulating text into a square British hole, another Conservative controversially tweeted "Thank God the athletes have arrived! Now we can move on from leftie multi-cultural crap. Bring back red arrows, Shakespeare and the Stones!"[24] In the face of such apparent narrow-minded nationalism, it is worth remembering the name of Shakespeare's theatre and the way his plays offer globes and globules, places and uncanny spaces, for thinking through past perspectives and future directions, even if invoking Shakespeare can sometimes be self-exposing, as in the case of the London Olympic ceremony. "Every historical period finds in him what it is looking for and what it wants to see", Jan Kott proposed in *Shakespeare Our Contemporary*.[25] Even so, Shakespeare's work is so

---

[19]Mannoni, 117. For Aimé Césaire's reading of O. Mannoni's own Prospero-like "conjuring tricks" with his book, see Césaire, 39.
[20]A quotation from Aidan Burley's tweet discussed below; see *BBC News*, "Aidan Burley."
[21]Woods.
[22]Ibid.
[23]*BBC News*, "London 2012."
[24]*BBC News*, "Aidan Burley."
[25]Kott, 5.

hospitable that it can also welcome thinking that we would not always care to admit. "I know that everything is in Shakespeare", affirmed Jacques Derrida, "everything and the rest, so everything or nearly."[26] Shakespeare (and theory) invites unexpected guests, but it also offers space for thinking through the potential of Shakespearean texts, their theatre, and the positions that we take, both critically and politically.

* * *

The essays in this issue invoke Shakespeare and theory in different ways. While all the essays seek to shed light on the potential of Shakespeare's texts, they also demonstrate how the Shakespearean text can be used as a touchstone—or space—to think through theories and problems. In doing so, they continue a tradition of "Shakespeare and theory", even as some of them question the way that theories have been represented and articulated in the past. Patricia Parker explained in *Shakespeare and the Question of Theory* that Shakespeare "has been not just the focus of a variety of divergent critical movements within recent years but also, increasingly, the locus of emerging debates within, and with, theory itself".[27] Theory, then, is not "a dangerous virus from which Shakespeare needs to be quarantined"[28]—at least, not unless by Shakespeare we mean nothing more than a playwright who *just* induces admiration or boredom. In *The Subjectivity Effect in Western Literary Tradition*, Joel Fineman comments that the "considerable overlap" between Shakespeare's work and contemporary theory "suggests either that Shakespeare was very theoretically acute or, instead, that contemporary theory is itself very Shakespearean."[29] But the open secret is that just as theory has been used to read Shakespeare, so Shakespeare has helped in the articulation and creation of theory as we know it. As Jonathan Gil Harris explains in his *Shakespeare and Literary Theory*, "[a]ll the major theoretical movements of the last century...have developed key aspects of their methods in dialogue with Shakespeare."[30] So, you might say, Shakespeare always already equals Shakespeare and theory. All the essays in this issue draw out some of the implications of this equation.

"If New Historicism was wise to insist on the proximity of *theory* and *theatre*," as Richard Wilson wrote in *Shakespeare in French Theory*, we can now acknowledge how "theorists have been emancipated by Shakespeare themselves."[31] Harris highlights just some of the thinkers who have been drawn to Shakespeare for their theory:

> To name just a few examples: Karl Marx was an avid reader of Shakespeare and used *Timon of Athens* to illustrate aspects of his economic theory; psychoanalytic theorists from Sigmund Freud to Jacques Lacan have explained some of their most axiomatic positions with reference to *Hamlet*; Michel Foucault's early theoretical writing on

---

[26]Derrida, 67.
[27]Parker, vii.
[28]Harris, 3. For a reading of this attitude, see Harris, 1–5.
[29]Fineman, 112.
[30]Harris, 3.
[31]Wilson, 3.

dreams and madness returns repeatedly to *Macbeth*; Jacques Derrida's deconstructive philosophy is articulated in dialogue with Shakespeare's plays, including *Romeo and Juliet*; French feminism's best-known essay is Hélène Cixous's meditation on *Antony and Cleopatra*; certain strands of queer theory derive their impetus from Eve Kosofsky Sedgewick's reading of the Sonnets; Gilles Deleuze alights on *Richard III* as an exemplary instance of his theory of the war machine; and postcolonial theory owes a large debt to Aimé Césaire's revision of *The Tempest*.[32]

It is one thing to celebrate Shakespeare as a British playwright, but as Harris's list attests, Shakespeare is much more than that. His plays have created a theatre for theory.

All the same, approaches to Shakespeare are always in danger of getting trammelled into certain fixed ways of thinking. Julia Reinhard Lupton explains in *Thinking with Shakespeare* that,

> [a]ll readings … risk turning into what Kott calls "costume drama", productions constrained by the corsets and laces of their own apparatus, whether the interpretation is flooded by too much context or left high and dry by too much concept.[33]

Like Kott's *Shakespeare Our Contemporary* and Lupton's book, the essays in this issue seek "to engage Shakespearean drama with a sense of playfulness, experiment, and historical awareness, but *without too much makeup*, in order to touch what is timely in Shakespeare."[34]

In the first essay of this special issue—"Shakespeare by Design: A Flight of Concepts"—Julia Reinhard Lupton and C. J. Gordon take four concepts from contemporary design theory and deploy them in readings of Shakespeare. Working from the premise that "Shakespeare's plays have something to tell us about our designed environments today", they use the concepts "affordances", "softscapes", "soundscapes" and "instant urbanism", and show how these work in *Romeo and Juliet*, *Macbeth*, *The Tempest* and *King Lear* respectively. In "Of Cause", Madhavi Menon draws on, and develops, queer theory in relation to Shakespeare's *Othello*: she postulates that the cause of the play's agonising finale is its queer causality, an absence of cause. For Menon, the play "propels us into a horrifying absence that is foundational for any appreciation of desire".

Étienne Poulard's "'After the Takeover': Shakespeare, Lacan, Žižek and the Interpassive Subject" also draws on psychoanalytic theory. The essay uses Shakespeare to think through "the principle of mediation that shapes our experience". Rather than celebrating an interactive subjectivity, Poulard considers the modern "interpassive" experience. Reading Shakespeare's *Hamlet*, *Macbeth* and *Henry V* to set this reflection on interpassivity in motion, the essay also shows how Slavoj Žižek looked awry through Shakespeare to underpin his interpretive method. "Wordplay in Shakespeare's

---

[32]Harris, 3.
[33]Lupton, 18. Cf. Kott, 65–6.
[34]Lupton, 18.

Hamlet and the Accusation of Derrida's 'Logical Phallusies'" returns, again, to the relationship between the work of Shakespeare and Jacques Derrida. Using Shakespeare's *Hamlet* as a starting point followed by the infamous letter to *The Times* that accused Derrida of "logical phallusies", Johann Gregory draws out some of the implications of acknowledging the play of all words, while reassessing the incrimination of Derrida's perceived punning. Christopher Pye's "Storm at Sea: *The Tempest*, Cultural Materialism, and the Early Modern Political Aesthetic" is the final essay in the issue. He points out that "[c]ritical reception of *The Tempest* has shifted over time from broadly aesthetic matters—the sublimating passage of matter into spirit, the work's self-conscious artfulness—to a concern with material context, particularly its status as colonial encounter". But he suggests that some "forms of cultural materialist analysis … have sought to historicize early modern works by bracketing the problem of the aesthetic". Pye's essay shows how *The Tempest*, itself, offers a timely theoretical corrective to readings of literature that exclude the aesthetic, concerned as the play is with aesthetic autonomy as well as the contingencies of material culture and history.

A second issue on "Shakespeare and Theory" follows in this same volume. It continues the project of showing *not* how theory might be applied to Shakespeare "in theory", but how Shakespeare acts on and through theory; how—after all the talk of the death of theory in Shakespeare criticism—we might learn to live finally with "this dreaded sight" (*Hamlet*, 1.1.23).

Acknowledgments

We would like to take this opportunity to express our unfathomable gratitude to the contributors of the essays in these special issues for their offerings, patience and support.

References

Allen, Kevin. *August Jaeger: Portrait of Nimrod: A Life in Letters and Other Writings*. Burlington, NH: Ashgate, 2000.

Ashcroft, Bill. *Caliban's Voice: The Transformation of English in Post-Colonial Literatures*. London: Routledge, 2009.

BBC News. "Aidan Burley Says 'Leftie Multi-Cultural' Tweet Misunderstood." 28 July 2012. [cited 10 December 2012]. Available from http://www.bbc.co.uk/news/uk-19025518.

———. "London 2012: Boris Johnson Dismisses 'Leftie' Complaint." 28 July 2012. [cited 10 December 2012]. Available from http://www.bbc.co.uk/news/uk-19029510.

Belsey, Catherine. *Shakespeare in Theory and Practice*. Edinburgh: Edinburgh University Press, 2010.

Bennett, Alan. *The History Boys*. London: Faber and Faber, 2004.

Bloomfield, Jem. "Caliban and Brunel: Kenneth Branagh's Speech at the Olympics Opening Ceremony." *quiteirregular~culture theatre, gender*. 29 July 2012. [cited 10 December 2012]. Available from http://quiteirregular.wordpress.com/2012/07/29/caliban-and-brunel-kenneth-branaghs-speech-at-the-olympics-opening-ceremony/.

Branagh, Kenneth, dir. *Henry V*. Produced by Bruce Sharman. 1989. Film.

Bretzius, Stephen. *Shakespeare in Theory: The Postmodern Academy and the Early Modern Theater.* Ann Arbor: University of Michigan Press, 1997.

Carroll, Lewis. *Alice's Adventures in Wonderland.* London: Macmillan, 1953.

Césaire, Aimé. *Discourse on Colonialism.* Translated by Joan Pinkham. New York: Monthly Review Press, 1972. (Published in French, 1955.)

Derrida, Jacques. "'This Strange Institution Called Literature': An Interview with Jacques Derrida." Translated by Geoffrey Bennington and Rachel Bowlby. In *Acts of Literature,* edited by Derek Attridge. London: Routledge, 1992.

Dominiczak, Peter. "London 2012 Olympics: Boris Johnson Left in Floods of Tears by 'Stupefyingly Brilliant' Opening Ceremony." *Evening Standard,* 28 July 2012. [cited 10 December 2012]. Available from http://www.standard.co.uk/olympics/olympic-news/london-2012-olympics-boris-johnson-left-in-floods-of-tears-by-stupefyingly-brilliant-opening-ceremony-7984659.html.

Faberman, Hilarie, and Philip McEvansoneya. "Isambard Kingdom Brunel's 'Shakespeare Room.'" *The Burlington Magazine* 137, no. 1103 (1995), 1–18.

Fineman, Joel. *The Subjectivity Effect in Western Literary Tradition: Essays Toward the Release of Shakespeare's Will.* Cambridge, MA: Massachusetts Institute of Technology Press, 1991.

Florek, Michael. "Shakespeare Passage Features in Opening Ceremony." *USA Today,* 27 July 2012. [cited 10 December 2012]. Available from http://usatoday30.usatoday.com/sports/olympics/london/story/2012-07-27/shakespeare-tempest-london-olympics-opening-ceremony/56548372/1.

Garber, Marjorie. *Shakespeare's Ghost Writers: Literature as Uncanny Causality.* Rev. ed. New York: Routledge, 2010.

Graff, Gerald, and James Phelan, eds. *William Shakespeare "The Tempest": A Case Study in Critical Controversy.* Boston, MA: Bedford, 2000.

Greenblatt, Stephen. *Learning to Curse: Essays in Early Modern Culture.* Rev ed. New York: Routledge, 2007.

Harris, Jonathan Gil. *Shakespeare and Literary Theory: Oxford Shakespeare Topics.* Oxford: Oxford University Press, 2010.

Hawkes, Terence. *Meaning by Shakespeare.* London: Routledge, 1992.

Kott, Jan. *Shakespeare Our Contemporary.* Translated by Boleslaw Taborski. New York: Norton, 1974. (Published in Polish, 1964.)

Lupton, Julia Rheinhard. *Thinking with Shakespeare: Essays on Politics and Life.* Chicago, IL: University of Chicago Press, 2012.

Mannoni, O. *Prospero and Caliban: The Psychology of Colonization.* Translated by Pamela Powesland. 2d ed. New York: Praeger, 1964. (Published in French, 1950.)

Parker, Patricia. "Introduction." In *Shakespeare and the Question of Theory,* edited by Patricia Parker and Geoffrey Hartman. New York. Methuen, 1985.

Royle, Nicholas. *How to Read Shakespeare.* London: Granta Books, 2005.

———. *The Uncanny.* Manchester: Manchester University Press, 2003.

Shakespeare, William. *The Norton Shakespeare: Based on the Oxford Edition.* Edited by Stephen Greenblatt, Walter Cohen, Jean E. Howard and Katherine Eisaman Maus. New York: Norton, 1997.

Wilson, Richard. *Shakespeare in French Theory: King of Shadows.* London: Routledge, 2007.

Woods, Eric Taylor. "What the Olympics didn't say about Britain's place in the world." *British Politics and Policy at LSE.* 30 August 2012. [cited 10 December 2012]. Available from http://blogs.lse.ac.uk/politicsandpolicy/archives/26348.

Shakespeare by Design: A Flight of Concepts

Julia Reinhard Lupton and C. J. Gordon

"Shakespeare by Design: A Flight of Concepts" develops four concepts that link the socio-spatial experimentation of Shakespearean drama to contemporary design discourse. We read affordances (how objects and environments cue and constrain behaviour) in Romeo and Juliet; softscapes (fabric spaces and textile properties) in Macbeth; soundscapes (acoustics as weapon and building material) in The Tempest; and instant urbanism (portable cities and occasional housing) in King Lear. Each of these scapes convenes elements of assembly, mobility, setting and action, place-making factors that bind together dramatic poetry, theatricality and design in order to assemble habitations for life, thought and art. Shakespeare's plays have something to tell us about our designed environments today, both because his world practised forms of husbandry, housekeeping and artisanal craft to which contemporary urban farmers, locavores and DIY self-fashioners are returning with a militant nostalgia, and because his friends and countrymen were already investing in the forms of enclosure, colonization, industrialization and global trade whose ashen apples we are harvesting now.

Introduction

Toasters, books, jackets, book jackets, public plazas, green cars, plastic straws, the Nike logo, your blog, as well as Romeo's glove, Macbeth's sleeve, Lear's luggage and Prospero's sound system: all of these are instances of design. In these pages, we probe the real, virtual and speculative spaces of Shakespearean drama by deploying live concepts in contemporary design, especially those that concern the disposition of environments in their mediated and spectacular as well as ecological and phenomenological dimensions.[1] We are especially interested in those design concepts and practices that reflect the saturation of contemporary place-making protocols by hyperactive

---

[1] We are pursuing two separate but related projects: C. J. Gordon is writing a dissertation entitled "Shakespeare's Landscape Futures: Designed Ecologies and Renaissance Conjectural Terrains." Julia Reinhard Lupton is writing a book currently entitled "Shakespeare by Design: Objects, Affordances, and Environments in Renaissance Drama."

communication economies and information overload, whether as aggravating cause or as chagrined *whaddafah* response. Although we draw on design as it is practised in a number of established subfields (especially architecture and urbanism, product design and industrial design, and landscapes and brandscapes), our emphasis falls on integrative practices that flow among several zones of contemporary design activity. Built environments and place-making efforts merge graphic, architectural and environmental systems; marketing and branding mix typographic, theatrical and product design; and contemporary landscape architecture integrates traffic patterns shared by people, air, water, flora, fauna and Wi-Fi. We have selected and modelled four concepts—affordance, softscape, soundscape and instant urbanism—that gauge the torsion of contemporary spaces by climate change, global recession and escalating fashion cycles, as well as by new social and expressive opportunities opened up by technologies both mass and micro. Shakespeare's plays, we are wagering, have something to tell us about our designed environments today, both because his world practised forms of husbandry, housekeeping and artisanal craft to which contemporary urban farmers, locavores and DIY self-fashioners are returning with a militant nostalgia, and because his friends and countrymen were already investing in the forms of enclosure, colonization, industrialization and global trade whose ashen apples we are harvesting now.

Although we necessarily draw on historical materials, we are uninterested in pursuing a critical course that would drain the speculative matter of the plays into the more familiar canals of historical context or intellectual genealogy. Instead, we have chosen to bind Shakespearean drama to contemporary design on a speculative plane open to the conjectural, indeed poetic quality of floating libertarian principalities and offshore data havens, tuned cities and drone landscapes, inflatable apartments and cryptoforests. There is an ecocritical dimension to this project; we draw on the microbially subverted humanity Robert Watson finds in *A Midsummer Night's Dream*, the perverse and uncanny supernature Gabriel Egan and Steve Mentz unfold in *King Lear* and *The Tempest*, and the animal architecture and parasitical ecologies Karen Raber finds slithering in the corners of *Romeo and Juliet* and *Hamlet*.[2] We are also inspired by the object-oriented cookery of Julian Yates; like Yates, the environments we want to consider are theatrical, imaginative, psychic and phenomenological as well as natural, and they are always atremble with the data streams and feedback loops of desire both queer and consumer.[3] Cultivating the easements among manifold forms of life, design in our project always takes its orientation from the fact of poesis, whether conducted by crowds, snails, robots or artisanal lollipop-makers.

If "Shakespeare by Design" is not ecocriticism, it's not theatre studies, either, because the design concepts that we bring to bear on the plays, though sometimes dovetailing with scenography, are borrowed from broader design practices that

---

[2] Egan; Mentz, 115–17; Raber, 13–32; Watson, 33–56.
[3] Yates. For more cookery, see Lupton, "Thinking with Things"; and Jem Boyle and Martin Foys.

include branding and marketing, urbanism and place-making, and industrial and product design. We are concerned as much with assembling unexpected vistas out of the image banks, proprioceptive memories, and speculative musings of each drama's imagined places and spaces as we are in the actual disposition of the stage, Shakespeare's or anyone else's. Some of the new technologies that backlight our work here—virtual reality gloves and sound art—have implications for theatre, however; whether because they bear on the theatricalization of life in the age of micro-fibres, nanochips and occupy hash tags, or because they develop techniques of projection, abstraction and assemblage that have become mainstays of modern stagecraft and whose impulses can be discerned in the design thinking at work in Shakespearean poetics.

Our flight of concepts, then, begins with *affordances*, a term used by designers to describe the action capacities latent in things and environments. We then move into three distinct but often overlapping forms of theatricalized architecture, each of which takes place and makes place by marshalling a manifold of affordances. The *soft-scape* concerns textile constructions that frame and shelter scenes of curtained slumber and domestic entertainment. *Soundscape* encompasses acoustic spaces and aural contexts that couch and enable, or retard and disallow, human action through the porches of the ear. *Instant urbanism* sets up portable cities and occasional housing in situations of travel, exile and military engagement, a form of responsive dwelling that often serves as a last-ditch cover for populations displaced by natural disasters and states of emergency. Each of these scapes convenes elements of assembly, mobility, setting and action, place-making factors that course among and bind together dramatic poetry, theatricality and design in order to assemble new habitations for life, thought and art.

Affordances

In *Romeo and Juliet,* Romeo muses on the light cast from the portal of Juliet's bedroom into the shady orchard below:

> But, soft, what light through yonder window breaks?
> It is the east, and Juliet is the sun.
> Arise, fair sun, and kill the envious moon,
> Who is already sick and pale with grief
> That thou, her maid, art far more fair than she:
> Be not her maid, since she is envious;
> Her vestal livery is but sick and green
> And none but fools do wear it; cast it off.
> It is my lady, O, it is my love!
> O that she knew she were!
> She speaks yet she says nothing; what of that?
> Her eye discourses, I will answer it.
> I am too bold, 'tis not to me she speaks:
> Two of the fairest stars in all the heaven,
> Having some business, do entreat her eyes

To twinkle in their spheres till they return.
What if her eyes were there, they in her head?
The brightness of her cheek would shame those stars,
As daylight doth a lamp; her eyes in heaven
Would through the airy region stream so bright
That birds would sing and think it were not night.
See how she leans her cheek upon her hand!
O that I were a glove upon that hand,
That I might touch that cheek! (*R&J* 2.2.2–25)[4]

Beginning with the comparison of Juliet and the sun, the extraordinary flight of the passage comes to an end in Romeo's positing of himself as a glove upon Juliet's hand. The appearance of the glove effects a number of spatial abridgements and rescalings in a scene in which distance is both problem and solution.[5] The lacing of chiastic exchanges around the points of light formed by Juliet's eyes and the twinkling stars in the passage's central conceit threaten to become matted and fibrous; thankfully, the nocturne of day birds, a phenomenon that belongs to one of the play's key audio tracks, keep open a patch of sky in the thickening weave of the poetry. In the figure of the glove, the vast distance of the cosmos shrinks to the kidskin interface between cheek and hand, and she who had been exalted to the point of dispersal into light-emitting diodes once again assumes body and form. The silken membrane of the glove preserves a layer of distance between hand and cheek; if the hand in the glove is a classic emblem of vaginal penetration, it also provides a primitive image of birth control. Romeo's glove simultaneously re-embodies Juliet, imagines physical congress with her, preserves her hymen, and obliquely proposes the possibility of non-reproductive satisfaction. Wow.

Affordance theory offers a framework for apprehending the real as well as dramatic and poetic functionalities of the glove in this passage. In design research, "affordances" refer to the possible uses of a particular object and the way in which those latencies are communicated by size, shape, texture, orientation or other indicators of utility. The concept of affordances was first developed by ecological psychologist James J. Gibson to describe the way in which animals perceive environmental features in relation to the opportunities for action borne by specific elements of their world. Donald Norman transferred affordances from ecology to design, including usability studies and human-computer interaction (HCI). Although this work has led to "user-friendly" innovations of the most precise and world-changing kind, it has often proceeded on a behaviourist model that reduces human action to the finger on the button or the hand on the handle, minimizing the affinity between affordances and phenomenology and masking the vibrant ecological field from which affordances

---

[4]All citations from Shakespeare are taken from *The Riverside Shakespeare* (Shakespeare). The following abbreviations are used: *AMND* (*A Midsummer Night's Dream*); *KL* (*King Lear*); *M* (*Macbeth*); *R&J* (*Romeo and Juliet*); and *TT* (*The Tempest*).

[5]On the subjectivizing role of distance and leave-taking in this scene and the play as a whole, see Kottman.

first emerged as a concept.[6] Many designers and architects today, responding to new environmental and economic constraints, are mining the history of affordances itself for ecological paradigms that might check the behaviourist and consumerist tendencies of their profession.[7] In Shakespeare studies, Evelyn B. Tribble has used affordances in tandem with distributed cognition in order to conceive of the space of the theatre as an "information architecture" that actively supports memory and movement across the stage.[8] W. B. Worthen has used affordances to shift the relationship between text and performance from a hermeneutic paradigm (the staging of a play interprets the script) to a model based on scenes of use (the play text affords its actualizations, which take shape under different regimes of technical and ideational possibility).[9]

In reaching for the glove as an implement of human contact, Romeo taps a range of affordances. Gloves are designed to protect the skin from heat and cold; if Juliet is the sun, such protection is warranted, and the image of the glove wards off the danger that Romeo already senses she poses to him. Thanks to its thinness and flexibility, however, a well-made glove, such as those that John Shakespeare might have manufactured in his Stratford workshop, is able to preserve the sense of touch while limiting the risks of direct contact with flesh or fluids. Romeo wants to be the glove on Juliet's hand and not, say, the hand in Juliet's glove, dissolving himself into the proprioceptive interface of erotic self-touching rather than inserting himself into the more legible space of sexual intercourse. Often made from animal skins, the glove is itself a second skin, a membrane that communicates information concerning size, shape, weight and portability in tandem with more ambient features such as temperature, wetness, viscosity and texture. (These communicative capacities are harnessed in the use of gloves as interfaces in virtual reality games as well as LED lightshows.) The glove, moreover, shares affordances with condoms: both are protective sheaths that facilitate the transfer of tactile stimulation while erecting a barrier against liquid flow. Renaissance condoms, designed to prevent both pregnancy and syphilis, were manufactured out of linen, animal intestines and bladders; intestines had also been used in glove-making since the thirteenth century.[10] Precisely because of the shared affordances of sheathing, the glove offers itself up for visual punning on sexual matters. Romeo's glove is both chaste *and* queer, at once the sumptuary marker of the most delicate gradations in status and the spontaneous carrier of bawdy intentions, nocturnal emissions and haptic flights of seeing feelingly.

---

[6]The work of Harry Heft is an exception. See Heft.

[7]*Design Ecologies* (a journal published by Eniatype, a group of architects based in London) looks at "the complex relationship between human activity and the environment," examining "the totality or pattern of linkages between drawing and environment." See *Design Ecologies*, "about this site." Other designers committed to rethinking affordances from an environmental perspective include Tony Dunne and Fiona Raby, principals of Dunne & Raby Studio and authors of *Design Noir: The Secret Life of Electronic Objects*. On affordance theory and the humanities, see Almquist and Lupton, 3–14.

[8]Tribble, 67–8. See also Lupton, "Making Room, Affording Hospitality."

[9]"Tools and technologies," writes W. B. Worthen, "exist in a dynamic equilibrium; tools afford different acts in different technologies, which redefine the *affordance* of the tool" (21).

[10]See Collier.

We focus on the affordances shared by gloves and condoms not in order to fortify an historical context that would hedge the play behind an ever greater forest of footnotes, but rather to begin to imagine environments of use that assemble different kinds of players (artisans, actors, stagehands, drabs, molls) within a common scene of tactile knowing and performance anxiety. What Richard Sennett has called the "tacit knowledge" of craftsmanship is also *known tacitly* by the plays, which tend to capture and avow artisanal work not in its dramatic plots and characters, where artisans figure only occasionally, but rather through the unconscious phenomenological recording device of the poetic image.[11] Tribble's emphasis on the cognitive affordances embedded in the architecture of the theatre might bid us to pay special attention to the role of the glove in both signalling a cue to the actor playing Juliet (rest head on hand, please!) as well as keeping track of the forms of space travel effected by the passage. Romeo's poetic conceit has vaulted the cosmos itself; now the lover grasps the image of the glove in order to regain his footing and to bring us gently back to earth, alighting for a moment at Juliet's window. Affordances invite us to consider not only the uses of gloves, but also the way in which the passage as a whole plays the vertical layers of the stage (plateau, gallery, canopy, open sky) as a mnemonic map of action and expression possibilities.[12]

James J. Gibson's ecological psychology would emphasize the formal features shared by gloves and condoms as well as tunnels, sleeves, hollow tree trunks and (that most Shakespearean of architectural orifices) chinks in the wall. We might tap contemporary designers' commitment to reclaiming the ecological framework of James J. Gibson's original affordance theory by considering how the night song of larks, evoked here as positive evidence of love's transformative capacities, can with just a little tweaking signal fundamental disturbances in seasonal rhythms. Romeo's birds that "sing and think it were not night", like lab animals trapped in a circadian study, are affined with Titania's vision of a climate-changed world in which

> the spring, the summer,
> The childing autumn, angry winter, change
> Their wonted liveries. (*AMND* 2.1.111–3)

Listening for the uncanny resonances in the larks' inverted evensong allows us to attend to the ecological disruptions that wrinkle Verona's various communicative systems, pushing the play towards considerations of urbanism as a network of flows among several species and forms of traffic.[13] The Friar's letter does not reach its destination because of an unexpected outbreak of plague, itself associated with theatrical congregation. (The judicious use of gloves and condoms might have helped stem the spread.) The accidents in communication that make the play feel capricious

---

[11]See Sennett, 50–2.

[12]"Action possibilities" is another gloss on affordances. See E. J. Gibson and Pick, 70.

[13]See Raber, 18, on animals and the "city economy."

from a narrative point of view manifest from the perspective of ecology the dependencies shared by postal delivery, theatrical performance and communicative diseases.

Friar Lawrence, the play's pre-eminent gardener and pharmacist, uses the word "virtue" in a manner akin to modern affordances. He says of his osier basket of plants, "Many for many virtues excellent, / None but for some, and yet all different" (*R&J* 2.3.13–14). "Virtue" here is denuded of its moral connotations in order to indicate the power or properties of things in the natural world, potentialities inherently disposed within scenes of use rather than considered, say, from the standpoint of their chemical composition. In classical rhetoric and ethics, the virtuous man is he who intuits and seizes the action possibilities latent in the *kairos* or moment. The Friar's enigmatic phrase "None but for some" (no plant has all virtues; what is an excellence for one agent in one action is not for another) emphasizes the dynamic quality of plant virtues as capacities that are both inherent in particular species and only manifested *as virtues* when they are put to use.

Compare James J. Gibson: "Ecologists have the concept of a *niche*. A species of animal is said to utilize or occupy a certain niche in the environment. This is not quite the same as the habitat of the species: a niche refers more to how an animal lives than to where it lives. I suggest that a niche is a set of affordances."[14] The ecological niche is not an identifiable location in the wilderness (cave, log, puddle), but rather the set of affordances that support the routines of a particular form of life. In her account of politics, Hannah Arendt construes the polis not as a specific location (Athens, Baltimore, Irvine) but rather as the set of communicative actions made possible by the fact of human assembly.[15] We would like to map Arendt's transitive and action-based account of place and place-making onto James J. Gibson's understanding of the ecological niche. Thus the Renaissance glove affords different actions for different actors in the niches of courtly love, artisanal labour and theatrical performance ("None but for some"), which only take shape as definable spaces through acts of dwelling and habitation. If for James J. Gibson, "a niche is a set of affordances", then the stage is always a niche, an open shelter composed of those capacities that support the peculiar life form called theatre. *Romeo and Juliet* assembles its own distinctive array of niches (sonnet, balconies, lanterns, graves) out of the various virtues of stage architecture, real and posited things, the play text, and its actualizations in speech, movement and scenography as well as imagination and recollection.

Softscape

With such thoughts in mind, let's take up another poetic image from another play:

> Methought I heard a voice cry, "Sleep no more!
> Macbeth does murther sleep"—the innocent sleep,
> Sleep that knits up the ravell'd sleave of care … (*M* 2.2.32–4)

---

[14] J. J. Gibson, 128.
[15] "Wherever you go, you will be a polis" (Arendt, 198).

Although "sleave" may refer to "a thin filament of silk made by ravelling a thicker thread", editor Nicholas Brooke prefers the garment sense of "sleeve": another protective sheathe, once again associated with clothing and artisanal craft.[16] Detached as sleeves often were in the Renaissance from a larger fabric construction, we glimpse in this image sleep knitting a tunnel of comforting darkness around the self-abandoning consciousness of a being undone by a day of care. We might even say that the image *yawns*, that it evokes the opening and closing of the throat through which consciousness releases its grasp on attention. "Ravel" meant both to entangle *and* to disentangle; it is thus one of those Freudian "antithetical words" which wraps around its opposite, twisting together opposite meanings in a single tensile thread. "Care" implies both the cares of the day that are shelved in the vulnerable security of sleep, and the forms of affective labour, including artisanal craft and the work of hospitality, in which knitting itself participates. If care names what is relinquished by the sleeper, care is exercised by the makers of beds and the singers of lullabies in the social work of slumber.

Manic Macbeth sloughs off this image in the process of acknowledging what it means to "murder sleep", taken as an assault against a vital bodily function wrapped up in intricate technologies of blanketing and curtaining enclosure. This crime against life as life function will issue in psychosomatic disturbances in nocturnal rhythms and spatial experience. Drawing on the padding, draping and light-shielding affordances of fabric, the image reminds us of the textile world that would have cloistered the king in his bed of state, a veritable fortress of bed clothes (mattress, linens, coverlets, bed curtains, canopy, all hung and elevated on a timber frame) that together form a magnificent "sleeve of care". The murder occurs offstage; we might imagine the deed taking place (and *destroying place*) in the curtained discovery space at the back of many Renaissance stages, whose veiled niche becomes an architectural alibi for the bed of state itself.

We have developed the concept of *softscape* in order to gather and map this series of exchanges among Renaissance home furnishings, the space of the stage, the political-theological architecture of the body, and the labile, proprioceptive volumes knit by poetic images. In landscape architecture, "softscape" refers to the plantings added to the "hardscape" composed by paths, retaining walls and land forms.[17] In "Shakespeare by Design", softscape collects what is makeshift, incomplete, mobile or transient in the spatial construction of human scenes of gathering, with a special attention to the marshalling of textile affordances in constructing the spaces of performance. Tapestry historian Laura Weigert argues that ambitious fabrics, which covered entire walls, were frequently hung and taken down, often wrapped around corners and sometimes reserved a membrane of open space between fabric and stone, were conceived in the

---

[16]Brooke, ed.

[17]Lupton develops the concept of the softscape in two essays on Renaissance tapestry: "Pauline Edifications"; and "Soft *Res Publica*."

Renaissance not simply as decorative surfaces but as architectural features in their own right.[18] The open-air amplitude of the Globe curtained music and discovery spaces, temporary stages built from fabric and timber, and canopied chairs and beds of state: in each case, portable or partial edifices support the collaborative fictions of theatre and life. Meanwhile, in contemporary environments, verandas, picnic blankets, kiosks, gazebos and pavilions continue to erect temporary commons, elastic spaces that render up our social relationships and environmental dependencies for symbolization and acknowledgement as well as resistance and disavowal.

The softscape is a congeries of fabric affordances, including the unfurling of images on or as surfaces; the topological torsion of such surfaces by billowing, folding, creasing, tying, stretching and tearing; the assembly of three-dimensional volumes out of two-dimensional fields; the ambient shaping of light and sound by fabric membranes; and the stretching, wrapping and folding of interior and exterior spaces in each other. Renaissance tapestries long ago ceded their glamour to the sharper achievements of panel painting, yet their periodic, space-shaping modes of display anticipate the techniques of projection, abstraction and assemblage that have become mainstays of modern scenography, as Aby Warburg already sensed in his brief comments on tapestry as a form of mechanical reproduction.[19] The softscape convenes connections between banners and billboards, between flags and signposts, and between tapestry cycles and video projections. In each of these convergences, the softscape harbours a special relationship to theatre: not only to front and back curtains and painted flats, but also to modern and post-modern investigations of space shaped by sound and light. Hung between modern and pre-modern scenographies, the softscape is aflutter with the movement of both history and thought, like the seismographic metaphor favoured by Warburg that, in François-Xavier Gleyzon's formulation, "captures the waves, the tides, the agitations that still *survive* buried in the depths of time."[20]

In developing her own account of fabric spaces, Weigert cites architectural theorist Gottfried Semper on the "shared etymology of *Gewand* (clothing), *Wand* (wall), and *winden* (to envelop)."[21] In the murder of sleep, bed clothes become winding sheets that harden around wounds or *Wunde*, and the sanctuary of sleep becomes a mausoleum. Macbeth's sleeve takes up residence alongside a host of textile references in the play in order to build the affordances of fabric into images of consciousness adrift in a landscape that keeps unmaking and remaking itself, like the operating system on your computer, or the mother in your kitchen. In *Romeo and Juliet*, larks behave like nightingales in a city of systems. In *Macbeth*, owls kill falcons and horses eat themselves (2.4), environmental symptoms of Macbeth's war against vitality. If we were to push Macbeth's ravelled sleeve for its environmental intersections with contemporary design, we might curate it in the same space as the Hyperbolic Crochet Coral Reef,

---

[18]Weigert, 317–36.
[19]Warburg, 314–23.
[20]Gleyzon, xviii.
[21]Weigert, 326.

a multiplex installation that bids participants to weave coral out of wool, reclaimed fibres and trash. Combining mathematics, marine biology, handicraft and community art practice in response to global warming and oceanic garbage, this extraordinary collaborative softscape knits together multiple communities of artisans and activists.[22] Created and curated by two sisters, Christine and Margaret Wertheim, this project manifests the extent to which crochet and coral are linked at the level of structure and process, as aggregative crowd-sourced ravellings.

Beyond its engagement with physical spaces and fashioned things, the softscape is supple enough to move between *the affordances of fabric* (folding, twisting, swaying, sheltering and so on) and *what those affordances afford* for dramatic poetry, the intricate topologies of consciousness disclosed in images like the ravelled sleeve of care and its disposition in a series of soft scenarios. Always bound up with fabric affordances are their metaphoric, phenomenological and psychological rapture in the roving images of dramatic poetry, not as a secondary reflection of material objects but as forms of thinking always implicated in the world of things.

Soundscape

When Prospero speaks of the "baseless fabric of this vision" (*TT* 4.1.151), he uses "fabric" to mean "a product of skilled workmanship" as well as an "edifice, a building".[23] Shakespeare's bewitching song translates the "baseless fabric" of liquid architecture into the sublime, hallucinatory heights of an intoxicating soundscape woven from the found matter of the island environment and the craft of Prospero's verse. Ensnared in the acoustic threads of Prospero's design, Ferdinand is teased and tortured by sounds emanating, it seems, from the landscape itself:

> Where should this music be? I' th' air, or th' earth?
> It sounds no more; and sure it waits upon
> Some god o' th' island. Sitting on a bank,
> Weeping again the King my father's wrack,
> This music crept by me upon the waters,
> Allaying both their fury and my passion
> With its sweet air; thence I have follow'd it,
> Or it hath drawn me, rather. But 'tis gone.
> No, it begins again
> .   .   .
> This is no mortal business, nor no sound
> That the earth owes. I hear it now above me. (*TT* 1.2.388–396, 407–8).

Ignoring the visual information that might provide topographical clues to his situation (say, tell-tale signs of deforestation and inhabitation), Ferdinand moves through the island landscape according to a strange process of echolocation. The song is both

---

[22]See *The Institute for Figuring.*
[23]"Fabric, n." (senses I and I.1), *The Oxford English Dictionary.*

orienting and disorienting: Ferdinand cannot determine whether he follows in the sound's wake as the siren song tempers the rough waters, or whether the unearthly tune shadows him as he fights his way to dry land. Is the prince pulled toward the land by the music's attractive power, or does it track with his emotions, as if it were the score in a movie starring the young prince, penetrating suddenly and awkwardly into the diegetic frame of the action? The question is not resolved when he reaches safety: Ferdinand remains utterly perplexed as to the obscure source of the sound, unable to fix upon either the natural sources or the offstage speakers that funnel the verse into his orbit. The rush of sensory impressions visited upon him seem to swell up at points from both earth and sky, shifting based on his position: the enrapturing sound rages during the tempest, fades, and then surges again as the prince approaches water, sitting on a bank and adding his sobs as yet another melancholy layer to the tempestuous mix. The sound is "more than the earth owes", too intense and complex and narratively specific to write off as the product of purely natural or ecological formations.[24] On the other hand, the prince hesitates before ascribing the song to some ill-defined human agency, an offstage presence manipulating him, supervising the scene, and directing the course of events. In a rush of negations that solves nothing, Ferdinand concludes that the sound stems from neither "mortal business" nor the earth, neither man nor nature.

Critics, by and large, have not lingered upon this moment of indecision but dismissed it. Ferdinand is caught up in his host's mean-spirited trap; we are not, and we know that this sound is at least in part a product of Prospero's versification, his remarkable, if not magical, capacity to manufacture scenes and create illusions like any good stage manager. And yet, the source of sonic agency is not so clear. The extent of Prospero's sovereign control over the elements is mediated by spirits of the land who, like the fairies of *A Midsummer Night's Dream*, personify the active and agental dimensions of the landscape.[25] Naturally, the island generates its own soundtrack, a point that has been recognized long since by Caliban, the character most attuned to the island's acoustic personality:

Be not afeard, the isle is full of noises,
Sounds, and sweet airs, that give delight and hurt not.
Sometimes a thousand twangling instruments
Will hum about mine ears; and sometimes voices… (*TT* 3.2.135–8)

Of course, Prospero appears to have mastered soporific songs and spells, and he exercises his sonic tricks to provide pleasure as well as pain; but these "sweet airs" seem to pre-date his presence on the isle, a sonic register of the forest's eerie vitality and potentially threatening activity. Caliban's observation resonates not so much with that of an

---

[24]Scott Trudell carefully tracks the mutual sonic exchanges between human language and environmental noise in "The Mediation of Poesie."

[25]Jane Bennett recuperates personification as a recognition of the agentic capacities of non-human actors, a first step in a more environmentally friendly and ethical politics in *Vibrant Matter*.

impressionable child or a deluded savage, but with the rather sophisticated reflections of Alexander von Humboldt, who, in his travels through Latin America, wrote long and lovingly of the sublime and unearthly soundscapes of the New World: "Yet amid these strange sounds, these wild forms of plants, and these prodigies of a new world, nature everywhere speaks to man in a voice familiar to him."[26] Or perhaps Caliban's sensibility is best captured by Brian Eno, whose ambient music took shape during a formative trip to Ghana which he devoted to recording atmospheric sounds, an experience that led him to reconceptualize his music as a dispersed sound-field rather than a fixed, structurally coherent composition.[27]

Ferdinand and Caliban's accounts of the intricately plaited sonic profile of the island suggest that we might address the confused source of the sound through the lens of acoustic ecology, a field that unpacks the tight weave of sonic relations between humans and their environment. All landscapes are also soundscapes, acoustic fields produced by a collaboration among human, animal, industrial, mechanical, vegetative and ecological factors. Sound is more than a constituent part of the landscape, an additional and extraneous element arising from environmental stimuli. A rippling disturbance, a viral transmission, sound is produced and warped by the media it passes through (dampened, reflected, attenuated, amplified). Sound is architectural, panoramic, a physical phenomenon and a material component of both the non-human wilderness and the built environment—indeed, soundscapes are the product of mutual incursions by multiple species staking out, belligerently defending, and constantly renegotiating their own niches. The city is a resonance machine, a tuned organism groaning with the sounds of engines and elevators, ringtones and gunfire, wailing infants and your neighbour's band practice.

But if the environment produces noise, sound reciprocally creates and defines spaces, weaving people together with one another and their environment through an acoustic fabric spun by the shared exposure to sound.[28] Georg Klein argues that acoustic art involves "installing a space within an already existing space" in a complex play that creates layered interiors, or interior soundspaces bounded within exterior hardscapes.[29] Softscapes and soundscapes are cut from the same cloth: as sound waves shiver through physical bodies, they draw listeners together in a space shaped by the physical and auditory dimensions of the sound, networking human and non-human bodies together in a makeshift assembly. The acoustic body produced by our gathering within the framing of a local soundscape may be empowering, the spontaneous production of a new collective from a dispersed series of unrelated elements.[30] Luke Fischbeck and Sarah Rara, of the Los Angeles-based electronic band Lucky Dragons, stage performances that embody the most generative and creative

---

[26]Quoted in Helferich, 73.
[27]Toop, 131.
[28]See the essays collected in LaBelle and Roden, eds.
[29]Klein, 108.
[30]Karen Tongson provides a thoughtful and edgy reading of the positive, queer valences of pop music as the foundation for "remote intimacies" (27).

dimensions of sound as environment rather than composition. By distributing analog instruments through the crowd and processing the signals generated from their unique combinations, Lucky Dragons creates a human circuit, wrapping the audience together in spontaneous and tactile formations of sound, light and bodies.

Even so, involuntary conscription into a sonorous body may embody the most insidious effects of interpellation and neoliberal subject-production. The Muzak company describes its product as "audio architecture", a structural and not incidental component to theatres of hospitality, commerce, healthcare, dining and finance. Catchy snatches of music are grist for the mill of capitalist identity formation: soundscapes are brandscapes, neoliberal niches that mould pliant and tractable consumers.[31] The collective spawned by an exposure to sound can easily take the shape of a brand community, a group recognition aligned with the goals and modes of what contemporary marketers call the experience economy.[32] And if these aural techniques of soft power fail to produce docile consumer-subjects, sound can be repurposed as a brutal instrument of state power, as when the police turn sound cannons on protestors, or when the CIA tortures suspected terrorists by blasting their cells with Metallica. And yet, as Drew Daniel argues, by exploiting the radical openness of the ear, sound can act as an "involuntary solvent of the self", triggering alternative, queer subject formations inassimilable to the neoliberal dictates of identity politics and brand recognition.[33] Music is sneakily subliminal, a penetrating and potentially de-individuating force whose playful reworking of subjectivity is the premise of both inane corporate jingles and grinding, abusive noise bands: Muzak and Merzbow operate according to the same principle.

As befits the play that boasts Shakespeare's most fully realized soundtrack, *The Tempest* explores both the transformative and empowering dimensions of the soundscape while probing its darker, exploitative, abusive potentials.[34] Prospero does not traffic in pure illusion, but manipulates, channels, loops, remixes, distorts and amplifies the sounds of the rushing sea and the wild island to stage scenes with his captive audience that walk a curiously fine line between pastoral romance and survivalist nightmare. A late and complex instance in a long line of kinky Shakespearean sadists, Prospero takes pleasure in punishing both his enemies and the objects of his affection. Unlike Iago's psychological torture, or Shylock's binding and cutting fantasies, or Oberon's species-transgressive bestiality scenarios, or Petruchio's camp-like taming regime, the vehicle of Prospero's preferred method of sensory stimulation and pain regulation is distinctly auditory. The pulsing, wave-like, periodic rhythms of Ariel's melody amplify and intensify the surge of the sea: song as a continuation of the storm by other means. Sound waves and salt water lick Ferdinand in nauseating

---

[31]Design collective Metahaven's recent projects chart new forms of combinatory urbanism arising from global capital as mediated by social networks, brand communities and Wikileaks. See van der Velden and Kruk.
[32]See Pine and Gilmore; and Klingmann.
[33]Daniel, 43–6.
[34]Neill, 36.

currents of noise that mentally and emotionally prepare the prince for his role as hunky male lead in the romantic plot of Prospero's crafting. The sickening swells tenderize him, mould him and prod him until he's receptive to direction. The sonic strategem works: Ferdinand is honestly, guilelessly staggered by the sight of Miranda, taking her name at face value and hailing her as a goddess, while we might reasonably wonder whether a home-schooled girl who had never seen another human besides her father and abusive stepbrother would be as ravishing were she presented at court.

Because, for better or worse, the character and quality of these scenes is mediated, curated and crafted by the acoustic field, we might say that the soundscape is fundamentally scenographic, a necessary component to stagecraft and the broader theatrical business of assembling, collecting and place-making in the service of both entertainment and incarceration. We are not unearthing acoustic ecologies in Shakespeare in order to flesh out our sense of the soundworld of Renaissance England, subtracting the channels of industrial noise and post-industrial Muzak, then adding a splash of church bells and cannon fire, cross-fading past and present to produce a purified sonic cartography of early modern terrain. That mix is worth a listen, and no one has produced a clearer sound image than Bruce R. Smith in his dazzling text on *The Acoustic World of Early Modern England*.[35] We prefer to tune in, however, to the resonances of Shakespeare's speculative soundscapes, tracking the passages between sonic architecture and the urban condition in the darkly utopian strands of *The Tempest*. The transformative magic of softscape and soundscape shapes the desolate domains of exile into inhabitable scenes of creepy domiciles, pastoral romance and even grudging hospitality. In our final concept, we put the affordances of softscape and soundscape into conversation with the shockingly modern and perfectly ancient projects of portable architecture (think: tent cities in the Old Testament and Tahrir Square). Here we turn to the ambling cities of courtly progress and the creeping cities of military invasion in *King Lear*, Shakespeare's most extended investigation into instant urbanism as a disastrous experiment in sovereign rule and household management.

Renaissance Instant Urbanism

Once the mobile city of King Lear's itinerant court has descended upon her estate, Goneril complains that her father's progress has exposed her manor to the architectural equivalent of venereal disease:

> Here do you keep a hundred knights and squires,
> Men so disorder'd, so debosh'd and bold,
> That this our court, infected with their manners,
> Shows like a riotous inn. Epicurism and lust
> Makes it more like a tavern or a brothel
> Than a grac'd palace. (*KL* 1.4.241–6)

---

[35]Smith. See also Folkerth.

This peculiar infection is unequivocally sexual in nature. Separated from their own homes and families on Lear's permanent road trip, the knights behave badly, taking advantage of the servants while spreading a rash of drunken disorder and, presumably, disease throughout their host's estate. But viewed from an ecological perspective, the infection in question is more broadly biological: Lear has endangered his host estate by introducing a swarm of parasites cultured in the liquid medium of alcohol, unleashing an opportunistic infection that threatens to consume the household's stores, subvert its regulatory mechanisms, upend its hormonal balance and disable its defences from within. The unbridled appetites of Lear's parasitical retinue upset the delicate homeostasis of the domestic environment conceived as a biological organism or corporate ecology.

Court, palace, inn, brothel, tavern: Goneril's castle incubates a world of building types that are differentiated by patterns of use as much as by physical construction. The causes as well as effects of this contagion are architectural in nature, and the structural damage to the estate arises in response to a specifically Renaissance form of instant urbanism: the court progress. The ambling city of royal progress was compiled from human, animal and microbial agents housed within portable, foldable, storable, makeshift edifices, temporary softscapes that could be added to the more permanent manors that opened themselves to royal visits, giving the beleaguered hosts and cluttered homes some extra breathing room after the locust-like descent of a few dozen (or a few hundred) high-maintenance guests.[36] These new living arrangements, which would have scattered the knights through rooms in the estate while parcelling their individual servants through tents and doubling up in servant's quarters, undeniably contributed to the sudden outbreak of sexual licentiousness. Curiously, the effects of the sexually transmitted epidemics, pregnancy, disease and drunken debauchery are not restricted to the bodies and skins of the staff, but ripple outward to mar the surfaces of the edifice with growths of trash piles, pock-marked walls and embarrassing leaks in the plumbing. It is as if the entire household, human inhabitants as well as their architectural shell, had contracted a series of degrading infections. So extensive and disfiguring are the changes undergone by the house, Goneril no longer recognizes it as a respectable domicile, a seat of state and a safe refuge. Although Goneril's complaint begins with an indictment of human misbehaviour, she concludes her summation with an account of transformations in the built environment: with the advent of Lear's company, the estate resembles a brothel or dive bar more than Downton Abbey, registering the less material changes in social standing, family politics and sexual dynamics with the accumulated waste of a week-long party.

Even more disconcertingly, the encampment itself served as a not-so-subtle reminder to the host family that a small battalion of soldiers were lodged dangerously close to

---

[36]With reference to *A Midsummer Night's Dream*, Robert Watson has argued that microbial elements refashion the human as a multi-tiered ecology (see Watson). Telescoping this claim, we might suggest that the walking cities of progress and invasion in *Lear* demonstrate that the city, too, is a complex ecology.

the bodies of the newly enfranchised sovereigns, a physical reminder of the precariousness of their station. It is a sign of practicality and not moral deficiency that leads Goneril to wonder whether

> 'Tis politic and safe to let him keep
> At point a hundred knights; yes, that on every dream,
> Each buzz, each fancy, each complaint, dislike,
> He may enguard his dotage with their pow'rs
> And hold our lives in mercy. (*KL* 1.4.323–7)

A slight failure in hospitality could quite literally transform the domestic sphere into a bloody battleground, as their jackbooted guests turn their considerable force to the utter destruction of the hosts. The descent of Lear's mobile dwellings upon the reluctant homes of his daughters climaxes in the theatre of hospitality bleeding into the theatre of war, transforming the home into the home front.

In the Renaissance, as today, instant urbanism served the occasional, ad-hoc needs of both entertainment and conflict. From the Mongolian yurt and Bedouin tent to the RV and the Marines' Forward Operating Base, portable architecture spans the history of the built environment, providing not only temporary housing but mobile support for military operations, medical emergencies, humanitarian catastrophes, festive affairs, holiday vacations and civic events.[37] The architectural theorist and urban futurist Geoff Manaugh is keenly attuned to how the world-making possibilities of instant urbanism are shadowed by their darker military and industrial doubles.[38] *Lear*, amazingly, documents the utter collapse of these categories: the tent cities of the play's first acts tease out the violent erotics and tedious impositions of seasonal family visits, while the late stages of the action feature Lear's hospitable reception in the mobilized encampments of the French invasion. Cordelia receives her much-subdued, broken father in tents that serve as reception chambers, temporary housing for troops and makeshift hospital. It doesn't take long for all the characters in *Lear* to be mobilized, as they either hide from unpleasant relatives, elope, run for their lives, or go to war.

Although the eco-friendly dimensions of flexible architecture have deepened its critical purchase and liberal respectability, the urban fabric of late capital translates the idiom of plug-in cities into vast stretches of identical, factory-made suburban homes, or mini-malls and food courts that look the same in Sulpher Springs and Baghdad. And yet, as tent cities spring up in public plazas and master-planned communities, we see an intensification of the potentials of instant urbanism on each end of the political spectrum. *Lear* reminds us that, as sites of makeshift encampments, temporary architecture can house scenes of both festivity and terror, oppositional and progressive organization as well as military entrenchment. Summer camps and

---

[37]For an introduction to portable architecture, see esp. Kronenburg, *Portable Architecture*; and Kronenburg, *Flexible*.

[38]See Manaugh.

refugee camps, Burning Man and Abu Ghraib, participate in a single architectural vernacular, all erecting the roughly equivalent seasonal, temporary, portable frameworks.

Conclusion

This brings us around to the convergence of our key themes. Whereas *affordances* concern the opportunities for action solicited by particular objects and settings, *softscapes*, *soundscapes* and *instant urbanisms* gather up and rezone manifold affordances for purposes ranging from conviviality and refuge to occupation and incarceration. In each case, these occasional assemblages stage architecture as event. Whereas architecture in its monumental mode aims to establish peace time and place through the tenacity of its pillars and pylons, architecture as event erects mobile frames that host occasions, enable assembly and, in its militarized modes, both instigate and respond to emergency. Pop-up cities exploit the foldable and portable affordances of fabric, while fabric's more ambient virtues—the ability of textiles to shape acoustical and lighting conditions—reveal softscape as soundscape. In *King Lear*, great halls and courtyards afford pomp, circumstance and the egregious testing of filial love, but also riot, shaming, torture and mutilation. The very openness of semi-public space in late medieval floor plans houses a multitude of possible uses and abuses whose actualization become the stuff of tragedy. And the mechanisms of such rezoning reside in the mobilia of temporary domicile, whether transported in the revolving wardrobe of the itinerant monarch or pulled out of storage by his nervous hosts like so many daggers in the air.

Design, urban planning and landscape architecture are engaged in forms of speculative poesis that share conceptual turf with drama, mapping the conjectural terrain of possible worlds and setting the stage for potential communities. Shakespearean drama, in the density of its figural operations and the luminosity of its spatial imaginings, helps us consider not only architecture's collusions with theatre, but also the passage between portable edifices and the movement of thought. Dramatic poetry records the exchanges that take place between ways of draping, shaping, moving, muting and sounding space, and the formations of affective and cognitive life, both interior and distributed, that such techniques support, disclose and sometimes disavow. "Shakespeare by Design" aims to account for the role of objects, settings and ambience in the poetics, politics and affective labour of Renaissance drama, with an eye to what these mixed scenes of assembly and assemblage might teach us about the frames for action today.

References

Almquist, Julka, and Julia Lupton. "Affording Meaning: Design-Oriented Research from the Humanities and Social Sciences." *Design Issues* 26, no. 1 (2010): 3–14.

Arendt, Hannah. *The Human Condition*. Chicago: University of Chicago Press, 1998.

Bennett, Jane. *Vibrant Matter: A Political Ecology of Things*. Durham, NC: Duke University Press, 2009.

Boyle, Jem and Martin Foys. "Editors' Introduction: Becoming Media." In "Becoming Media. Special issue, edited by Jem Boyle and Martin Foys, *postmedieval* 3, no. 1 (2002): 1–6.

Brooke, Nicholas, ed. *Macbeth.* Oxford: Oxford University Press, 1990.

Collier, Aine. *The Humble Little Condom: A History.* New York: Prometheus Books, 2007.

Daniel, Drew. "All Sound is Queer." *The Wire* 33, no. 3 (2011): 43–6.

Design Ecologies. [cited 11 March 2012] Available from http://www.eniatype.com/index.php?/about-this-site/.

Dunne, Tony, and Fiona Raby. *Design Noir: The Secret Life of Electronic Objects.* London: August Media, 2001

Egan, Gabriel. *Green Shakespeare: From Ecopolitics to Ecocriticism.* London: Routledge, 2006.

Folkerth, Wes. *The Sound of Shakespeare.* New York: Routledge, 2002.

Gibson, Eleanor J., and Anne D. Pick. *An Ecological Approach to Perceptual Learning and Development.* Oxford: Oxford University Press, 2000.

Gibson, James J. *Ecological Approach to Visual Perception.* Hillsdale, NJ: Lawrence Erlbaum, 1986.

Gleyzon, François-Xavier. *Shakespeare's Spiral: Tracing the Snail in* King Lear *and Renaissance Painting.* Lanham, MD: University Press of America, 2010.

Heft, Harry. *Ecological Psychology in Context: James Gibson, Roger Barker, and the Legacy of William James' Radical Empiricism.* Mahwah, NJ: Lawrence Erlbaum, 2001.

Helferich, Gerard. *Humboldt's Cosmos: Alexander von Humboldt and the Latin American Journey that Changed the Way We See the World.* New York: Gotham, 2004.

The Institute for Figuring. "Hyperbolic Crochet Coral Reef." [cited 11 March 2012]. Available from http://crochetcoralreef.org/about/index.php.

Klein, Georg. "Site-Sounds: On Strategies of Sound Art in Public Space." *Organized Sound* 14, no. 1 (2009): 101–8.

Klingmann, Andrea. *Brandscapes: Architecture in the Experience Economy.* Cambridge, MA: Massachusetts Institute of Technology Press, 2007.

Kottman, Paul. "Defying the Stars: Tragic Love as the Struggle for Freedom in *Romeo and Juliet.*" *Shakespeare Quarterly* 63, no. 1 (2012): 1–38.

Kronenburg, Robert. *Flexible: Architecture that Responds to Change.* London: Laurence King Publishing, 2007.

———. *Portable Architecture.* 3d ed. Oxford: Elsevier/Architectural Press, 2003.

LaBelle, Brandon, and Steve Roden, eds. *Site of Sound #2: Of Architecture and the Ear.* Los Angeles, CA: Errant Bodies Press, 2011.

Lupton, Julia Reinhard. "Making Room, Affording Hospitality: Environments of Entertainment in *Romeo and Juliet.*" *Journal of Medieval and Early Modern Drama* 43, no. 1 (2013): 145–72.

———. "Pauline Edifications: Staging the Sovereign Softscape in Renaissance England." In *Political Theology and Early Modernity*, edited by Graham Hammill and Julia Reinhard Lupton. Chicago, IL: University of Chicago Press, 2012.

———. "Soft *Res Publica*: On the Assembly and Disassembly of Courtly Space." *Republics of Letters* 2, no. 2 (2011): 95–113. [cited 10 March 2012]. Available from http://rofl.stanford.edu/node/96.

———. "Thinking with Things: Hannah Woolley to Hannah Arendt." Special issue, *postmedieval* 3, no. 1 (2002): 63–79.

Manaugh, Geoff. *The BLDGBLOG Book: Architectural Conjecture, Urban Speculation, Landscape Futures.* San Francisco, CA: Chronicle Books, 2009.

Mentz, Steve. "Tongues in the Storm: Shakespeare, Ecological Crisis, and the Resources of Genre." In *Ecocritical Shakespeare*, edited by Lynne Bruckner and Dan Brayton. Burlington, VT: Ashgate, 2011.

Neill, Michael. "'Noises, / Sounds, and Sweet Airs': The Burden of Shakespeare's Tempest." *Shakespeare Quarterly* 59, no. 1 (2008): 36.

Oxford English Dictionary. 2d ed. *OED Online.* Oxford University Press. [cited 10 March 2012]. Available from http://dictionary.oed.com.

Pine, B. Joseph II, and James H Gilmore. *The Experience Economy: Work is Theater & Every Business is a Stage.* Cambridge, MA: Harvard University Press, 1999.

Raber, Karen. "Vermin and Parasites: Shakespeare's Animal Architectures." In *Ecocritical Shakespeare,* edited by Lynne Bruckner and Dan Brayton. Burlington, VT: Ashgate, 2011.

Sennett, Richard. *The Craftsman.* New Haven, CT: Yale University Press, 2008.

Shakespeare, William. *The Riverside Shakespeare.* Edited by G. Blakemore Evans and J. J. M. Tobin. 2d ed. Boston: Houghton Mifflin, 1997.

Smith, Bruce R. *The Acoustic World of Early Modern England: Attending to the O-Factor.* Chicago, IL: University of Chicago Press, 1999.

Tongson, Karen. *Relocations: Queer Suburban Imaginaries.* New York: New York University Press, 2011.

Toop, David. *Ocean of Sound.* London: Serpent's Tail, 1995.

Tribble, Evelyn B. *Cognition in the Globe: Attention and Memory in Shakespeare's Theatre.* New York: Palgrave Macmillan, 2011.

Trudell, Scott. "The Mediation of Poesie: Ophelia's Orphic Song." *Shakespeare Quarterly* 63, no. 1 (2012): 46–76.

Velden, Daniel van der, and Vinca Kruk. *Uncorporate Identity.* Baden: Lars Müller Publishers, 2010.

Warburg, Aby. "Peasants at Work in Burgundian Tapestries." In *The Renewal of Pagan Antiquity.* Los Angeles, CA: Getty Research Institute, 1999.

Watson, Robert. "The Ecology of Self in *Midsummer Night's Dream.*" In *Ecocritical Shakespeare,* edited by Lynne Bruckner and Dan Brayton. Burlington, VT: Ashgate, 2011.

Weigert, Laura. "Chambres d'amour: Tapestries of Love and the Texturing of Space." *Oxford Art Journal* 31, no. 3 (2008): 317–36.

Worthen, W. B. *Drama Between Poetry and Performance.* Chichester: Wiley-Blackwell, 2010.

Yates, Julian. "Shakespeare's Kitchen Archives." In *Speculative Medievalisms,* edited by Nicola Masciandro and Eileen Joy. New York: Punctum Books, in press.

Of Cause

Madhavi Menon

This essay asks why the closing scene in Othello *is so often viewed with horror: what differentiates this scene of murder from others in Shakespeare plays like* Hamlet *or* Macbeth? *What causes this "unutterable agony"? Thinking through the thread of desire in the play, this essay suggests one response to this question. The final scene in* Othello *is agonising because the play repeatedly refuses to give us a cause for it: the cause of the final scene's agony is the causelessness of the final scene. Or rather, the final scene presents a queer cause that removes causality from the realm of ontological certainty and logical explanation. This propels us into a horrifying absence that is foundational for any appreciation of desire.*

Othello is an agonising play. H. H. Furness, for example, admits:

> I do not shrink from saying that I wish this Tragedy had never been written. The pleasure, however keen or elevated, which the inexhaustible poetry of the preceding Acts can bestow, cannot possibly to my temperament, countervail, it does but increase, the unutterable agony of this closing scene.[1]

The closing scene of the play—Act 5 Scene 2—is when Othello murders Desdemona, and where the folly of his behaviour implacably unfolds after the murder has been committed. But what makes this scene "unutterabl[y]" agonising? After all, several Shakespeare plays end with murder and bloodshed—one can think of *Macbeth*, and *Hamlet*, to name only two. Why does Othello's murder of Desdemona excite more agony than, say, Laertes's murder of Hamlet? This essay will suggest one response to this question. The final scene in *Othello* is agonising because the play repeatedly refuses to give us a cause for it: the cause of the final scene's agony is the causelessness of the final scene. Or rather, the final scene presents a queer cause that removes causality from the realm of ontological certainty—a progenitor that explains its offspring—or logical explanation—if *x*, then *y*—and propels us instead into an absence that is foundational.

---

[1]H. H. Furness, quoted in Siemon, 39.

I borrow this idea of a foundational absence from Alain Badiou who, in *Saint Paul: The Foundation of Universalism*, theorises the ways in which we can think differently about desire and identity. He argues that:

> There is no doubt that universalism, and hence the existence of any truth whatsoever, requires the destitution of established differences and the initiation of a subject divided in itself by the challenge of having nothing but *the vanished event* to face up to.[2]

The "subject divided in itself" is divided also from its desire; the "vanished event" is not about an originary cause for that desire so much as an absence that is the foundational event of desire. Outlining the effects of the "vanished event" does not in itself constitute a search for the event that has vanished (from memory, from the record). Rather, it insists that an event might not have an antecedent, an effect might not have a cause. Even though for Saint Paul, the protagonist of Badiou's book, the event is the Resurrection of Christ, Badiou makes it clear that the event is that thing that calls into question our protocols of ontology and epistemology, and need not be an actual occurrence at all—"[l]et us emphasize once more that … the event that [Paul] takes to identify the real *is not* real (because the Resurrection is a fable)";[3] rather, it is a queer turn that allows us to see things differently. The queerness of the event is that it invalidates all that we have hitherto considered normal. And for Badiou, one of the realms in which this queerness registers is desire: "what is at issue [in theorising the event] is desire."[4] *Othello* is queer in a Badiousian register, then, not only because there is no explanation for desire in the play, but also because there *can be none*. The event of Desdemona's murder in the last scene of the play is agonising because it asks for an antecedent that can only be recuperated as a vanished event, that is as something to which we have no access, but which nonetheless propels the play. The name for that vanished event is desire. And in *Othello*, it bears no satisfactory relation to cause.

Queer *Othello*

The relation between desire and cause has fomented one of the most important debates in queer theory today. Is there a cause for desire? And if so, then do certain bodies more properly embody its effects than others? Indeed, the question of what is and is not "properly" queer focuses on what a body *does* sexually. Whose desire is queer? How do we count sexual identities? Does sexual desire have to be acted on in order to be classified as identity? Is homosexuality a lifelong characteristic? Do lapsed heterosexuals count? Are desires constant? Should a literary queer theory only speak of

---

[2]Badiou, 58; emphasis mine.
[3]Ibid.
[4]Ibid., 79. This essay's indebtedness to Alain Badiou's radical rereading of Paul to reread *Othello* does not amount to an attempt to map Paul, even a Badiousian Paul, onto the play. Rather, I have attempted to tease out some of the queer implications of what Badiou says, via Paul, about desire. However, for an excellent Pauline reading of *Othello*, see Lupton.

orientations embodied by characters in texts? For long considered a theory about gay and lesbian identity, one strand of queer theory has recently and forcefully moved away from an identitarian politics of sexuality based in the body to a politics of desire in the Badiousian sense.[5] Moved, that is, from an identifiable cause of desire—embodied same-sex attraction—to the surprising ways in which desire plays itself out in literature and politics—the vanished event that nonetheless has forceful effects. In an interview, Lee Edelman elaborates on this relation between queer theory and sexuality:

> What an impossibly large question: queer theory's relation to sexuality! To respond to it adequately, one would first have to specify what exactly we mean by "sexuality" in order to clarify that queer theory has an historic, but by no means essential, relation to the fields once defined as lesbian and gay studies. That relation is vexed insofar as queer theory, though first enabled by the politicization of sexual orientation, operates as a resistance to the identitarianism produced by such a poli- tics. ... [L]esbian and gay liberation participates in the endless proliferation of iden- tities, all of which have their value in contesting the fixity of the social order, but all of which do so while harboring investments in a categorical fixity of their own. Queer theory, though also susceptible to such positivistic appropriations, undertakes to uncouple itself from identitarian moorings by focusing, instead, on resistances to social normativity and on the political, philosophical, aesthetic, and affective conse- quences those resistances entail. But the construction of a stigmatized category of those identifiable as "queer"—even when not conflated with the politics of lesbian, gay, bisexual, transgender, or intersex identities (all of which, as social movements, seek institutional normalization and protection by the state)—does not escape inflection by a relation to sexuality. For stigma—and stigma, not self- affirmation, properly registers queerness—reflects the operation of a libidinal economy in which enjoyment and disgust are endlessly braided in the making of a norm. Queer theory, then, retains its indicative association with sexuality precisely in its attention to the libidinal politics that normativity compels—a libidinal politics whose consequences extend beyond sexual identity, but which remains bound up with the subject's relation to narcissism, abjection, and enjoyment.[6]

While this essay is certainly interested in the sexual dynamics of *Othello* (according to Arthur Kirsch, "*Othello* poses a peculiar difficulty for critics because its preoccupations are so unremittingly sexual"[7]), it is even more invested in a queerness that does not necessarily involve the sexual orientation, explicit or implied, of any character in the text. *Othello* is not a queer play if we want to identify characters in it who are gay or lesbian (I say this despite the powerful reading of the exchange between Othello and Iago in Act 3 as a marriage scene). Rather, as a text fully committed to showing us the force of desire, *Othello* tracks what Edelman calls the "libidinal politics" of

---

[5]For an overview of debates within queer theory, see Jagose. Queer theorists tend to be divided along theoretical lines on the status of the body: historical materialists will prioritise the ontological truth of the body, whereas the- orists more inclined towards deconstruction and psychoanalysis call it into question as the basis for their theorisation.

[6]Edelman, interview.

[7]Kirsch, 721.

queerness, and what Badiou terms the "superabundance" of desire.[8] This libidinal politics suggests that desire is a senseless pulsation defying rationality and causality, taking no prisoners, and leaving a carnage in its wake. *Othello* brings to the fore desire's relation to doom: in the play that relation is borne out by Othello, Desdemona and Iago. By the play's end, two of the three are dead, and the third one refuses to speak any more. None of them is queer from the standpoint of identitarian sexuality. But all of them are queer because their textual positions are made to bear the weight of causeless desire, a too-muchness that cannot be explained, and that proves utterly disastrous to all who encounter it.

If the field of queer theory is divided along the lines of how much sexual identity should be at the core of its theorisations, then *Othello*'s response to that debate is none at all. The play instead has too much desire and too little identity. In Badiou's formulation of Paul's thinking about identity, desire

> points toward a theory of the subjective unconscious, structured through the opposition life/death. The law's prohibition is that through which the desire of the object can realize itself "involuntarily", unconsciously [Paul terms this state "what I do not want, *ho ou thelō*"]—which is to say, as life of sin. As a result of which the subject, de-centred from this desire, crosses over to the side of death.[9]

The subject is separated from its desire because there is no founding event, no cause, for that desire; the subject thus does not own a sexual identity. Instead, desire passes through him, unconsciously. This automatic action of desire, separate from the self, is what Paul calls *ho ou thelō*. We can, of course, hear Othello's very name in this Greek formulation,[10] but even more, we can hear what Sigmund Freud termed the "death drive", which Edelman has made the core of his queer theorisation, and to which I will return later in this essay. Identifying the source of desire is impossible; the only way in which we can desire is by not specifying the object of our desire, by transgressing against the law that demands a cause. Othello, both character and play, inscribe the causeless superabundance of desire that continually frustrates legal prohibition and the attempt to codify desire within the logic of cause and effect. We do not know if Othello and Iago are gay or straight; we do not know if Emilia and Desdemona are attracted to one another. Far from being a rhetorical sleight of hand, this lack of clarity allows us to appreciate the full force of a desire that acts without naming itself. Too much language, too much desire, not enough reason, not enough cause. *Othello* insists on the insistence of desire despite marriage and despite war. It theorises the relation between desire and identity, putting paid to our desire *for* identity by presenting to us the incompatibility between the two. Insofar as identity desires containment, identity cannot contain desire. And insofar as desire outstrips identity, it embodies without embodiment what it means to be in the grip of too much.

---

[8]Badiou, 64.

[9]Ibid., 80.

[10]For a brilliant essay on the many implications of Othello's name, see Fineman.

Off Course

Queer theory is thus riven by the question of embodied cause: is same-sex desire the cause of queerness, or does queerness flit in more unexpected places? Can the expectation that desire must *have* a cause be queered, turning us away from understanding desire to reading it? Understanding desire would insist on a bodily cause for desire, and insist also on the causality *of* desire for bodies—for instance, those who have sex with people of similarly marked bodies are homosexuals. Alternatively, reading desire would make no such presumption and have no such expectation of cause, bodily or otherwise. Instead, reading desire would—and this is the very nature of reading—insist on the "vanished event" that refuses to provide a cause even as it might serve up several. If queerness does not *have* a cause, then it cannot form the basis for an identitarian theory. And this is what is queer about *Othello*: repeated searches for cause turn up empty. A play that is obsessed with desire is obsessed also with cause, but no matter how hard it tries, it cannot build a bridge from the one to the other. *Othello* uncouples for us, in a deadly way, the relationship between causality and desire.

Indeed, even before critics have noted the lack of causality in the play, characters in the play have commented on it. From Bianca, who understands that cause is always retrospective, and exclaims after Cassio has given her Desdemona's handkerchief to copy the work—"O, Cassio, whence came this? / This is some token from a newer friend. / To the felt absence now I feel a cause" (3.4.205–7)—to Cassio at the end of the play when he learns that Othello has colluded in the plan to murder him—"Dear General, I never gave you cause" (5.2.351), the text repeatedly tries to understand the cause of actions, the motive for passions, and the reason for disasters.[11] And each time it insists on coming up with nothing. Even so prosaic an event as the attack by the Turks early in the play has neither rhyme nor reason. But still, the senators in Venice grasp for a cause despite the manifest uncertainty surrounding the machinations of the Turks. "'Tis certain, then" (1.3.50), the Duke says even as neither the cause nor the course of the Turks seems clear: not the number of ships they have, nor the destination of their fleet. This search for cause is noticeably absent at the end of the play when Iago refuses to explain the cause of his actions —"Demand me nothing. What you know, you know. / From this time forth I never will speak word" (5.2.355–6). *Othello* ends with a vanished event, and with questions that continue to remain unanswered: why does Iago lie to Othello? Why does Othello believe him? Why does Desdemona allow herself to be killed? Why does Desdemona desire Othello rather than Roderigo, a man whom her upbringing would seemingly have better prepared her to accept? Why does Emilia desire to please Iago despite disliking him intensely? Why does Iago hate Othello as much as he does?

In this play, and in each of these instances, not knowing the cause of desire is of paramount importance. So much so that even Iago's attempts at letting us know his reasons

---

[11]Shakespeare. All citations are given in text. Quotations are taken from the Folger Shakespeare Library edition.

for hating Othello during the course of the play have drawn flak from his critics, prime among them Samuel Taylor Coleridge. Commenting on the unclear relationship between (Iago's) cause and action, Coleridge says that Iago is Shakespeare's only presentation of "utter monstrosity", arguing that this utter monstrosity "depends on the … absence of causes": Iago performs the "motive-hunting of motiveless malignity …. [i]n itself fiendish."[12] Rather than faulting Iago for *being* motivelessly malignant (as is commonly understood), Coleridge blames him for hunting after motives, for seeking for causes where none might exist; in other words, for not sufficiently accepting the motivelessness *of* his malignity. Iago should embrace motiveless malignity, according to Coleridge, not look to cure it, because his particular brand of malignity can only *be* motiveless. In this, and without knowing it, Coleridge echoes Badiou's insistence on the vanished event of desire, that which will always exceed causality.

Indeed, because it cannot be identified with certainty—neither Brabantio nor Othello seems to know where Desdemona's desire lies, for instance—and because it cannot be contained within set parameters—whether of marriage or family—desire provides fertile ground for Iago's machinations in the play. So does a reading of causeless desire in the play automatically become an Iago-ist reading? Perhaps, though not for that reason embodied by Iago alone. Othello, for instance, enters the "unutterabl[y] agon[ising]" last scene of his play with these words:

> It is the cause, it is the cause, my soul.
> Let me not name it to you, you chaste stars.
> It is the cause. (5.2.1–3)

He has determined to kill Desdemona after believing Iago's version of her infidelity. But what *is* the cause to which he is referring here? Is it the handkerchief—that token apparently given to Othello's mother by a wise Egyptian woman as a means of ensuring Othello's father's love and fidelity, and later stolen from Desdemona? Is it the account of Cassio's dream that Iago has fabricated? Is it an internalised racism that has convinced him he cannot hold Desdemona's desire for long?

We do not know. The cause is presented at the beginning of this climactic scene as the single most important reason why the play is going to end as it does. Yet—and this is also the first word of the next line—we do not know what that cause is. "It" is clearly important, yet we do not have a referent for it. What is the cause to which Othello refers, and of what is it the cause? It does not help, of course, that Othello refuses to name it. Rather, the text seems to assume that the audience already knows the cause to which he refers,[13] which is why Othello can depend on being understood without having to make his meaning plain.

---

[12]Barnet, 19.

[13]This is exactly the kind of "probable" knowledge that Joel Altman exfoliates in "Preposterous Conclusions." The essay then went on to become the locus of his book, *The Improbability of Othello*. Noting that "[*Othello*] is informed by an economy of desire that is, in the deepest sense, improbable" ("Preposterous Conclusions," 134), Altman points out that the characters in the play trade on knowledge that seems probable to one another even though it is not grounded in cause.

Indeed, the audience's understanding can be counted upon because we automatically associate desire with causality. Othello "knows" that we will come up with our own version—whatever it might be—of the cause for his jealousy and Desdemona's murder; the text has given us several options, and we will pick one. The only option we will not pick, which is also the most agonising one, is no cause at all. We will always *presume* a cause that can explain things rather than acknowledge a vanished event that changes our ways of knowing and seeing. *Othello* exposes our protocols of demanding the cause of desire as hollow and phobic. Meanwhile, the event that has changed our method of knowing can itself never be known—is it the play as a whole? Iago's rhetoric? Racial miscegenation? Cause is no longer about ontology or epistemology: it cannot be conjured up in the service of knowledge because it is always the thing that exceeds the knowable. The audience might thus think it *knows* the cause—surely something that has been repeated thrice must have some foundation—but what it knows is its desire for a cause of desire.

Except, of course, that desire can take no recourse to cause, and the play insists on this repeatedly. When Othello very publicly starts acting impatiently and irrationally towards Desdemona, for instance, she simply cannot understand the reason why. Later in conversation with her mistress, Emilia broaches what seems to be increasingly obvious:

> EMILIA   Pray heaven it be
> State matters, as you think, and no conception
> Nor no jealous toy concerning you.
>
> DESDEMONA   Alas the day, I never gave him cause!
>
> EMILIA   But jealous souls will not be answered so.
> They are not ever jealous for the cause,
> But jealous for they're jealous. It is a monster
> Begot upon itself, born on itself. (3.4.175–82)

Emilia's conception of jealousy suggests it does not have a cause. Even though she begins her speech by looking for an *alternative* cause to the one that seems most apparent, Emilia ends this conversation by saying it is futile to look for a cause in matters of jealousy. Jealousy is as jealousy does, one might say. For Emilia, trying to pin down jealousy's cause is an impossible endeavour because jealousy is always in bed with desire. As such, one can never tell whether it has no cause or too many.

So what is "the cause" of which Othello boasts in the play's final scene? By way of addressing this question, let us consider briefly what Freud has to say about a neighbour who borrows a kettle and is then accused of having returned it with a hole.[14] According to Freud, the accused neighbour comes up with three contradictory explanations: first that he never borrowed the kettle, second that the kettle did not have a hole in it when it was returned, and third, that the kettle was damaged at the time of borrowing. For Freud, this is a classic example of overdetermination—when no one reason will suffice to explain an occurrence and so multiple reasons are adduced for it.

---

[14]Freud, 143–4.

Overdetermination draws attention to a fundamental feature of language: that it is always open to misunderstanding, especially when reaching for an explanatory cause. Each of the three explanations for the damaged kettle is plausible in itself, but all three hastily cobbled together are mutually contradictory. The more one tries to stop up the holes in one's lie, the more meaning leaks out of words, seeps through characters, and washes out syllables. Freud's interest in this seepage is psychic: what does an unfixed language do for a psyche that tries to fix its identity by linguistic means—using names, epithets, adjectives? Every lie seems to require another one to make it more secure. Freud's point, of course, is that such security can never be achieved, especially when no cause is involved. This is less a moral claim and more an indicator of how language always takes us away from rather than closer to cause. In Badiou's formulation, "one of the phenomena by which one recognizes an event is that the former is like a point of the real ... *that puts language into deadlock.*"[15] In this Lacanian formulation, the real is that which can never be known, and which produces reality as a poor substitute. Cause occurs in the realm of reality, not in the domain of the real. And the best indicator of that domain of the non-causal real is the functioning of language: its deadlocks suggest an absence of causality in the very medium that we use to generate cause.

Especially when what demands a cause is desire. *Othello* echoes this "point of the real" at which language is put into deadlock by adding to verbal lying the Biblical association with desire. In yet another attempt to provide Othello with proof of his wife's infidelity, Iago reports a conversation he has allegedly had with Cassio:

OTHELLO	Hath he said anything?
IAGO	He hath, my lord, but be you well assured, No more than he'll unswear.
OTHELLO	What hath he said?
IAGO	(Faith,) that he did—I know not what he did.
OTHELLO	What? What?
IAGO	Lie—
OTHELLO	With her?
IAGO	With her—on her—what you will.
OTHELLO	Lie with her? Lie on her? We say "lie on her" when they belie her. Lie with her—(Zounds,) that's fulsome! (4.1.34–42)

Led expertly by Iago, Othello makes the inevitable link here between lying as sexual act and lying as telling an untruth; to add to the linguistic deadlock, he also throws in a third intensified version of lie with "belie". The lie of language is about the act of lying; the lie of language is that desire has a cause. In this play, the excess (and therefore

---

[15]Badiou, 46.

paucity) of causes is paralleled only by excessive "lies". The play knows what its protagonist in this passage is unable to read.

Even Iago generates a version of the Freudian kettle story and the Badiousian linguistic deadlock when he tries to explain his animosity towards Othello ("I do hate him as I do hell (pains)" [1.1.171]). First, in conversation with Roderigo, he refers to the fact of Cassio having been preferred over him by Othello to the position of lieutenant, then he simply repeats to Roderigo: "I have told thee often, and I retell thee again and again, I hate the Moor" (1.3.407–9). And then he lies about lying:

> I hate the Moor,
> And it is thought abroad that 'twixt my sheets
> 'Has done my office. I know not if 't be true
> But I, for mere suspicion in that kind,
> Will do as if for surety. (1.3.429–33)

These several utterances, these multiple causes, are what drove Coleridge to inveigh against Iago's "motive-hunting". None of them, of course, is the whole truth because as Iago knows, the truth of his desire has vanished and cannot be found. Even as the list begins with a professional slight, it quickly devolves into sexual suspicion and then stays there. The trajectory of Iago's "cause" moves ineluctably towards the malignancy of desire, no matter how much and with what justification he tries to present it as being noble. Like the borrower of the kettle, the more Iago tries to stop up the holes in his logic, the more he betrays a lack of causality.

Of Course

Both Iago and Othello, then, share one thing in common: they speak much too much and convey very little. This very little, though, is a queer reconfiguration of cause as logical explanation. It generates effects that can never specify their antecedents. Even if we say that Othello's gulling by Iago is such that he determines to murder Desdemona is the Pauline "event" of the play, it does not suffice to serve as cause since it in turn begs questions about its own cause: why would Othello believe Iago? Why would Iago want Desdemona dead? How come Desdemona does not know what is going on until it is too late? The cause has vanished in *Othello*, not because characters do not ascribe causes to their actions, but because the play cannot support those ascriptions.

This lack of causal support, though not consciously in the queer vein I am teasing out, looms large in Thomas Rymer's excoriating early review of *Othello*, a play he disliked intensely for straining the limits of our credulity. In a complaint picked up later by T. S. Eliot in his critique of *Hamlet* as lacking an "objective correlative" sufficient to bear the weight of the play's emotion, Rymer suggests *Othello* is improbable because it doles out its punishments (Desdemona's murder) and rewards (Othello's elevation to captain of the Venetian fleet) on the flimsiest of circumstances. The loss of a handkerchief leads to a murder, he scoffs, and a black man is made a Venetian captain: how improbable! Rymer does not explicitly mention the problem of desire even as everything he writes (including the improbability of Desdemona being attracted to Othello) points towards it. Part of his sarcastic dismissal of the play involves outlining what he terms the "moral" of the text:

> First, This may be a caution to all Maidens of Quality how,
> without their Parents consent, they run away with Blackamoors.
> Secondly, This may be a warning to all good Wives, that they look
> well to their Linnen.
> Thirdly, This may be a lesson to Husbands, that before their
> Jealousie be Tragical, the proofs may be Mathematical.[16]

Clearly these are ridiculous morals for a tragedy worth its salt, and that is Rymer's point. Nonetheless, his mock-morals are of interest to readers of the play because he draws not one but three of them: one racist (white women should not elope with black men), one sexist (women should look after their household linen more carefully), and the third scientific (men should have mathematical proof before murdering their wives). Not one moral but three. Despite not using the word "cause", then, Rymer too cannot seem to pin down the meaning of the play; even his dismissal comes up with too many reasons why. It is almost as though the moral of the tale cannot get over Desdemona's "excessive" desire in the first instance, and simply rambles on after that. Because surely if you do not run away against your parents' wishes—Moral 1—then you need not have too much care of your linen closet—Moral 2—since there will be no grounds for suspicion, which means the husband will not need to have mathematical proof because he will not be in the business of murdering his wife, thus putting paid to Moral 3. Despite his satiric tone, then, Rymer intends the play to have only one moral: do not cross any boundaries in your desire and all will be well in the world.

But the only identifying mark of desire is that it crosses boundaries: this is why governments and individuals alike scramble to try and contain it in marriage, with little success. Desire is also universal, by which I mean not only that everyone experiences it—which may or may not be true—but rather that everyone suffers its effects without knowing for sure their causes. This is why what one does with one's own body can never be the entirety of one's desire; desire exceeds bodily containment in a way that makes the question of "sexual orientation" an impossible one to answer. Desire both does and does not belong to a "one" that can be defined on the basis of that desire. This is probably why Othello says further on in his speech about cause:

> Yet I'll not shed her blood,
> Nor scar that whiter skin of hers than snow,
> And smooth as monumental alabaster.
> Yet she must die, else she'll betray more men (5.2.3–6)

---

[16]Zimansky, ed., 132.

It is not only a matter of what Othello and Desdemona have done to and with one another, but rather, it is a question of what their desire has unleashed upon the world of the play. Othello is murdering Desdemona on the suspicion that she has been unfaithful to him. *And* that she might be unfaithful to other men in the future. This speech is thus both oddly personal and impersonal: my wife has betrayed me but even more, she might betray nameless and faceless other men. The cause of Desdemona's murder is both very close and far removed, immediate and distant at once, personal and universal. Desdemona's desire both does and does not belong to Othello. And this is why he murders her.

In *No Future: Queer Theory and the Death Drive*, Edelman speaks in a psychoanalytic register about the causelessness that constitutes the death drive:

> As the name for a force of mechanistic compulsion whose formal excess supersedes any end toward which it might seem to be aimed, the death drive refuses identity or the absolute privilege of any goal. Such a goal, such an end, could never be "it"; achieved, it could never satisfy. For the drive as such can only insist, and every end toward which we mistakenly interpret its insistence to pertain is a sort of grammatical placeholder, one that tempts us to read as transitive a pulsion that attains through insistence alone the satisfaction no end ever holds. Engaged in circulation around an object never adequate to fulfill it, the drive enacts the repetition that characterizes what Judith Butler has called "the repetitive propulsionality of sexuality."[17]

For Edelman, the death drive names that which cannot be named—it is the queer cause that defies logical causality. At once the thing that moves us towards an end and that insists no end is satisfactory, the death drive makes murderers of us all. Not literally— queer theory's interest in this play is not because Desdemona is murdered, but because both Othello's gulling and Desdemona's murder point to the one thing that the death drive insists on: the vanished event of desire. This desire is the embodiment of too-muchness, the remainder that persists even after all causes have been laid bare. No matter how many reasons Othello lines up to explain Desdemona's murder, they will never be enough. And no matter how many reasons Iago gives for hating Othello, they do not add up. This is why the murder scene in the play is considered so horrific by critics—not because Desdemona is murdered, but because there is no cause that can contain and explain that murder. Othello fears that Desdemona's desire is excessive, but then again, so is his own. It is the ubiquitousness of excessive desire from which Othello turns away his face in this scene.

Lest this excess be folded back into placebos about the "mysterious workings" of the heart—desire that cannot be understood because it is ineffable—with which we continually bombard ourselves, let me hasten to add that for *Othello* the working of desire is less ineffable than inevitable. It is desire's universal course towards destruction that guarantees the "grammatical placeholder" with which we explain desire cannot help us achieve

---

[17]Edelman, *No Future*, 22.

the satisfaction we are lured into thinking is possible. A causeless desire may not have an origin, but it has a destination, and it is to keep that destination at bay that we fabricate lies about love lasting forever, until death do us part. What Shakespeare (and an impressive divorce rate) suggests instead about desire is that it is always marked by the senseless pulsation of the death drive—something that cannot be accounted for in the best planned weddings. Whether that senseless pulsation throbs in Desdemona's desire to have Othello, Iago's desire to be Othello, Othello's desire to save his honour, or our desire to avert the agony of the last scene, desire always creates the desire to *understand*: Desdemona thinks she understands Othello's appeal, Iago is sure he understands his own motives, Othello is convinced he understands the extent of Desdemona's infidelity, and we assume we understand the play. The death drive, then, exists most forcefully in our desire to make sense, to understand rather than read. This means that the minute we pick up the play to read, we are in the grip of the desire to know. And once desire has been let into the house, it can only burn down the entire edifice. To a certain extent, this is true of all texts. But *Othello* turns the screws on us much more agonisingly, giving us multiple causes for desire all the while knowing that it can only end with the thrice-repeated, thrice-empty "cause". It is not Othello or Desdemona or Iago, then, who embodies the death drive in the play, it is desire itself, ours every bit as much as the text's. Rather than waiting until death do us part, desire introduces death into our lives—whether in the form of decentring the subject in relation to desire, or hurtling us towards the impossibility of understanding desire—even and especially when it promises only good things. Badiou, Edelman and Shakespeare speak in the same voice when they speak of this universal aspect of desire.

Brabantio is one of the few characters in the play who eventually understands this aspect, although his knowledge does not help him cope any better with his daughter's preposterous desire. Initially, when faced with the reality of the Othello–Desdemona marriage, he states perplexedly:

> For nature so prepost'rously to err—
> Being not deficient, blind, or lame of sense—
> Sans witchcraft could not. (1.3.75–7)

Desire must be understood; it needs to flow in orderly channels, otherwise the world as we know it will be at an end. Because we tend to follow in the footsteps of Brabantio's logic, the audience too can be counted on to pick a "cause" for Desdemona's desire and then murder. But his daughter's marriage to Othello is an indicator late in Brabantio's life that desire can never be kept in check, especially by marriage. This is why the father, after being overruled in his objection to the daughter's marriage, says spitefully to Othello: "Look to her, Moor, if thou hast eyes to see. / She has deceived her father, and may thee" (1.3.333–4). In an early echo of what Othello will bring up later in his "cause" speech, Brabantio talks about deceptions both near and far, of himself and of someone else, personal and universal. Desdemona's desire will kill. But desire kills, whether it is embodied by Desdemona or Othello or no one at all: that is its job.

Whether or not Desdemona is unfaithful to Othello is thus entirely beside the point in this play. *Othello* suggests a reading of desire in which desire is always excessive, and refers only to a vanished event that is as unknowable as it is excessive. Desire in this play keeps increasing but it never adds up. And this is how *Othello* theorises queerness: by giving us a pulsing and decentred desire that refuses identitarian specificity (there are no gay characters in the play who own their desire), by declining to provide desire with either a ground or a body (no reason can sufficiently explain desire in the text; no single body can contain the demands of desire), and by presenting us with an absence that is the foundational event of desire (many effects and no single cause). Three queers instead of one cause: the play suggests that there are always three causes when there are none. *Othello* thus allows us to invert Othello's thrice-repeated formulation of "it is the cause" so that it reads, in queer fashion, that "the cause" is never "it".

References

Altman, Joel. *The Improbability of Othello: Rhetorical Anthropology and Shakespearean Selfhood.* Chicago, IL: Chicago University Press, 2010.

———. "'Preposterous Conclusions': Eros, Enargeia, and the Composition of Othello." *Representations* 18 (spring 1987): 1–57.

Badiou, Alain. *Saint Paul: The Foundation of Universalism.* Translated by Ray Brassier. Stanford, CA: Stanford University Press, 2003.

Barnet, Sylvan. "Coleridge on Shakespeare's Villains." *Shakespeare Quarterly* 7, no. 1 (1956): 9–20.

Edelman, Lee. Interviewed by Madhavi Menon, 2011. [cited 10 January 2012]. Available from http:// shakespearequarterly.wordpress.com/2011/08/02/queer-theory-and-hamlet/.

———. *No Future: Queer Theory and the Death Drive.* Durham, NC: Duke University Press, 2004.

Fineman, Joel. "The Sound of O in *Othello*: The Real of the Tragedy of Desire." *October* 45 (summer 1988): 76–96.

Freud, Sigmund. *The Interpretation of Dreams: The Complete and Definitive Text.* Translated and edited by James Strachey. New York: Basic Books, 2010.

Jagose, Annamarie. *Queer Theory: An Introduction.* New York: New York University Press, 1997.

Kirsch, Arthur. "The Polarisation of Erotic Love in 'Othello'." *The Modern Language Review* 73, no. 4 (1978): 721–40.

Lupton, Julia Reinhard. "Othello Circumcised." In *Citizen Saints: Shakespeare and Political Theology.* Chicago, IL: Chicago University Press, 2005.

Shakespeare, William. *The Tragedy of Othello, the Moor of Venice: Folger Shakespeare Library.* Edited by Barbara Mowat and Paul Werstine. New York: Simon and Schuster, 1993.

Siemon, James. "'Nay That's Not Next: Othello V.ii in Performance 1760–1900." *Shakespeare Quarterly* 37, no. 1 (1986): 38–51.

Zimansky, Curt, (ed.), *The Critical Works of Thomas Rymer.* New Haven, CT: Yale University Press, 1956.

"After the Takeover": Shakespeare, Lacan, Žižek and the Interpassive Subject

Étienne Poulard

The starting point for this essay is the sense that we live in a world that is, perhaps more than ever before, intensely mediated. In many ways, the rise of electronic information technology in the so-called "developed world" has reinforced the principle of mediation that shapes our experience of reality. The ubiquity of information technology in our everyday lives also provides us with invaluable tools to contextualise our position as mediated subjects. In recent theoretical debates, the mediation of subjectivity has been addressed through the concept of "interpassivity". Drawing on Lacanian psychoanalysis, Slavoj Žižek uses interpassivity to conceptualise the intrinsic displacement that defines the experience of enjoyment. Interpassivity describes how enjoyment is always, by essence, displaced onto another instance (the "big Other"). The essay explores the manifestations and implications of interpassivity in technologically advanced twenty-first-century societies. Shakespearean drama provides a key entry point into the topic: Hamlet, Macbeth and Henry V throw a new light on the big Other qua symbolic instance that regulates social interactions. The Chorus of Henry V, in particular, illustrates the kernel of mediation underlying mass entertainment and opens up a reflection on the role of the media in the distribution and control of information.

They put an off button on the TV for a reason. Turn it off …[1]

Introduction

In *Shakespeare in the Present*, Terence Hawkes points out that facts and texts "don't speak at all unless and until they are inserted into and perceived as part of specific discourses which impose their own shaping requirements and agendas." Such an approach entails a recognition that facts and texts do not exist on their own, as free-floating entities. Rather, they are the result of critical operations in a specific present—that of the critic, *our* present. "We choose the facts. We choose the texts.

---

[1]President George W. Bush quoted in *C-SPAN Video Library*.

We do the inserting. We do the perceiving. Facts and texts, that is to say, don't simply speak, don't merely mean. *We* speak, *we* mean, *by* them", Hawkes insists.[2]

The idea that literary texts always crystallise contemporary preoccupations is central in the present article, whose treatment of Shakespeare reflects this notion. This is not an essay on Shakespeare though. Shakespearean drama here features as a springboard, as something to be looked through. The main topic at hand is the notion of interpassivity, made popular by Slavoj Žižek in the late 1990s.[3] While interpassivity sets the critical agenda, some of Shakespeare's plays provide an entry point into the discussion as well as a crucial platform to illustrate the displaced dynamics of interpassive subjectivity. Žižek's own considerations on *Richard II* in the light of Lacanian psychoanalysis, addressed at the beginning of the essay, pave the way for a reflection on the decentred optics of *Hamlet* and *Macbeth*.

In many different ways, Shakespearean drama can be said to stage the Lacanian notion that subjectivity is haunted by a supplementary figure, that of the "big Other"—"the agency that decides instead of us, in our place", as Žižek defines it.[4] A key feature of Žižek's theory of interpassivity, the big Other testifies to the structural alienation that shapes the subject/object relation. At the very core of interpassivity is the sensation that the object deprives us of our emotional content and takes over the process of enjoyment for us. The interpassive chorus of *Henry V*, discussed in the essay, illustrates the extent to which this constitutive displacement underlies the dynamics of enjoyment in mass entertainment.

Approached through the contemporary topic of interpassivity, Shakespearean drama provides a fascinating perspective to look at the objectification of the viewer and the cult of interactivity in the modern media. Inevitably, the essay reaches a point where it parts ways with Shakespeare, which remains a means to my theoretical ends—for the critical focus here is the present. "A Shakespeare criticism which takes that on board will aim scrupulously to seek out salient aspects of the present as a crucial trigger for its investigations", Hawkes suggests. "Reversing, to some degree, the stratagems of new historicism, it will deliberately begin with the material present and allow that to set its interrogative agenda. It will not only yearn to speak with the dead. It will aim, in the end, to talk to the living."[5]

I. Uncanny Perspectives: Shakespeare's Lacanian Optics

In the preface to *Looking Awry*, Žižek announces that Shakespeare is to be "read strictly as [a] kitsch author".[6] This "kitsch Shakespeare" turns out to be a key platform in his examination of Lacanian psychoanalysis. A few pages into the book, Žižek asserts that

---

[2]Hawkes, 3.

[3]"Interpassivity" as the act of projecting one's own self or emotions onto exterior objects was first used by the Austrian philosopher Robert Pfaller. Slavoj Žižek traces Pfaller's first use of the term to a 1996 symposium in Linz (Austria), *Die Dinge lachen an unsere Stelle* (Žižek, *The Plague of Fantasies*, 144n). See also Pfaller.

[4]Žižek, *Looking Awry*, 77.

[5]Grady and Hawkes, eds., 4.

[6]Žižek, *Looking Awry*, vii.

"*Richard II* proves beyond any doubt that Shakespeare had read Lacan."[7] He then goes on to look at his favourite passage in the play. After King Richard's departure for Ireland, the distraught Queen shares her grief with one of Richard's followers. Unexpectedly, Bushy's attempt at comforting the Queen develops into an elaborate speech on perspective:

> Each substance of a grief hath twenty shadows
> Which shows like grief itself but is not so.
> For sorrow's eye, glazèd with blinding tears,
> Divides one thing entire to many objects—
> Like perspectives, which, rightly gazed upon,
> Show nothing but confusion; eyed awry,
> Distinguish form. So your sweet majesty,
> Looking awry upon your lord's departure,
> Find shapes of grief more than himself to wail,
> Which, looked on as it is, is naught but shadows
> Of what it is not. (*RII* 2.2.14–24)[8]

This speech lays the very foundation for Žižek's interpretive method, which relies on the sense that a shift in the viewer's position can make a familiar concept radically unfamiliar. "Looking awry", to use Shakespeare's original phrase, implies that we shift our perspective in order to "distinguish form", that is to produce meaning.[9] In *Looking Awry* (named after *Richard II*), Žižek deliberately skews his critical position in order to provide a fresh outlook on Lacanian theory: "this way of 'looking awry' at Lacan makes it possible to discern features that usually escape a 'straightforward' academic look", he suggests.[10]

Repeatedly emphasised in recent scholarship, the uncanny affinity between Lacanian psychoanalysis and Shakespearean drama also stands the test of other works.[11] *Hamlet*, for instance, toys insistently with the notion of a sideways gaze that decentres subjectivity. This idea climaxes in the elaborate optics of the play within the play in Act III. While King Claudius is watching "*The Mousetrap*", a bigger play is taking place: a play that is about Hamlet watching Claudius watch another play—"I'll observe his looks", the prince had announced previously (*H* 3.2.217; 2.2.573). But Hamlet himself is under the constant scrutiny of invisible eyes posted everywhere. Although his original plan is to observe the king's looks, he is himself branded "Th'observed of all observers" by Ophelia (*H* 3.1.153). And the prince is indeed being looked at from everywhere—by Claudius' secret agents, by an inscrutable ghost, but also by audiences potentially

---

[7]Ibid., 9. For an account of the pairing of Shakespearean drama and Lacanian psychoanalysis in recent criticism, see Harris, 91–106.

[8]All references to Shakespeare's plays are from *The Norton Shakespeare* (Greenblatt et al., eds.) and are given in the text. The following abbreviations are used: *AYLI* (*As You Like It*); *H* (*Hamlet*); *HV* (*Henry V*); *M* (*Macbeth*); *O* (*Othello*); and *RII* (*Richard II*).

[9]For a detailed reading of this speech and how it can be said to inform Žižek's ideology critique, see Poulard.

[10]Žižek, *Looking Awry*, vii–viii.

[11]On this topic, see notably Reinhard Lupton and Reinhard; and Armstrong, *Shakespeare in Psychoanalysis*.

watching or reading *Hamlet*. From a Lacanian perspective, the interest of the play within the play lies in its staging of an endlessly shifting gaze: the subject's conviction of being in control of its field of vision is systematically undermined by the presence of a supplementary gaze lurking in the margins. While Claudius' central position as an observer is decentred by Hamlet's "special observance", the prince's own vantage point in the theatre in Elsinore is destabilised by a multitude of invisible eyes coming from all sides (*H* 3.2.17). The notion that the gaze manifests itself from a point that is always already elsewhere is a typical Lacanian locus: "in the scopic field, the gaze is outside, I am looked at, that is to say, I am a picture", Jacques Lacan remarked in his famous seminar on the gaze.[12] Thus, Hamlet's seemingly privileged position as a looking subject in the theatre renders him oblivious to the fact that he is also part of the picture—"the picture, certainly, is in my eye. But I am in the picture", as Lacan put it.[13] This primordial scopic estrangement also mirrors our own precarious position as viewers (readers and playgoers alike) of *Hamlet*. As the play illustrates, theatrical representation fundamentally destabilises how we see ourselves in relation to the world. Although we might like to think of ourselves as comfortably uninvolved observers, we (like Claudius) sooner or later realise that we too are in the spotlight: "we are beings who are looked at, in the spectacle of the world."[14]

The play within the play in *Hamlet* can be read as a metadramatic comment on the precarious situation of the viewer, not only in the theatre, but in the world at large. The presence of an ever-shifting gaze circumscribing the subject makes vision a fundamentally alienating experience. What destabilises subjectivity, according to Lacan, is "the pre-existence of a gaze", which testifies to the sensation that "I see only from one point, but in my existence I am looked at from all sides."[15] In *Hamlet*, the pre-existence of a gaze is epitomised in the figure of the ghost, which always already precedes the subject in the scopic field. The ghost's decentring function is dramatised at the

---

[12]Lacan, "Of the Gaze as *Objet Petit a*," 106. Martin Jay specifically locates Jacques Lacan's optics within the larger context of an "antiocularcentric discourse" in twentieth-century French philosophy and psychoanalysis (16).

[13]My own translation. Sheridan's English translation of the seminar contains a serious mistake—it reads: "the picture, certainly, is in my eye. But I am *not* in the picture" (Lacan, "Of the Gaze as *Objet Petit a*," 96). This is a problematic reversal of Lacan's original aphorism: "le tableau, certes, est dans mon œil. Mais moi, je suis dans le tableau" (*Les quatre concepts fondamentaux*, 111). Anne Marsh suggests that

> this translation has influenced the way in which Lacan has been read in the English speaking world. To be "not in the picture" means that the subject has no agency. It is similar to the way in which Foucault has been read through secondary adaptations as a determinist. Neither Lacan nor Foucault are determinist theorists but their work in translation has often been read as such. For Lacan the gaze and desire are entwined and entangled so as to produce a complex web of looking and being looked at. (47)

[14]Lacan, "Of the Gaze as *Objet Petit a*," 75. Lacan develops this locus in his seminar on *Hamlet*, "a tragedy of desire that establishes the subject in dependence on the signifier." Thus, "Hamlet is suspended in the time of the Other," and "whatever he does is only at the time of the Other" (Lacan, "Desire," 11–52).

[15]Lacan, "Of the Gaze as *Objet Petit a*," 72.

beginning of the play when one of the sentinels posted on the battlements inquires: "What, has this thing appeared again?" (*H* 1.1.19). What fascinated Jacques Derrida about this particular line in the play is that the *thing* in question has not "appeared" yet—it is literally the first reference to the ghost in the play. Thus, the first scene of *Hamlet* confronts us in effect with a *thing* that "comes back, so to speak, for the first time", Derrida points out in *Specters of Marx*.[16] The fact that the ghost's first apparition is itself haunted establishes the pre-existence of a gaze in the play. The ghost stands for the asymmetrical dialectic between the subject's eye and the objectifying gaze to which it is subjected—after all, Lacan defined the experience of "*seeing*" as that to "which I am subjected in an original way".[17] In this sense, it can be said that *Hamlet* maps out a visual regime where seeing is intrinsically obscene because it involves a radical form of exhibitionism. The ghost symbolises an omniscient gaze that comes from all sides; and although it "fixe[s] [its] eyes upon [us] … Most constantly", such a gaze cannot be allocated a point of origin because, from the beginning (and before—*especially* before), it comes from elsewhere (*H* 1.3.232–3). Derrida's thought-provoking analysis of the play suggests that the ghost, *qua* pure gaze, is at once all-seeing and unseen (presence *and* absence):

> This Thing meanwhile looks at us and sees us not see it even when it is there. A spectral asymmetry interrupts here all specularity. It de-synchronizes, it recalls us to anachrony. We will call this the *visor effect*: we do not see who looks at us.[18]

Powerfully dramatised in *Hamlet*, the desynchronising function of the gaze is a recurring Shakespearean locus. The spooky sense that we do not see who looks at us, in spite of being looked at from all sides, runs like a guiding thread in Shakespeare's Jacobean dramas—from the dark paranoia of *Measure for Measure* to the bleak panopticism of *The Tempest*.[19]

---

[16]Derrida, 4.

[17]Lacan, "Of the Gaze as *Objet Petit a*," 72.

[18]Derrida, 6–7.

[19]There is consistent debate around the issue of whether Lacan's discourse on optics is compatible with other French theories of vision, and notably Michel Foucault's reflections on panopticism. Thus, Marsh notes that

> critics have often … tended to read Jacques Lacan through the existential philosophy of Jean-Paul Sartre and combined these two interpretations of the gaze to support a Foucauldian panoptic analysis. It is therefore necessary to re-examine Lacan's thesis on the gaze in order to undermine this panoptic determinism and to recuperate a subject who is always part of the picture, especially as it is being made. In Lacan's thesis, the subject becomes a kind of virus infecting the picture. (42)

Jay (381–4) traces this ongoing panopticisation of Lacan to an essay by Jacques-Alain Miller—Lacan's son-in-law and the editor of the French journal of psychoanalysis *Ornicar?*. First published in 1975 as "Le despotisme de l'utile: la machine panoptique de Jeremy Bentham," the essay examines Bentham's 1791 treatise on a model prison. Considering the concept of the panopticon, Miller suggests that "this configuration sets up a brutal dissymmetry of visibility. The enclosed space lacks depth; it is spread out and open to a single, solitary central eye. It is bathed in light. Nothing and no one can be hidden inside it—except the gaze itself, the invisible omnivoyeur.

In *Macbeth*, the witches occupy the same οὐτόπος ("non-space") as the ghost in *Hamlet*: they epitomise the pre-existence of a gaze that lurks in the margins of theatricality.[20] Their desynchronising function transpires in the first scene of the play, as the French poet Stéphane Mallarmé pointed out in "La fausse entrée des sorcières dans *Macbeth*". In the essay, Mallarmé suggests that the witches' supposed entrance—"*Enter three WITCHES*"—is not really an entrance (*M* 1.1.0). Instead, they seem to be already present before the performance starts: it is "as if the curtain has simply risen a minute too soon, betraying fateful goings-on."[21] In this sense, the untimely rising of the curtain (*lever de rideau*) lets us peek at something that should have remained hidden: the extra-dramatic presence of a gaze that stares back at us from the gaping darkness of the stage. Rehearsing Mallarmé's insight, Jean-Michel Rabaté notes that "the curtain that separates us from the mystery has been raised too early, forcing us to peep through a darkness that was not meant for us."[22] In the theatre, the curtain embodies (although it is also supposed to hide it) the "darkness that was not meant for us", which corresponds to the inscrutable moment that precedes representation. But in *Macbeth*, the curtain is by definition *always* lifted too early, letting us "peep through the blanket of the dark" (*M* 1.5.51). Instead of entering the page/stage, the witches become visible, suddenly and intermittently, in the epileptic blink of lightning

---

Surveillance confiscates the gaze for its own profit, appropriates it, and submits the inmate to it" (Miller, 4). But, as Jay notes, "Miller was not the first to criticize the coercive implications of Bentham's panoptic dream. ... Nor was his critique the most influential, that honor going to Michel Foucault's more extensive discussion in *Discipline and Punish*" (383)—also published in 1975. While "Jacques-Alain Miller was the first psychoanalyst to see the panoptic model as the architectural embodiment of Lacan's theory of the eye and the gaze," Marsh argues that "Miller really offers a psycho-social reading, much like Foucault's. There is no direct reference to Lacan and the question of the subject's desire, which is fundamental to psychoanalysis, is not addressed." By contrast, "the field of vision explored by Lacan is full of traps, it is a labyrinth rather than a panopticon" (Marsh, 42 and 46). However, Jay points out (in relation to both Miller and Louis Althusser) that "the psychological analysis of vision in Lacan could easily be absorbed into a social and political critique in which *voir* was linked with both *savoir* and *pouvoir*" (383). And indeed, "Lacanian and Foucauldian positions have been confounded by an unstable theoretical marriage," Marsh observes. "The geometric scheme, embodied by the panopticon, is about *space* and does not adequately explain the function of the eye, let alone the gaze which is active within the relationship between the eye and light, enmeshed within a complex corporeal and psychological space." In contrast with Foucauldian optics, "Lacan's concept of the subject as blind spot, a stain within representation, allows for a more complex and less homogenous interpretation and understanding of visual representation," Marsh claims (42, 46 and 48). In his seminar on "The Line and the Light," Lacan remarks: "if I am anything in the picture, it is always in the form of the screen, which I earlier called the stain, the spot" ("The Line and the Light", 97).

[20]Terry Eagleton makes a similar point when he argues that "the witches figure as the 'unconscious' of the drama" (2).

[21]"*Ouverture sur un chef-d'œuvre : comme, en le chef-d'œuvre, le* rideau *s'est* simplement *levé, une minute,* trop tôt, *trahissant des menées fatidiques*" (Mallarmé, 348). Translated from the French by Barbara Johnson and cited in Garber, 123–4.

[22]Rabaté, 73.

strokes—"*Thunder and lightning*" (*M* 1.1.0).[23] Following Mallarmé, Marjorie Garber remarks that "the witches do not *enter*, are not described as entering the scene in the ordinary way of actors—instead they *appear: extra-scéniquement*, uncannily present."[24] What the witches stand for in the first scene of *Macbeth* is a presence that precedes all presence, an "extra-scénique" gaze that transcends the spatio-temporal boundaries of the stage and decentres the subject's fantasised ontological centre. This oblique gaze does not only address the characters in the play; it also circumscribes potential audiences: "the spectator of the play *Macbeth*, and Macbeth himself as spectator of the witches' play, are both thereby subjected to a gaze, *photographed* as components within the spectacle", Philip Armstrong observes.[25] Thus, the peripheral gaze of the witches imparts the sense that we are not only spectators of the play: crucially, we are also part of the performance. From the beginning, even *before* the play starts, we are unwittingly "*photographed* as components within the spectacle". When we go to the theatre, we obey a scopic drive that makes us want to "look at things" compulsively: we watch the world as spectacle.[26] However, the originary split between the subject's eye and the object's gaze posited by Lacan guarantees that we are fundamentally looked at in the spectacle of the world. Rephrasing this foundational axiom of Lacanian psychoanalysis, Žižek writes: "when I look at an object, the object is always already gazing at me, and from a point at which I cannot see it."[27]

The dramatic status of the witches in *Macbeth* is strikingly unclear: although they are characters in the play (they are listed in the *dramatis personæ*), they also function as a metadramatic commentary, in the manner of a chorus. Such hybridity is apparent in the first scene, where they figure not so much as characters but rather as narrators introducing the play in a few words.

FIRST WITCH	When shall we three meet again? In thunder, lightning, or in rain?
SECOND WITCH	When the hurly-burly's done, When the battle's lost and won.
THIRD WITCH	That will be ere the set of the sun.
FIRST WITCH	Where the place?

[23]"A lightning flash is composed of a series of strokes with an average of about four. The length and duration of each lightning stroke vary, but typically average about 30 microseconds (the average peak power per stroke is about 10^{12} watts)" (Christian and Cook, n.p.).

[24]Garber, 123.

[25]Armstrong, "Guilty Creatures," 245. See also Armstrong, *Shakespeare's Visual Regime.*

[26]Although Freud had suggested oral, anal, and genital drives, Lacan added the scopic drive to the main categories of drive: "it is not, after all, for nothing that analysis is not carried out face to face. The split between eye and gaze will enable us, you will see, to add the scopic drive to the list of the drives" (Lacan, "Of the Gaze as *Objet Petit a.*", 78).

[27]Žižek, *Looking Awry*, 109.

SECOND WITCH   Upon the heath.

THIRD WITCH   There to meet with Macbeth (*M* 1.1.1–7)

The whole plot of *Macbeth* is here summarised in the space of seven lines: recalling those two-minute comic adaptations by the Reduced Shakespeare Company, the first scene of the play is a bit of a narratorial joke, anticipating subsequent subversions of the play.[28] The reference to the main protagonist—"There to meet with Macbeth"—announces the fateful encounter that is to take place later in the same act. Like a chorus, the witches speak catachronically (their utterances appear in a different order from that of the narrative which unfolds for audiences): in this way, they give us glimpses of the action to come. But are they merely anticipating the action in a descriptive mode or are they actually instigating the play performatively? The strong performative dimension of the witches' utterances suggests that they hold a form of authorial agency. Such performativity is encapsulated in the third witch's impatient injunction, "Anon" (meaning "right now" or "at once" in Shakespeare's English), the aim of which, it seems, is to conjure up immediate dramatic presence (*M* 1.1.8). So, does the witches' famous aphorism, "Fair is foul, and foul is fair", crystallise the play's reversal of established values or is it a generative statement (performative) that engenders the play *de facto* (*M* 1.1.10)? There is no ready-made answer to this question: *Macbeth* famously keeps the mystery intact regarding the origin and agency of its witches, whose dramatic intervention is, in their own words, "a deed without a name" (*M* 4.1.65). While the witches are part of *Macbeth* as we may read it or watch it, their position in the scopic field is constantly shifting, which conveys an uncanny effect of presence as absence (just like the ghost in *Hamlet*). The primordial ontological shift that the witches embody is precisely what makes *Macbeth* so relevant to contemporary reflections on subjectivity. Their role as metadramatic commentary originates in the empty dramatic space (οὐτόπος) from which they speak. In a Žižekian sense, what the witches symbolise is the necessary perspective, the "awry" view that allows the observer to "distinguish form". Readers and viewers of *Macbeth* often wonder what the witches actually "do" in the play. On the level of dramatic enjoyment, at least, it is clear: they tell us *how to enjoy* the play. Like the chorus of Greek tragedy, the witches are the managers of enjoyment.

II. Interpassivity: On the Displacement of Subjectivity in Mass Entertainment

In *The Ethics of Psychoanalysis*, Lacan comments on the role of the classical chorus in the theatrical economy of enjoyment:

> When you go to the theatre in the evening, you are preoccupied by the affairs of the day, by the pen that you lost, by the check that you will have to sign the next day. You

---

[28] *The Reduced Shakespeare Company: The Complete Works of William Shakespeare (Abridged)* is available on DVD. See their two-minute rendition of *Macbeth* on YouTube (The Reduced Shakespeare Company).

shouldn't give yourselves too much credit. Your emotions are taken charge of by the healthy order displayed on the stage. The Chorus takes care of them. The emotional commentary is done for you. ... Therefore, you don't have to worry; even if you don't feel anything, the Chorus will feel in your stead.[29]

As Lacan points out, the theatrical chorus displaces subjectivity by taking charge of the audience's emotions. Not only are we told what to feel but *it* feels for us; we are "felt for", so to speak. Nowhere in Shakespeare's plays is this idea better illustrated than in *Henry V*, whose coercive chorus epitomises the Lacanian big Other (as Žižek remarks, "the 'big Other' designates precisely the agency that decides instead of us, in our place"). One of the most fascinating aspects of *Henry V* lies in the Chorus' strategy of objectification of (what it sees as) its audience. Let us pretend for a while that we are in the position of the imaginary audience under address. At all times, the Chorus' dizzying melodramatic logorrhoea ensures that the emotional commentary is done for us: all we are required to do, it seems, is to watch the Chorus enjoy the play in our stead. In Act IV, for instance, it insists on the need for us to "sit patiently and inly ruminate", to "sit and see"—meanwhile, the emotional content is taken charge of (*HV* 4.0.24; 4.0.52). Each choric intervention is an occasion to bombard us with repetitive orders apparently aimed at depriving us of our free will. While the Chorus revels in the bombastic grandeur of its historical narrative, we are constantly asked to "suppose" or "imagine" that we actively participate in the dramatic deployment. Specifically, the Chorus repeatedly demands that we "behold" or "see" the visions it invokes—the two verbs recur ten and five times respectively over the six short choruses. The numerous appeals to the spectators create a powerful sense of interactivity; we are given a central role in the dramatic process. However, the situation in which the object carries out the emotional commentary for "me" is the exact opposite of interactivity, as Žižek explains:

> The other side of this interactivity is interpassivity. The obverse of interacting with the object (instead of just passively following the show) is the situation in which the object itself takes from me, deprives me of, my own passivity, so that it is the object itself that enjoys the show instead of me, relieving me of the duty to enjoy myself.[30]

In *Henry V*, the deprivation of the viewer's passivity is enacted by the Chorus taking over the process of enjoyment. In this sense, the Chorus appears as the ultimate symbol of interpassivity. Thus, when the Chorus enjoys for me, "*I am passive through the Other.*"[31] The most disturbing aspect of interpassivity lies in the way the object can experience emotions in my place: "it is as if some figure of the other—in this case, the Chorus—can take over from us and experience for us our innermost and most spontaneous feelings and attitudes, inclusive of crying and laughing",

---

[29]Lacan, *The Ethics of Psychoanalysis*, 310.
[30]Žižek, *How to Read Lacan*, 24.
[31]Ibid., 26.

Žižek writes.[32] In *Henry V*, the Chorus exults, manifestly intoxicated by its own narrative: "now sits expectation in the air" (*HV* 2.0.8). As the feeling of anticipation is experienced for us by "some figure of the other", we are deprived of our emotional content. The main effect of being "felt for" in this way is that the status of the audience *qua* positively invested subject is cancelled. In Lacanian terminology, the matheme $ refers to the inherently barred or split status of the subject, which is constituted through a lack. Thus, "the very fact that I can be deprived of even my innermost psychic ('mental') content, that the big Other (or fetish) can laugh for me, and so on, is what makes me $, the barred subject, the pure void with no positive substantial content."[33] A modern equivalent of the theatrical chorus would be canned laughter—artificial audience laughter inserted into TV programmes. Canned laughter was first devised by the American sound engineer Charles Rolland Douglass in the 1950s, when the need to simulate live audiences became pressing due to the ever-increasing costs of live TV sitcoms.[34] The "Laff Box", as it was then dubbed, was a huge tape machine which stood "more than two feet tall, operated like an organ, with a keyboard to select the style, sex and age of the laugh as well as a foot pedal to time the length of the reaction."[35] On a purely mechanical level, canned laughter emulates the "genuine" (or rather expected) emotional response of an audience. However, its most far-reaching effect is that it ultimately supplants the so-called genuine emotion it purports to stage. In this sense, it is not sufficient to say that canned laughter imitates human feelings; rather, it literally takes the place of them. For Žižek, the process of emotional substitution that canned laughter activates epitomises the interpassive process.

> When I come home in the evening too exhausted to engage in meaningful activity, I just tune in to a TV sitcom; even if I do not laugh, but simply stare at the screen, tired after a hard day's work, I nonetheless feel relieved after the show. It is as if the TV were literally laughing in my place, instead of me.[36]

Canned laughter empties me of my emotional content: it enjoys for me when I am too tired to think or engage with whatever I am watching (which is no longer relevant). As such, it highlights a central function of mass entertainment, which is to relieve me of the duty to enjoy myself.[37]

Another TV-related example of interpassivity is the practice that consists in recording films (or other programmes) and storing them for future viewing—"for which, of course, there is almost never time", Žižek points out:

---

[32]Ibid., 22.
[33]Žižek, *The Plague of Fantasies*, 159.
[34]Cellania.
[35]Bernstein.
[36]Žižek, "Will You Laugh."
[37]In a paper called "The Enjoying Machine," Mladen Dolar offers "a glance into the prehistory of interpassivity" in the arts (136–47). The paper was given at a conference in Istanbul in 2010.

> Although I do not actually watch the films, the very awareness that the films I love are stored in my video library gives me a profound satisfaction, and occasionally enables me to simply relax and indulge in the exquisite art of *far niente*—as if the VCR is in a way *watching them for me, in my place.*[38]

Video recording is a significant modern instance that illustrates the extent to which mass entertainment relies on a big Other figure enjoying in my place. Thus, when the video player is watching the films for me, I can afford to do nothing: I can truly relax. *At last*, I can watch TV in peace because I know that the "important stuff" is taken care of by the Other—here again, I am being "felt for". Far from being an empowering activity, watching TV fundamentally implies that *I am being watched*. The ultimate example for the idea that enjoyment relies, at heart, on the displacement of subjectivity is pornography, which functions more and more in an interpassive way, Žižek implies. Thus, "X-rated films are no longer primarily the means to excite the user for his (or her) solitary masturbatory activity—just staring at the screen where 'the action takes place' is sufficient, it is enough for me to observe how others enjoy in the place of me."[39] In effect, pornography magnifies the core principle of alienation that underlies the whole experience of watching television. If pornography is so unnerving, it is precisely because it takes us too close to this principle by bringing to the surface the kernel of obscenity that sustains mass entertainment.[40]

Ultimately, what pornography helps us realise is the extent to which mediated entertainment in all its forms is inherently pornographic. Taking the example of Shakespeare again, the intrinsic obscenity of the modern industry of large-scale entertainment can be read in the very geography of Elizabethan London. In Shakespeare's time, playhouses were typically relegated to the outskirts of the city, along with brothels. This significant geographical determination asserts theatricality's elective affinity with pornography—from the Greek *pornē*, literally meaning "prostitution". The prostitutive nature of theatre is dramatised in *Henry V*, with a promiscuous Chorus that flirts with its audience relentlessly:

> ...the scene
> Is now transported, gentles, to Southampton.

---

[38]Žižek, *How to Read Lacan*, 24.

[39]Ibid.

[40]This kind of close-up effect can be found elsewhere in popular culture—and most notably in David Lynch's films, when the camera typically zooms in on an apparently insignificant detail and suddenly reveals the primordial substance of life, swarming with disgusting larvae. A famous example would be that of *Blue Velvet*, which opens on an idyllic image of American suburbs: blue sky, red poppies, white fences, waving firemen and well-groomed kids crossing the street. The scene's dream-like quality culminates in the figure of a middle-aged man watering his garden. However, the harmonious feeling soon disintegrates when the man suddenly suffers a stroke and collapses. The camera then zooms in on the grass, revealing a multitude of cockroaches crawling about. In the next scene, the main protagonist Jeffrey Beaumont (Kyle MacLachlan) finds a severed ear in a field; a close up reveals it to be infested with ants. For Žižek's analysis of *Blue Velvet*, see "David Lynch, or, the Feminine Depression," 113–29. For an extensive discussion of *Blue Velvet* in view of Žižek's theories, see McGowan, 90–109.

There is the playhouse now, there must you sit,
And thence to France shall we convey you safe,
And bring you back, charming the narrow seas
To give you gentle pass—for if we may
We'll not offend one stomach with our play. (*HV* 2.0.34–40)

Throughout *Henry V*, the Chorus refers to its audience as "gentles"—which, in Shakespeare's time, was synonymous with "well-born", "honourable" or "noble". However, this systematic gentrification is only a preliminary stage in the lewd flirtatious strategy of the Chorus, which then offers to take its spectators to France, "charming the narrow seas" to give them "gentle pass". The proclaimed destination gives us a clue as to how the proposition should be read: the French word *passe*, a euphemism for sexual gratification, is generally used in the expression *maison de passe* (literally "brothel"). So the Chorus' figurative pledge to "give ... gentle pass" to its audience is also a straightforward proposition to pleasure them in a sexual way—as well as a very convincing demonstration that from being "felt for" to being "felt up" there is a very fine line. We are in the presence of a sexually aggressive Chorus that "makes a pass" at us. It flirts with us, chats us up, comes on to us. *Il nous drague!* (as the French would say). The expression is very appropriate here as it nails down two essential features of the Chorus' naughty flirtation with its fantasised audience: while coming on to us in an overtly sexual way, it also "drags" us quite literally—a double function that recalls that of the prostitute, who has to be promiscuous and engaging in order to attract customers. Thus, in *Henry V*, the Chorus drags its audience to a performance by making explicit promises of sexual gratification. Such a perverted little dramatic strategy illustrates the extent to which theatre is the pornographic institution *par excellence*.

Ultimately, pornography crystallises the extent to which staged entertainment relies on the viewer being assigned the status of an object.

> Contrary to the commonplace according to which, in pornography, the other (the person shown on the screen) is degraded to an object of our voyeuristic pleasure, we must stress that it is the spectator himself who effectively occupies the position of the object. The real subjects are the actors on the screen trying to rouse us sexually, while we, the spectators, are reduced to a paralyzed object-gaze.[41]

Žižek's insight prompts the sense that pornography is nothing but a metonymy for mass entertainment. What pornography does, in effect, is magnify the obscene dynamics of enjoyment underlying theatre, television or cinema. In other words, it makes apparent something that is already *there* in the visual arts. Likewise, the anti-ocularcentric play within the play of *Hamlet* and the Chorus *dragueur* of *Henry V* both testify to theatre's capacity to reflect on its own alienating function in relation to the viewer's eye. The "paralysed object-gaze" that Žižek locates on the side of the viewer in pornography is also a favourite locus of contemporary film. The idea that vision is at heart an alienating

---

[41] Žižek, *Looking Awry*, 110.

experience for the subject is staged in one of the most memorable episodes of Stanley Kubrick's film adaptation from Anthony Burgess' novel, *A Clockwork Orange*.[42] Psychopathic delinquent Alex DeLarge is the leader of a small band of thugs whose main occupation is to indulge in "ultra-violence". After murdering a woman in her house, Alex is captured by the police and sentenced to fourteen years in prison. Two years into his sentence, he is offered an alternative procedure: the Ludovico technique—an experimental aversion therapy which aims at rehabilitating criminals within two weeks. The "therapy" consists in forcing the subject to watch violent images for protracted periods of time while under the effect of nausea-inducing drugs; the use of iron specula guarantees that the victim's eyes remain open at all times. It is probably not a coincidence that the scene bears striking similarities with the play within the play in *Hamlet*. Does not Alex's "paralysed object-gaze" in the experimental scientific cinema exactly match Hamlet's position as "the observed of all observers" in the theatre in Elsinore? In both situations, the subject is staged as deprived of its privileged viewing position. In *A Clockwork Orange*, the possibility of such a vantage point is undermined by the doctors' ubiquitous gaze, coming from all sides and circumscribing their patient. The dehumanising effect of this medical gaze, all-seeing but unseen, is implied by the spectral presence of the doctors at the back of the cinema: merged in the blinding halo of the projector's light, they are hardly discernable, except for their ghost-like white coats.

III. A New Media Order: The Cult of Interactivity

While films and theatre plays occasionally give us fleeting glimpses of the principle of alienation underlying mediated representation, the objectification of the viewing subject culminates in TV adverts, which offer a concentrated version of this principle. The notion of a *vox ex machina* that takes charge of our most intimate emotions is staged to perfection in adverts, which almost invariably feature a voice coming out of nowhere uttering the most random injunctions. Žižek emphasises the extent to which this ghostly voice is another hallmark of interpassivity: "Do we not witness 'interpassivity' in a great number of today's publicity spots or posters which, as it were, passively enjoy the product instead of us? (Coke cans containing the inscription 'Ooh! Ooh! What taste!' emulate the ideal customer's reaction in advance.)"[43] Most advertising comments come across as gratuitous and utterly random. However, from a theoretical point of view, it can be said that a key function of the floating advertising voice is that it passively *enjoys* the product instead of us.[44] The presence of the big Other in advertisement manifests itself as a God-like voice coming from nowhere and everywhere at the same time and regulating consumer enjoyment. Ultimately, TV

---

[42]Kubrick.

[43]Žižek, *The Plague of Fantasies*, 145.

[44]It is certainly no accident that the communication strategy of big multinational companies like Coca-Cola revolves around the very notion of enjoyment. See one of their relatively recent press releases: "'Open Happiness' and Enjoy Life's Simple Pleasures With Coca-Cola" (The Coca-Cola Company).

adverts testify to the fact that even the most intimate emotions have the potential to be transferred onto others without losing their sincerity. In this sense, the hovering advertising voice reminds us that the emotional commentary provided by the TV set is nothing but an updated version of the classical chorus that not only urges us to enjoy but literally enjoys for us.[45]

For Žižek, adverts, pornography and canned laughter are specific symptoms of capitalism and the way it shapes our everyday reality through the small screen. Canned laughter, in particular, appears as a typical symptom in that its function is that of an obscene supplement that cannot be elucidated. As such, it stands for the cryptic *objet petit a* of Lacanian psychoanalysis, which constitutes the point at which the observer is already inscribed in the observed scene. Canned laughter is based on the assumption that it is possible to emulate the ideal customer's reaction in advance. Paradoxically, it is well known that canned laughter irrupts in the most arbitrary ways in the middle of TV series and does not even make sense most of the time—which is precisely what makes it so traumatic and profoundly alienating. The most puzzling aspect of canned laughter lies in the way it always fulfils its function of taking charge of the audience's emotional response, especially when we know that its structural arbitrariness is a widely accepted fact that remains oddly unquestioned. If canned laughter "works" so well, Žižek explains, it is because it conditions the relation of interpassivity between the TV set and its viewer:

---

[45]The pervasive commenting voice in televised football matches represents another hallmark of interpassivity that could be explored in parallel with the practice of sweetening—for "even live sports presentations are sweetened now, with augmented boos, gasps, and cheers from the crowd" (Cellania). In terms of communication strategy, every TV programme addresses a target audience, at which a specific message is aimed. In this sense, what marks the point of origin of a TV programme is the anticipation of the desire of an imagined audience. The wedding of Prince William and Catherine Middleton, which took place on 29 April 2011 in Westminster Abbey, offers a significant example of interpassive anticipation. What is striking about this "event" is *not* the fact that it was supposedly appropriated by the media; rather, we must recognise that it was the media that literally brought it into existence. Unanimously referred to as "The Royal Wedding" by journalists across the world, this so-called "event" was invested with international implications from the very beginning—that is, even before it took place. Underlying the superficial universalism of the phrase "The Royal Wedding" is a disturbing message of Western logocentrism. The naming of an event, which often pre-dates the event itself, is a very important step in the strategy of the mainstream media, whose key role in determining our empirical knowledge of "the world" is too often overlooked. Anticipatory naming is a good example of the extent to which a mediatised event always starts before it actually takes place. Although it has been pointed out, over and over in fact, that the celebration attracted an estimated TV audience of two billion people (i.e. more than a third of the entire world population), the figure has been fiercely challenged (news.com.au). Provided by the Conservative Culture Secretary Jeremy Hunt (who, unsurprisingly, turned out to be in charge of the "event"), the two-billion figure was announced more than three weeks before the wedding (REUTERS). Reports following the wedding differed widely though, suggesting an actual TV audience of 300 million (*sportingintelligence*). This huge discrepancy testifies to the media's absolute power to create an event *ex nihilo*. The mediatisation, advertising and broadcasting of "The Royal Wedding" epitomise the interpassive experience whereby the TV set takes charge and by the same token deprives us of our emotions. Characteristically, the mediatisation of this super-event relied on the creation of an "ideal viewer"—in this case, the whole world. The main effect of such large-scale audience foreclosure is the negation of individual free will: such a globalised media strategy relies on the disturbing notion that our most intimate desires can be anticipated and acted out with implacable precision.

After some supposedly funny or witty remark, you can hear the laughter and the applause included in the soundtrack of the show itself. Here we have the exact counterpart of the Chorus in antique tragedy; it's here that we have to look for "living Antiquity". That is to say, why this laughter? The first possible answer— that it serves to remind us when to laugh—is interesting enough because it implies the paradox that laughter is a matter of duty and not of some spontaneous feeling. But this answer isn't sufficient, because usually we don't laugh. The only correct answer would then be that the other—embodied in the TV set—is relieving us even of our duty to laugh, i.e., is laughing instead of us. So, even if, tired from the hard day's stupid work, we did nothing all evening but gaze drowsily into the TV screen, we can say afterwards that objectively, through the medium of the other, we had a really good time.[46]

As Žižek points out, canned laughter always seems to intervene at the wrong time. In fact, there is a strange untimeliness that guarantees that whenever the TV set is laughing we are not laughing. The trademark arbitrariness of canned laughter (and the practice of sweetening in general) is explored in David Lynch's series of short films *Rabbits*.[47] The series stages three humanoid rabbits (Suzie, Jane and Jack) in a room. Their terse conversation is punctuated by traumatic outbreaks of canned laughter. The general atmosphere, sustained by Angelo Badalamenti's cataleptic soundtrack, is deliberately gloomy and fraught with an implicit sense of menace. The tagline that introduces *Rabbits* on Lynch's website sets the tone: "In a nameless city, deluged by a continuous rain, three rabbits live with a fearful mystery."[48] There is clearly a sense of disjunction between the "fearful mystery" and the explosive bouts of canned laughter, seemingly triggered by some of the lines spoken by Jane (Laura Harring)—for example, "What time is it?", "There have been no calls today", "Do not forget that today is Friday" or "There is something I would like to say to you, Suzie."[49] Whenever Jack (Scott Coffey) enters the room, the fake audience whoops, cheers and applauds at great length. It is most unlikely that we, the so-called "real" audience, will be laughing, whooping, cheering and applauding while watching *Rabbits* though. Superimposed on traumatic incursions, including the sudden appearance of a burning hole in the wall or the intrusion of a demonic voice talking backwards, canned laughter has the potential to reduce spectators to a paralyzed object-gaze.

But does interpassivity, insofar as it is a key aspect of modern subjectivity, necessarily have to be a disempowering mechanism? In *The Plague of Fantasies*, Žižek insists on the coexistence of two seemingly contradictory aspects of the interpassive subject: while on the one hand the big Other deprives us of our individual capacity to enjoy, it also takes over the mechanical, repetitive, and alienating functions inherent to the process of enjoyment.[50] Far from being antagonistic, these two aspects of interpassivity

---

[46]Žižek, "The Lacanian Real."
[47]Lynch, *Rabbits*. Most of *Rabbits* features on *The Lime Green Set* DVD collection. Some of the footage also appears in Lynch's film *Inland Empire*. See also, *LynchNet: The David Lynch Resource*.
[48]*LynchNet: The David Lynch Resource*.
[49]See episode one from Lynch, *Rabbits*.
[50]Žižek, *The Plague of Fantasies*, 147.

complement and generate each other in a circular movement; this uncanny reversibility challenges the typical postmodern impasse of the disarticulated subject. Žižek insists on the liberating potential contained within the interpassive process:

> By surrendering my innermost content, including my dreams and anxieties, to the Other, a space opens up in which I am free to breathe: when the Other laughs for me, I am free to take a rest; when the Other is sacrificed instead of me, I am free to go on living with the awareness that I did atone for my guilt; and so on.[51]

The relieving function of the big Other is evident in the context of mediated entertainment: when the TV set is laughing for me I am relieved of the burden to enjoy. Obviously, this feature culminates when the TV is turned off. In place of the usual monotonous voice telling me what and how to enjoy, there is suddenly silence and the possibility for peaceful introspection: "a space opens up in which I am free to breathe". For this space to open, the most basic requirement is awareness—and specifically, awareness that the big Other is taking charge of the enjoyment, at this very moment, as when I record films for future viewing. The simple knowledge that the films are stored in my video library and that the Other is watching them for me gives rise to a profound sense of satisfaction (which lasts as long as I make sure *never* to watch the films). Thus, the liberating potential of interpassivity can be activated through the symbolic recognition of the deferral of enjoyment effected by the big Other.[52]

Such awareness causes the ubiquitous injunction to enjoy to be temporarily suspended. As Žižek notes,

> the only way really to account for the satisfaction and liberating potential of being able to enjoy through the Other—of being relieved of one's enjoyment and displacing it on to the Other—is to accept that enjoyment is not an immediate spontaneous state, but is sustained by a superego imperative: as Lacan emphasized again and again, the ultimate content of the superego injunction is "Enjoy!"[53]

The displacement of enjoyment can be viewed in two different lights: either as an ineluctable symptom of alienation inherent to mass entertainment or as the opening of a space of relative freedom where (for a change) nothing is expected of me. By "looking awry", it is possible to recognise the intrinsically mediated structure of enjoyment. To start with, we need to accept that there is no such thing as unmediated enjoyment, that it is not a spontaneous state. The recognition that I always enjoy through the Other is a first step in circumventing the superego injunction that tells us to enjoy at all

---

[51]Ibid., 141.

[52]See Stephen Collins' cartoon, "After the Takeover," reproduced in this article (Figure 1). From the perspective of Pete-the-screen, the humanoid "Fleshbag 5" is "so boring it really frees [him] up to live [his] life." Perhaps the most thought-provoking aspect of the cartoon lies in its reversal of the conventional relation between humans and technology. By turning their human off, the walking screens are finally able to live their lives to the full—for Pete and Vince, this means they are free to "go and have sex in a field."

[53]Žižek, *The Plague of Fantasies*, 147.

Figure 1 "After the Takeover", by Stephen Collins (reproduced with the permission of the cartoonist: originally appeared in *The Guardian*, 28 September 2012).

times. If we shift our view, we may realise that there is no need to run anxiously after enjoyment (as most humans do) for the good reason that it cannot be attained. Through this recognition, Žižek concludes, "one is relieved of the monstrous *duty* to enjoy."[54]

One of the most common threats associated with the modern media is that they turn us into mindless puppets, that they stop us from thinking by cramming our heads with lies all day long. Such a threat implies that the ubiquitous mediatic voice takes over our personal thinking space, decides for us and ultimately prevents us from taking action. In recent times, the paranoiac motif of an overarching governmental conspiracy arguably climaxed during the Cold War period. George Orwell's famous novel *Nineteen Eighty-Four* offers a graphic account of how the masses can be turned into obedient passive consumers through media control.[55] As a result of the obsession with security and information control in our so-called "developed" societies, Orwell's panoptic nightmare has become an everyday reality for many human beings. The systematic centralisation of the media by giant corporations over the last few decades tends to corroborate the visionary quality of his narrative.[56] The ongoing mediatisation of our private space has also profoundly altered the way we relate to knowledge—notably through the emergence of widely available alternative sources of information online. In technologically advanced societies, information is now available everywhere, at all times, with an almost infinite range of points of view. The fact is that "we", technologically advanced subjects, are constantly bombarded with messages coming from everywhere.

---

[54]Ibid., 148.

[55]Orwell.

[56]In 1983, the vast majority of the news media in the United States was controlled by approximately fifty corporations. By contrast, the ownership of the news media is now concentrated in the hands of six monolithic corporations: Time Warner, Walt Disney, Viacom, News Corporation, CBS Corporation and NBC Universal. See *The Economic Collapse*.

Besides giving us an illusion of democratic freedom, the sheer excess of points of view can easily make us feel overwhelmed. There is often a looming sense that all the interactive demands surrounding us may overtake us, should we fail to respond to them. Far from limiting our field of action, such overabundance opens up so many possibilities that it robs us of our passivity, Žižek argues:

> In contrast to the commonplace according to which the new media turn us into passive consumers who just stare blindly at the screen, one should claim that the so-called threat of the new media lies in the fact that they deprive us of our passivity, of our authentic passive experience, and thus prepare us for the mindless frenetic activity.[57]

A key characteristic of the new media is their reliance on interactivity, namely the fact that we are constantly invited to participate in the making and passing on of information. The flip side of this fashionable interactivity is, of course, interpassivity, through which we are ultimately deprived of our "authentic passive experience". In other words, the pervasive proximity of information provokes a maddening urge to participate—this cause/effect relation is a core feature of the new media order. By keeping us from being passive, the media "prepare us for the mindless frenetic activity": from everywhere now, we are pressed not only to have an opinion about everything but also to share it within a dazzling multitude of cyber-communities. Social networking platforms such as *Facebook* or *Twitter* relentlessly perpetuate the cult of interactivity (although these services only represent the tip of the iceberg). The injunction to participate or to take action also manifests itself in the form of ubiquitous online comment bars inviting users to give their opinion on the most insignificant topics. Like the Chorus of *Henry V*, comment bars project a fashionable illusion of democracy. Feedback is indeed a crucial feature of the new media order in which we live: customer complaint services, in particular, epitomise the cult of interactivity. The possibility to complain conveys the powerful message that every single individual can make a difference in the way the world works. The new media train us to be active at all times by ensuring that we are kept busy doing "something". And *what* we are actually doing does not really matter, Žižek observes—as long as we carry on thinking (within the boundaries of the established media order) and contributing to the great interactive dream:

> Even in much of today's progressive politics, the danger is not passivity but pseudo-activity, the urge to be active and participate. People intervene all the time, attempting to "do something", academics participate in meaningless debates; the truly difficult thing is to step back and withdraw from it. Those in power often prefer even a critical participation to silence—just to engage us in a dialogue, to make sure that our ominous passivity is broken. Against such an interpassive mode, in which we are active all the time to make sure that nothing will really change, the first truly critical step is to *withdraw into passivity* and to refuse to participate.[58]

---

[57] Žižek, *The Plague of Fantasies*, 159.
[58] Žižek, *How to Read Lacan*, 26–7.

By engaging us at all times, the new media order guarantees that our "ominous passivity" is kept in check. The superimposition of informational voices creates psychic chaos and confusion: it makes us oblivious to the intrinsic quality of silence and the value of non-engagement.

Conclusion

By way of a conclusion, returning to Shakespeare one more time might prove helpful. Shakespearean drama features some key characters that deliberately refuse to embrace the staged resolution. A significant figure, in that respect, is that of Jaques in *As You Like It*. As the play draws to a close, the melancholic lord declines the invitation to take part in the festivities, preferring the quiet of an "abandoned cave".

JAQUES	– So, to your pleasures; I am for other than for dancing measures.
DUKE SENIOR	Stay, Jaques, stay.
JAQUES	To see no pastime, I. What you would have I'll stay to know at your abandoned cave. (*AYLI* 5.4.181–5)

Although mildly disruptive, Jaques' refusal to return to court after the pastoral interlude is relatively harmless to the established order. By contrast, Iago's obstinate silence at the end of *Othello* exposes a more disturbing and radical side of non-engagement.

> Demand me nothing. What you know, you know.
> From this time forth I never will speak word. (*O* 5.2.309–10)

While his clever scheming leads Othello to kill his beloved Desdemona, Iago refuses to account for his radically antisocial behaviour, in spite of being threatened by those in power—"Torments will ope your lips", the Venetian senators warn him (in other words, torture will make you speak) (*O* 5.2.312). As a reaction to pressing demands from the establishment, Iago's silence promotes a form of passive terror.

Generally viewed as reprehensible and morally wrong, Iago's behaviour also suggests that silence can be used as a powerful tool of mass resistance. Although primarily directed against social and economic inequalities, the "Occupy" movement that started in New York at the end of the summer 2011 was characterised by the absence of a clear political message or demand. Against the all-inclusive politics of interactivity that prevail, the unnerving silence of the protesters was remarkable. "All we say now can be taken from us—everything except our silence", Žižek wrote on behalf of the protesters at the peak of the "occupation" in October 2011: "this silence, this rejection of dialogue, of all forms of clinching, is our 'terror', ominous and threatening as it should be."[59] But whether this "terrifying" silence should be politicised or not remains for each individual to decide.

---

[59] Žižek, "Occupy First."

References

Armstrong, Philip. "Guilty Creatures: The Visual Regime of Shakespeare's Later Tragedies." PhD thesis, University of Wales, College of Cardiff, 1995.

———. *Shakespeare in Psychoanalysis*. London: Routledge, 2001.

———. *Shakespeare's Visual Regime: Tragedy, Psychoanalysis and the Gaze*. New York: Palgrave Macmillan, 2000.

Bernstein, Adam. "Charles Douglass, 93; Gave TV Its Laugh Track." *The Washington Post*, 24 April 2003, B06.

Cellania, Miss. "Artificially Sweetened: The Story of Canned Laughter." Neatorama. 22 August 2012. [cited 24 December 2012]. Available from http://www.neatorama.com/2012/08/22/Artificially-Sweetened-The-Story-of-Canned-Laughter/.

Christian, Hugh J., and Melanie A. Cook. "A Lightning Primer: Characteristics of a Storm." Lightning & Atmospheric Electricity Research at the GHCC (NASA). [cited 31 August 2011]. Available from http://thunder.nsstc.nasa.gov/primer/primer2.html.

The Coca-Cola Company. "'Open Happiness' and Enjoy Life's Simple Pleasures with Coca-Cola." 21 January 2009. [cited 12 September 2011]. Available from http://www.thecocacolacompany.com/dynamic/press_center/2009/01/open-happiness.html.

Collins, Stephen. "After the Takeover." *The Guardian*, 28 September 2012. [cited 28 September 2012]. Available from http://www.guardian.co.uk/lifeandstyle/cartoon/2012/sep/28/1.

C-SPAN Video Library. "Q&A with President George W. Bush." 28 January 2005. [cited 16 January 2012]. Available from http://www.c-spanvideo.org/program/185341-1.

Derrida, Jacques. *Specters of Marx: The State of the Debt, the Work of Mourning, and the New International*. Translated by Peggy Kamuf. New York: Routledge, 1994.

Dolar, Mladen. "The Enjoying Machine." *"Interpasif Persona": Amber'08 Arts and Technology Festival*. Istanbul, 2010. [cited 18 January 2012]. Available from http://www.scribd.com/doc/59669927/amber-08-Art-and-Technology-Festival.

Eagleton, Terry. *William Shakespeare*. Oxford: Oxford University Press, 1986.

The Economic Collapse: Are You Prepared for the Coming Economic Collapse and the Next Great Depression? "Who Owns The Media? The 6 Monolithic Corporations That Control Almost Everything We Watch, Hear And Read." 4 October 2010. [cited 18 January 2011]. Available from http://theeconomiccollapseblog.com/archives/who-owns-the-media-the-6-monolithic-corporations-that-control-almost-everything-we-watch-hear-and-read.

Garber, Marjorie. *Shakespeare's Ghost Writers: Literature as Uncanny Causality*. New York: Routledge, 2010.

Grady, Hugh, and Terence Hawkes, eds. *Presentist Shakespeares*. Oxford: Routledge, 2007.

Greenblatt, Stephen, Walter Cohen, Jean Elizabeth Howard, and Katharine Eisaman Maus, eds. *The Norton Shakespeare*. New York: Norton, 1997.

Harris, Jonathan Gil. *Shakespeare and Literary Theory: Oxford Shakespeare Topics*. Oxford: Oxford University Press, 2010.

Hawkes, Terence. *Shakespeare in the Present*. London: Routledge, 2002.

Jay, Martin. *Downcast Eyes: The Denigration of Vision in Twentieth-Century French Thought*. Berkeley: University of California Press, 1994.

Kubrick, Stanley, dir. *A Clockwork Orange*. Screenplay by Stanley Kubrick based on *A Clockwork Orange* by Anthony Burgess. Warner Bros., 1971. Film.

Lacan, Jacques. "Desire and the Interpretation of Desire in *Hamlet*." Edited by Jacques-Alain Miller and translated by James Hulbert. *Yale French Studies* 55, no. 6 (1977): 11–52.

———. *The Ethics of Psychoanalysis. The Seminar of Jacques Lacan: Book VII*. Edited by Jacques-Alain Miller and translated by Dennis Porter. London: Routledge, 2008.

———. "The Line and the Light." In *The Four Fundamental Concepts of Psycho-Analysis*, edited by Jacques-Alain Miller and translated by Alan Sheridan. Harmondsworth: Penguin Books, 1977.

———. "Of the Gaze as *Objet Petit a*." In *The Four Fundamental Concepts of Psycho-analysis*, edited by Jacques-Alain Miller and translated by Alan Sheridan. Harmondsworth: Penguin Books, 1977.

———. *Les quatre concepts fondamentaux de la psychoanalyse*. Edited by Jacques-Alain Miller. Paris: Éditions du Seuil, 1973.

Lynch, David. *Blue Velvet*. Directed by David Lynch. Entertainment Group, 1986. Film.

———. *Inland Empire*. Directed by David Lynch. Absurda, 2006. Film.

———. *Rabbits*. In *The Lime Green Set*. Directed by David Lynch. Absurda, 2008. DVD. (Originally released 2002.)

LynchNet: The David Lynch Resource. "Rabbits." [cited 20 September 2011]. Available from http://www.lynchnet.com/rabbits/.

Mallarmé, Stéphane. "La fausse entrée des sorcières dans *Macbeth*." In *Oeuvres complètes*. Paris: Pléiade, 1945. (Originally written 1897.)

Marsh, Anne. *The Darkroom: Photography and the Theatre of Desire*. Victoria: Macmillan, 2003.

McGowan, Todd. "Fantasizing the Father in *Blue Velvet*." In *The Impossible David Lynch*. New York: Columbia University Press, 2007.

Miller, Jacques-Alain. "Jeremy Bentham's Panoptic Device." *October* 41 (summer 1987): 3–29.

news.com.au. "2 billion tune in to Royal Wedding." [cited 20 September 2011]. Available from http://www.news.com.au/business/billion-tune-in-to-royal-wedding/story-fn7mjon9-1226047685517.

Orwell, George. *Nineteen Eighty-Four*. London: Secker and Warburg, 1949.

Pfaller, Robert. *Die Illusionen der anderen: Über das Lustprinzip in der Kultur*. Frankfurt: Suhrkamp, 2002.

Poulard, Étienne. "Shakespeare's Politics of Invisibility: Power and Ideology in *The Tempest*." *International Journal of Žižek Studies* [online] 4, no. 1 (2010). Available from http://zizekstudies.org/index.php/ijzs/article/view/225/327.

Rabaté, Jean-Michel. *Given: 1 Art, 2 Crime: Modernity, Murder and Mass Culture*. Brighton: Sussex Academic Press, 2006.

The Reduced Shakespeare Company. "RSC Macbeth." [cited 3 November 2011]. Available from http://www.youtube.com/watch?v=pQk4Y6Q69u8.

The Reduced Shakespeare Company: The Complete Works of William Shakespeare (Abridged). Acorn Media Publishing Inc, 2003. DVD. (Originally released 2000.)

Reinhard Lupton, Julia, and Kenneth Reinhard. *After Oedipus: Shakespeare in Psychoanalysis*. Ithaca, NY: Cornell University Press, 1993.

REUTERS. "UK Minister Says 2 Billion to Watch Royal Wedding." [cited 20 September 2011]. Available from http://www.reuters.com/article/2011/04/06/us-britain-wedding-audience-idUSTRE73542Y20110406.

sportingintelligence: Original thinking, Informed comment, No froth, No spin. "REVEALED: Royal Wedding TV Audience Closer to 300m than 2bn (Because Sport, Not Royalty, Reigns)." [cited 20 September 2011]. Available from http://www.sportingintelligence.com/2011/05/08/revealed-royal-wedding%E2%80%99s-real-tv-audience-closer-to-300m-than-2bn-because-sport-not-royalty-reigns-080501/.

Žižek, Slavoj. "David Lynch, or, the Feminine Depression." In *The Metastases of Enjoyment: On Women and Causality*. London: Verso, 1994.

———. *How to Read Lacan*. London: Granta Books, 2006.

———. "The Lacanian Real: *Television*." *Symptom* 9 (2008). lacan dot com. [cited 9 September 2011]. Available from http://www.lacan.com/symptom/?p=38#_ftn1.

———. *Looking Awry: An Introduction to Jacques Lacan through Popular Culture*. Cambridge, MA: MIT Press, 1991.

————. "Occupy First. Demands Come Later." *The Guardian*, 26 October 2011. [cited 28 October 2011]. Available from http://www.guardian.co.uk/commentisfree/2011/oct/26/occupy-protesters-bill-clinton?newsfeed=true.

————. *The Plague of Fantasies*. 2d ed. London: Verso, 2008.

————. "Will You Laugh for Me, Please?" *In These Times*, 18 July 2003. [cited 6 September 2011]. Available from http://inthesetimes.com/article/88.

Wordplay in Shakespeare's *Hamlet* and the Accusation of Derrida's "Logical Phallusies"

Johann Gregory

That "Derrida's writing borders on being unreadable" has been maintained by several academics, journalists and students. This essay considers this reaction to Jacques Derrida's writing in relation to a broader history of wordplay and puns. Using Shakespeare's Hamlet *as a starting point followed by the infamous letter to* The Times *that accused Derrida of "logical phallusies", it argues that if Derrida's writing does border on being unreadable, then, this is the condition of all writing. The essay suggests that rather than suppressing the spectres of Derrida in Shakespeare studies, we should welcome back the aspects of his work that help us to "read and write in the space or heritage of Shakespeare".*

—Shakespeare's *Hamlet*: now there's an example of British English. Isn't it?
I mean, wasn't it? I mean, would it have been?
—You are not being serious.[1]

"[A]n untranslatable play on words" right and accurately note the translators. This wordplay is not one wordplay among other possible ones. It is the play that makes all plays possible.[2]

Shakespeare and Derrida, Again

Despite those who harbour a desire to suppress the relationship between William Shakespeare and Jacques Derrida,[3] it seems entirely possible that this relationship is only starting to be thought through. As Nicholas Royle suggested just last year, "we are really only at the beginning of reckoning with how Derrida's work illuminates Shakespeare's, and Shakespeare's illuminates Derrida's".[4] Neema Parvini summarises

---

[1]Royle, "Jacques Derrida's Language," 98.
[2]Derrida, *GLAS*, 30.
[3]On the desire to exclude French theory from Shakespeare studies, see especially Wilson, 4–7.
[4]Royle, "Prologue," vi.

that "deconstruction ... never really established itself in Shakespeare studies as anything more than a minor or ancillary movement that seemed to peter out sometime in the late 1980s".[5] But if deconstruction never established itself as a school or "ism", this does not mean that Shakespeare and Derrida stopped being read in relation to each other.[6] After all, Parvini's comment comes not long after *Shakespeare in French Theory*, *Shakespeare and Literary Theory*, and an international conference on Shakespeare and Derrida.[7] The year 2012 also saw a journal special issue devoted to Shakespeare and Derrida,[8] and a volume of essays on Shakespeare edited by a critic concerned with Derrida (Ivan Callus) and a translator of Derrida (Stefan Herbrechter); this book, *Posthumanist Shakespeares*, contains essays by another Derrida translator (Laurent Milesi) and other critics—such as Mark Robson and Mareile Pfannebecker—who are not so quick to sound the death knell of Derrida's work in relation to Shakespeare.[9]

I am not simply suggesting here that, to paraphrase Karl Marx, there is a spectre haunting Shakespeare studies—the spectre of Derrida. But it now seems obvious that the attempt to put a stopper on Derrida's haunting of Shakespeare studies, perhaps before Derrida's influence has "really established itself", is almost certainly doomed to failure: this failure seems even more likely when the exorcisms of the spectres of Derrida and deconstruction are articulated so absolutely, as when, for example, Brian Vickers argued in 1993 that "the balance of opinion [on deconstruction] has shifted, I believe decisively, to the critical side"[10]—and I believe "critical" is meant to be read in a negative sense.[11] Spectres, by Shakespearean definition, come back *again*, as Derrida argues for the spectres of Marx. "What, has this thing appeared again tonight?" asks Marcellus at the start of *Hamlet* (1.1.19).[12] "Look where it comes again" (1.1.38).

Derrida used Shakespeare's *Hamlet* in *Specters of Marx* to consider what facets of Marx's thinking—what spectres of Marx—should be followed or welcomed: his book was partly a question of inheritance, or what to accept or sign for. Before writing on *Hamlet*, Derrida exclaimed in an interview: "I would very much like to read and write in the space or heritage of Shakespeare, in relation to whom I have infinite admiration and gratitude; I would like to become (alas, it's pretty late) a 'Shakespeare expert'".[13] However, Derrida also professed to always "place [him]self

---

[5]Parvini, 38.

[6]On "Defining Deconstruction," see Royle, *Jacques Derrida*, 23–5.

[7]For these books, see Wilson; and Harris. For the conference, see the webpage, *Shakespeare and Derrida*.

[8]For the Shakespeare and Derrida journal special issue, see Royle "Prologue."

[9]See Herbrechter and Callus, eds.

[10]Vickers, 167.

[11]Brian Vickers's issue in his "monumental diatribe" seems to be not so much with the French thinkers, but with the way they had been affiliated with Shakespeare (Wilson, 267, n. 26).

[12]Shakespeare. All quotations from Shakespeare's plays are taken from *The Norton Shakespeare*, and citations are given in text.

[13]Derrida, "This Strange Institution Called Literature," 67.

in relation to philosophy" in his work so that it should be understood that his writing follows a larger philosophical tradition even as he questions many of its premises.[14] For a literary critic, this means that one has to be especially careful or responsible in reading Derrida and to decide, in turn, what aspects of his vast work to follow.

In his "last interview", Derrida made a pronouncement on the survival of his work which implicitly draws on his thinking on inheritance in terms of *Hamlet* and the spectres of Marx:

> At my age, I am ready to entertain the most contradictory hypotheses in this regard: I have simultaneously—I ask you to believe me on this—the *double feeling* that, on the one hand, to put it playfully and with a certain immodesty, one has not yet begun to read me, that even though there are, to be sure, many very good readers (a few dozen in the world perhaps, people who are also writer-thinkers, poets), in the end it is later on that all this has a chance of appearing; but also, on the other hand, and thus simultaneously, I have a feeling that two weeks or a month from after my death *there will be nothing left*. Nothing except what has been copyrighted and deposited in libraries. I swear to you, I believe sincerely and simultaneously in these two hypotheses.[15]

Derrida's double feeling echoes Hamlet's own when he asks Horatio to "tell my story" while proclaiming with his dying breath "The rest is silence" (5.3.291, 5.3.300). In writing an essay here concerning Derrida and Shakespeare, the move is to consider a reaction to Derrida's work in order to argue that the significance of his work for reading Shakespeare should not be ruled out, as it seems to have been done in various quarters prematurely. I would also like to go some way in following Christopher Norris and others in arguing that Derrida's work does not aim to use wordplay gratuitously or irresponsibly, as has often been declared.[16] Just as Derrida used the possibility of grammar to express a double feeling regarding the survival of his work—feelings that put together seem logically impossible—so Derrida's work employs language(s) to consider how certain writings and issues could be considered otherwise.

Writing that "Borders on Being Unreadable"

In a recent handbook entitled *Shakespeare and Contemporary Theory*, Parvini presents six pages on deconstruction in relation to Shakespeare studies for his chapter "Before New Historicism and Cultural Materialism". He declares:

---

[14]Derrida, "*Honoris Causa*," 412. Jacques Derrida says of his writing that "[s]ome are, I hope, recognizable as being philosophical in a very classical way; others try to change the norms of philosophical discussion from inside philosophy; still others bear philosophical traits without being limited to that" (ibid.).

[15]Derrida, *Learning to Live Finally*, 33–4. This extract is also quoted as the final lines of Benoît Peeters's major biography of Derrida and so is likely to be read by a wider audience in the future (542).

[16]I am grateful to Christopher Norris for commenting on a draft of my essay and allowing me to attend his seminars on "Deconstruction" and "Philosophy and Literary Theory" a few years ago. I am also grateful to him for giving me a copy of his forthcoming essay, "Provoking Philosophy." See also Norris, "Extraordinary Language."

> Few words make some literary academics ... recoil in fear quite like "Derrida" and "deconstruction". This is because, to put it frankly, Derrida's writing borders on being unreadable, especially for exponents of the Plain English Campaign. It is frustratingly abstract, dense, diffuse, loaded with esoteric jargon and demands a working knowledge of Plato, the development of Western philosophy, Nietzsche and Heidegger to understand that many students of literature plainly lack.[17]

While seeking to draw out some of the relations between the work of Shakespeare and Derrida, a function of my essay is to analyse this reaction to Derrida's writing that Parvini describes.

There is something extremely funny about imagining Derrida being feared by exponents of the Plain English Campaign.[18] This is because, on the one hand, Derrida wrote in French and so it would be outrageous to accuse him of not writing in Plain English, and, on the other hand, Derrida is probably one of the most exacting writers when it comes to using grammar and language responsibly. Part of Derrida's work was to show that, even when we think we are speaking in "Plain English", communication is not as straightforward as we might assume. The failure—even for someone trying very hard—to speak in totally plain English might be analogous to a condition of British English. Royle asks, "British English? That always makes me smile. Isn't it a term that came into existence just at the point of having to acknowledge its disappearance?"[19] Derrida's work shows how all writing is potentially unreadable, even when we think it is an example of plain, familiar, British English.

In the writing that follows I hope to lean on Parvini's assertion that "Derrida's writing borders on being unreadable" to show that this response is more appropriate than Parvini might be imagined to have meant. The essay considers the wordplay in the representation of Hamlet's character before looking at how Derrida has been accused of using puns. This dual writing will involve the reading of wordplay in *Hamlet* and Derrida's pronouncement that one of his most playful books does not contain a single pun. By isolating what is often considered to be a trivial issue of wordplay, I aim to make a bolder claim for the synergies of Shakespeare's and Derrida's work, and the way that both their writing could be understood to "border on being unreadable" in a way that is not finally disabling.

"Ask for me tomorrow", says the dying Mercutio in *Romeo and Juliet*, "and you shall find me a grave man" (3.1.93–4).[20] Shakespeare seems to have a devilish delight in making punning jokes at inappropriate moments. "A quibble was to him the fatal

---

[17]Parvini, 33–4. I am citing Neema Parvini here because he summarises a certain position people have taken, not because I especially want to take issue with his "purposes" (34) which it must be understood are expressed in the context of a Shakespeare and theory handbook. On the whole, I agree with his premise that "although the idea of 'Theory' is increasingly frowned upon by many within the academy, its influence endures hidden, disavowed and unquestioned" (Parvini, 3).

[18]The Plain English Campaign has been "Fighting for crystal-clear communication since 1979." See Plain English Campaign.

[19]Royle, "Jacques Derrida's Language," 97.

[20]On Shakespeare's use of the pun, see also Czerniecki; and Lopez.

Cleopatra for which Shakespeare lost the world and was content to lose it"[21] fretted the eighteenth-century editor, Samuel Johnson, stigmatising Shakespeare's wordplay. As Norris observes,

> Johnson is keen to assert his disapproval of Shakespeare's frequent running ... toward a style of profligate linguistic licence which threatens not only the principles of literary decorum but also those of the English language as a medium of well-conducted communicative discourse and, beyond that, the very bases of social, civil and political order.[22]

Both Derrida and *Hamlet* challenge received ideas about "communicative discourse", and this has had far reaching consequences. The lines of Shakespeare's characters can, on occasion, be delivered to make people laugh—at times because the audience is nervous and it appears to be irreverent to make punning jokes at moments of crisis. One of the worst culprits is Hamlet. As Margreta de Grazia phrases it, "Hamlet has more puns to his credit than any other Shakespearean character, no less than ninety".[23] Guildenstern exclaims in frustration at Hamlet's wordplay: "Good my lord, put your discourse in some frame, and start not so wildly from my affair" (3.2.282–3). Hamlet often seems to be deliberately punning—usually to the distaste of those around him—in that play that is now referred to with a title that might be considered a pun, the name of the prince, name of his father, and the name of the play.[24] To orally communicate "*Hamlet*", in fact, one is sometimes required to say "Hamlet the play", rather like saying "difference with an 'a'". But the question of when a pun is intended, or when a word is a pun, brings us to a larger problem of communication and our relationship to language, issues that the texts of Shakespeare and Derrida explore time and again.

"How to read Shakespeare is a question of how to think about wordplay" writes Royle.[25] His attention to wordplay might indicate an interest in Shakespearean puns, but following Derrida, he writes:

> Yet "pun" and "quibble" are not Shakespearean words. The only instance of the word "pun" in Shakespeare is in the sense of the verb "to pound": "He would pun thee into shivers with his fist, as a sailor breaks a biscuit" (*Troilus and Cressida*, 2.1.37–8). Likewise, the word "quibble" appears nowhere in Shakespeare. ... These terms ("pun" and "quibble") tend to carry with them a kind of artificial and trivializing effect that is in fact quite foreign to what is going on in a given passage of Shakespeare. They connote a certain frivolity, a momentary bubble of fun,

---

[21]Johnson, 68.

[22]Norris, "Extraordinary Language," 161.

[23]de Grazia, 183. Cf. Mahood, 166.

[24]The word "Hamlet" may have had an uncanny, ghostly, echo for Shakespeare too. Stephen Greenblatt notes that "[p]erhaps, too, Shakespeare's sensitivity to the status of the dead was intensified by the death in 1596 of his son Hamnet (a name virtually interchangeable with Hamlet in the period's public records)" (248). I am grateful to Étienne Poulard for reminding me of this Hamlet, and for commenting on a draft of my essay.

[25]Royle, *How to Read Shakespeare*, 13.

something contained and under control, a kind of calculated but ultimately pointless exhibition of playfulness.[26]

Royle's reading is historically astute. And yet, sometimes, readings of Shakespeare seem to hinge on the significance of a few words. Much rests on Hamlet's famous last words: "The rest is silence" (5.2.300). Could an interpretation of Hamlet's ambiguous words in the play rely on the pun "rest"? The play cannot rest: the rest of the play is not silent, but continues with the entrance of Fortinbras and his army with its drummer. Royle suggests that "[o]f all Shakespeare's works, Hamlet is perhaps the least restful".[27] Possibly the rest of Hamlet's character is supplemented by the Ghost, also called "Hamlet" (1.4.25), who arrested his attention in the first act. "The rest is silence" now that the vengeance arresting the Ghost and Hamlet is finally over by the killing enacted at the end of the play: "Rest, rest, perturbèd spirit" says Hamlet (2.1.183). Maybe the rest for Hamlet is the past that haunts him, accounting for his restlessness in the play. On the other hand, the rest might be still to come: after his mother's remarriage and his father's death, he cannot prevent his interest in the royal succession, what the rest will be, or how to rest with it, how to wrestle with the rest. The rest suggests both fulfilment and non-fulfilment, the restive experience of reading a text like *Hamlet*.[28] The play seems to ask "how can we rest?", but making sense of the answer, like the question, involves coming to terms with the uncanny ability of language to say one thing *and another*. "The time is out of joint" (1.5.189) exclaims Hamlet who cannot get to grips with the imperatives of a ghost that remain undecidable.[29] He needs a rest, but for the living, born before we know it, time will not rest. Likewise, in *Hamlet*, the meaning of time—or a word in time—will not be put to rest. The word "rest" speaks to the rest of the play, but it is unwise to say that it is because of a contained pun, a simple ambivalent double meaning. With a pun, we cannot ultimately tell which definition is the primary one, and which definitions are supplementary ones ghosting.[30] The "rest" in *Hamlet* produces echoes from the grave, of the remainder or supplement, which in fact challenges any chance of people or wordplay being laid to rest properly in the play. *Hamlet* seems unwilling to rest in peace or to rest assured. Its language will not come to rest and be finally restored. In fact, you might say that the wordplay of *Hamlet* "borders on being unreadable". Trying to foreground wordplay is often irresistible, sometimes irritating. Perhaps I had better try to give it a rest?

---

[26]Ibid.

[27]Ibid., 57.

[28]William Empson writes "of the mental sophistication required to use a word which covers its own opposite" giving "restive" as an example: "(a 'restive' horse, for instance is a horse which is restless because it has been resting for too long)" (195).

[29]For Derrida's reflection on Hamlet's quotation and the political, see his essay "The Time is Out of Joint."

[30]Marjorie Garber explains that a "useful analogue for the concept of a *ghost* … can be found in what Jacques Derrida has called the 'logic of the supplement.' The word 'supplement,' in French, means both a substitute and an addition" (19). Cf. Derrida, *Of Grammatology*, 141–64.

Representing Hamlet

Hamlet's first lines in the play all contain what scholars usually declare to be a pun, although, as Royle might be quick to point out, these lines do not exactly constitute a "bubble of fun". It is impossible, for example, to gauge how playful the prince is being here and in what ways Hamlet, as represented, might be thought to be conscious of his punning:

KING CLAUDIUS   But now, my cousin Hamlet, and my son—

HAMLET   A little more than kin and less than kind.

KING CLAUDIUS   How is it that the clouds still hang on you?

HAMLET   Not so, my lord, I am too much i'th' sun. (1.2.64–7)

Hamlet's line plays on the proverb: "The nearer in kin the less in kindness". Even though it is a proverb constructed in the past, however, the phrase also looks forward: traditionally a proverb contains a truth, almost a kind of truism that is supposed to be true in the future. The proverb, though, is rather cynical, and (like all proverbs) begs the question, who is the proverb true for? What is more, Hamlet twists the proverb to mean something different. His line plays on King Claudius's staged generosity, but also the recent marriage of Claudius, his dead father's brother, to his mother Gertrude. Hamlet's lines suggest that Claudius is "A little more than kin" (1.2.65) for his liking, implicitly indicating Hamlet's concern that his mother has had an incestuous marriage that might cut him out of the royal succession. Hamlet says he is "too much i'th' sun" (1.2.67), but the implied pun on the homonym "sun"/son suggests that he does not wish to be recognised as Claudius's son. As de Grazia points out in *"Hamlet" without Hamlet*, it was not really until the nineteenth century that Hamlet's wordplay was identified especially to be symptomatic of a disturbed psychology.[31] As de Grazia argues, "the ruse of being *non compos mentis* does more than deflect suspicion. It gives Hamlet license to express equivocally what it would have been fatal to express directly: his resentment at having been defrauded of his imperial expectation."[32] Hamlet's wordplay can be read on two levels: the play shows how wordplay can be seen as irrational or trivial, but also how it can be perceived to be unsafe or culpable. Wordplay, then, has been seen historically in two lights.[33] On the one hand, wordplay is seen as trivial and innocuous, while on the other it is viewed to represent a challenge to communication and social order.[34]

---

[31]de Grazia, 15.

[32]Ibid., 175.

[33]For a book-length history of the pun, see Redfern. For a recent BBC appraisal of the pun, see Davies.

[34]Noting "Shakespeare's flamboyant punning, troping and riddling", Terry Eagleton argues that the playwright's "belief in social stability is jeopardized by the very language in which it is articulated" (1). Unfortunately, there is not room here to consider Hamlet's confrontation with the gravediggers where wordplay is viewed as being both cause for macabre laughter and as dangerous to class order: Hamlet complains in relation to the "absolute" gravedigger that "The age is grown so picked that the toe of the peasant comes so near the heal of the courtier he galls his kibe" (5.1.126, 5.1.128–30).

To consider intentions in relation to theatre and the pun is of course to open a can of worms: did they mean what they said? Were they pretending? Were they being ironic, non-serious, or speaking in jest?[35] Royle considers the pun in relation to characterisation: "To talk about a character's punning or quibbling is also a way of conveniently forgetting the fact that the character is, in turn, fundamentally Shakespeare's verbal creation: wordplay precedes character."[36] Aside from whether Shakespeare was even conscious of some of the puns in his plays, Royle points out that it is hazardous to assume too much about the self-conscious punning of characters.[37] What is apparent in the play of words, nevertheless, is that Hamlet's first lines project a character who has an equivocal or especially troubled relationship with words, and that his character finds complexity, and indeed meaning, through the different ways his language could be read. For those within *Hamlet*, wordplay paradoxically both hinders and allows for representation and communication.

Ghosting and "Différance"

The Ghost haunts Hamlet, but it also haunts the language of the play. We might say that ghostliness is like the meanings that come to bear with wordplay because it is not always easy to tell whether another meaning of a word is present or absent:

HAMLET	Whither wilt thou lead me? Speak. I'll go no further.
GHOST	Mark me.
HAMLET	I will.
. . . .	
HAMLET	Speak, I am bound to hear.
GHOST	So art thou to revenge when thou shalt hear.
HAMLET	What?
GHOST	I am thy father's spirit (1.5.1–2, 1.5.6–9)

Hamlet affirms "I will", and yet for the rest of the play Hamlet struggles with how he "will" mark the Ghost's words. He is unsure "whither" it will lead him or, even, whether it is best to be led by a ghost at all. He says he will "go no further" but Hamlet recognises that he is "bound to hear" the Ghost's story of the past. The

---

[35]For a consideration of intentions in relation to communication, see Derrida, *Limited Inc*. Although my essay is indebted to this work, unfortunately there is not room to make more explicit links with it here. The exchange between Derrida and John R. Searle might be said to hinge on Derrida's reading of J. L. Austin's suggestion that "a performative utterance will, for example, be *in peculiar way* hollow or void if said by an actor on the stage, or if introduced in a poem, or spoken in soliloquy" (cited in Derrida, *Limited Inc*, 16) and Derrida's response that this "risk [is] rather [language's] internal and positive condition of possibility" (ibid., 17).
[36]Royle, *How to Read Shakespeare*, 13–14.
[37]Nicholas Royle discusses the embarrassment of Freud's reading of *Hamlet* and "literary psychobiography" (*After Derrida*, 93).

Ghost's rejoinder that Hamlet is also bound to act on his words by "revenge" is met with Hamlet's ambiguous interrogative: "What?" Does Hamlet question what it is he shall hear, or his binding to his father's words? There is, in effect, a double entendre, even a double bind for Hamlet if he wishes to act responsibly. Is Hamlet speaking to the very spirit, essence, of his father or is it just a spirit, shadow, of his father, maybe his father's darker side that still remains behind? The problem of the "spirit" is more complex than a word labelled a "pun" might suggest.

Royle considers the duplicity of ghosts in a reading of *Julius Caesar*. He writes "Double is the ghost, the ghost is always (at least) double".[38] Derrida uses the instability of the word "ghost" as a basis for reading the "specters" of Marx. That is, he uses the wordplay around the terms "spirit" and "ghost" in *Hamlet* to host and ghost his thinking on Marx. For Derrida, Marx was "often inspired" by the "experience of the specter" in Shakespeare when he "diagnosed a certain dramaturgy of modern Europe".[39] *Specters of Marx* began as a lecture in two sessions for a conference entitled "Wither Marxism?", the second session being on Shakespeare's "official" birthday, April 23.[40] Derrida draws on the resources of Shakespeare's writing, just at Marx had done, to think through the question of the conference, considering forms of Marx and Marxism as spectres. It is here that I would like to propose that Derrida's *Specters of Marx* offers a brilliant illustration of how we might think with Shakespeare.[41] Furthermore, we can also think with Derrida in order to read Shakespeare with more care and innovation.

Take "Différance": Derrida's neologism might be seen as nothing more than an elaborate pun by his cynical critics, and yet difference with an "a" seems to have a spectral, even spectacular, significance in *Hamlet*. In his essay "Différance", Derrida plays incessantly on the meaning of "différance" to negotiate active, passive, differing and deferring meanings of the word in French, and to show how the written word impinges on speech: "différance" "will refer irreducibly to a written text" (rather like "*Hamlet*" in italics maybe).[42] To anyone who reads Shakespeare's plays, the written element in the spoken word is usually taken for granted. Most audiences of *Hamlet* know that the play relies, to a certain extent, on a script. Royle writes that "[l]ike the nonpresent remainder or the supplement, difference is the 'concept' of what makes concepts possible".[43] The Ghost might, like "différance", be seen as a "nonpresent remainder" throughout the remaining action and language of *Hamlet*. In a similar way to the Ghost's meaning that haunts the later action of the play, the strange plurality of meaning in *Hamlet* relies on the "différance" of each word, the potential for each word to be played against or through another.

---

[38]Royle, "The Poet," 54.

[39]Derrida, *Specters of Marx*, 4–5.

[40]See ibid., xiii.

[41]For more on the notion of thinking with Shakespeare, see Lupton.

[42]Derrida, "Différance," 132.

[43]Royle, *Jacques Derrida*, 76.

This understanding of wordplay in a broader sense—working across the whole text rather than at just isolated moments—helps us to realise that another problem with the idea of puns in *Hamlet* is that nearly any word might be considered ambiguous. With reference to the Ghost's "questionable shape" (1.4.24), for example, Molly Mahood suggests that "[q]*uestionable* means not only 'that I may question' but also 'doubtful, uncertain', and *shape*, besides being the essential form of something, has commonly in Shakespeare the meaning of a theatrical costume or disguise".[44] The significance of the Ghost, and the word "shape", is "always (at least) double" to use Royle's phrase. The question of the Ghost's shape is supplemented on stage by its armour too. The armour gives the spirit a shape which shows and hides the spirit's nature in a "fair and warlike form" (1.1.45). Warren Montag points out that "the veil reveals only another veil: inside the body of the armor [of the Ghost] is only another body, the inside of the outside is only another outside".[45] Inside the helmet is a "face" (1.3.228). Even the Ghost, then, has a kind of body but this spectral body is, for Derrida, like the body of Marx's texts: Derrida writes that part of the "work of mourning" is to "*identify* the bodily remains".[46] Arguably the work of reading both texts and contexts is also a case of "*identifying* the bodily remains" which involves exploring the different meanings surrounding the body of the text, and listening or looking out for the other texts haunting them. Derrida's "différance", as the "nonpresent remainder" is a way of comprehending wordplay, but is also like the Ghost's face, a "veil [that] reveals only another veil". Words are just a veil, but maybe a partially revealing veil too. In this way, Derrida's "différance" with an "a" bears a striking resemblance to Hamlet's Ghost.

In *Specters of Marx*, Derrida used the neologism "hauntology" partly to express the "to be or not to be" ontology of spectres, "Derrida's coinage for the study of phenomena that bear the spectral traces of what are supposedly dead and gone".[47] But the ghostly wordplay of *Hamlet* shows us that there is a hauntology at play in words. We might hope to will into existence the intended meaning of our communication, or we may try to infer the meaning of any given word or sentence from context, but there are always already other supplementary meanings haunting these attempts. To admit that these other meanings are around can be spooky, uncanny, because "the supplement is what neither Nature nor Reason can tolerate".[48] This feeling of unnatural or unreasonable extra/loss when it comes to Shakespeare's and Derrida's wordplay—a wordplay that is often seen erroneously as *merely* supplementary[49]—has no doubt contributed to the reaction that a dangerous game is being played with language. These writers explore how we are not quite at home with "our" language. Their work

---

[44]Mahood, 123.

[45]Montag, 79.

[46]Derrida, *Specters of Marx*, 9.

[47]Ibid., 10; Harris, 168.

[48]Derrida, *Of Grammatology*, 148. I am grateful to Chris Müller for bringing this passage to my attention, and for his comments on an earlier draft of my essay.

[49]For a nuanced consideration of "supplementary value, [and] the linguistic extravagancies of neologism" in relation to Shakespeare, see Tudeau-Clayton, 176.

invites us to question "whether it is ever possible to simply say what one thinks, as if one were not already protected and determined by words and conceptions which one cannot own and did not invent."[50] If their uncanny writing "borders on being unreadable", then, this is because their language points out this ghost in the room when we would often rather keep to the straight and narrow notion of communicative discourse.

The "Cambridge Affair"

The issue of communication might be said to be one of Derrida's most pressing concerns, so there is a certain irony to the fact that he has often been accused of being wilfully obscure in his writing.[51] This accusation is not only one that has been voiced by some philosophers, but one that has become part of a certain popular notion of Derrida's writing. For example, while considering the perceived unreadability of his work, a quasi-obituary of Derrida in the *American Spectator* announced:

> If Derrida's works are not widely read it is because of a ponderous style that makes them all but unreadable. What in God's name is the man getting at, and why on Earth doesn't he just say it and have done with it?[52]

The accusations of Derrida's wilful obscurity seem to have come about not so much because people have carefully read an essay or book by Derrida, but because they have not read Derrida's work carefully or not at all (as Derrida bemoaned a number of times). Occasionally, this notion of Derrida's writing being obscure might come about due to the way that his work is presented in new contexts where fresh conflicts, tensions or even new obscurities have come to bear. But much worse, often Derrida is seen to be wilfully obscure simply due to representations such as those in the *American Spectator* and elsewhere in the media. However, Derrida was quick to point out that these media representations have not come out of the blue, but that, at least in one case, they could be traced back to academics: "it is academics, certain academics, who are responsible for these stereotypes, and who pass them on to journalists".[53]

Part of the problem that some people have had with Derrida's writing is not only what Derrida has said about language, but the way that he has gone about writing. There seems to be a larger historical and political dimension here which is related to a concern with communication, the crossover between different discourses or disciplines, and the perception of wordplay. Arguments are accused of getting bogged down in language when they challenge the Enlightenment aspiration for clear and

---

[50]Müller, 160. Müller comments in his reading of Heidegger's style that "Unhomeliness is ... the very essence of language" (149).

[51]For Foucault's alleged notion of Derrida's prose style being "obscurantisme terroriste" or even "obscurantisme terrioristc" as this alleged allegation was misquoted, see Derrida, *Limited Inc*, 158–9, n. 12.

[52]Orlet, n.p.

[53]Derrida, "*Honoris Causa*," 401.

distinct ideas by appearing to muddy the waters of crystal-clear communication. To sum up this reaction, you might say that Derrida is accused of being something of an antisocial, nihilistic, punning Hamlet-like antic, a figure that has endangered the articulation and future of philosophical and academic discourse. Perhaps the most famous example of this representation surfaced during the so-called "Cambridge Affair" in 1992. Academics at Cambridge University were considering whether to award Derrida an honorary doctorate while other academics (none of whom were at Cambridge University) took it upon themselves to publish a letter in *The Times* with the heading "Derrida Degree a Question of Honour". Not just because "this is *also* extremely funny",[54] I will quote some of the more serious accusations:

> In the eyes of philosophers ... M. Derrida's work does not meet accepted standards of clarity and rigour.
>
> ...
>
> M. Derrida's career had its roots in the heady days of the 1960s and his writings continue to reveal their origins in that period. Many of them seem to consist in no small part of elaborate jokes and the puns "logical phallusies" and the like, and M. Derrida seems to us to have come close to making a career out of what we regard as translating into the academic sphere tricks and gimmicks similar to those of the Dadaists or of the concrete poets.
>
> ...
>
> Many French philosophers see in M. Derrida only cause for silent embarrassment, his antics having contributed significantly to the widespread impression that contemporary French philosophy is little more than an object of ridicule.[55]

The pun "phallusies" was apparently a reaction to Derrida's neologism "phallocentrism" to refer to the historical privileging of the masculine in the construction of meaning.[56] It would not be so pressing to consider this accusation of "logical phallusies" if it was not for the fact that this kind of disparagement is still prevalent, putting off many who might benefit from carefully reading Derrida—and more overtly theoretical or philosophical writing generally—while potentially tarnishing in advance those who write in relation to Derrida.[57]

As Benoît Peeters narrates in relation to the affair, "[o]ver the following weeks, the polemic was widely publicized, in Britain and elsewhere. In order to stigmatize Derrida's style and thought, a perfectly imaginary formula ('logical phalluses' [*sic*]) was attributed to him".[58] As the Freudian slip of the typographical error in the quotation in the biography further emphasises, the point of the accusation and the pun on

---

[54]Ibid., 404.

[55]Smith et al., 420. This letter was first published in *The Times* (London), 9 May 1992 with nineteen signatories.

[56]It is worth noting that while Shakespeare is now often celebrated for his neologisms, similar voices condemn Derrida for his.

[57]An example of the legacies of this letter can be seen in the *American Spectator* obituary that repeated, twelve years later, several of the accusations voiced in the letter, right down to Derrida's work's supposed links with Dadaists, "the Dadists [*sic*] with their urinals" (Orlet, n. p.).

[58]Peeters, 447.

phallus/fallacy worked to suggest that Derrida was basically dicking around. This being the case, it is supremely ironic that this is in fact exactly what the *accusers* end up doing with language and scholarly protocol. Derrida was invited to respond in the *Cambridge Review* of 1992 after Cambridge had finally voted to award him the honorary doctorate. His reaction to this pun was to "challenge anyone to find in my writings the expression 'logical phallusies,' by which the signatories of this document, in what is a serious and dogmatic abuse of their authority in the press, try to discredit me."[59] These academics aimed in effect to ridicule Derrida as someone whose language was not only fraudulent, as the pun connoting fallacies suggests, but to represent him as a trickster, punster or malcontent. The letter argues that "where coherent assertions are being made at all, these are either false or trivial".[60] Echoes might be heard here of Royle's point on the perceived "trivializing effect" associated with puns. In *Hamlet* the prince uses word-play to perform an "antic disposition" (2.1.173) so that he can say what he likes without being held responsible. Accordingly, the signatories frame Derrida as someone not to be taken seriously, or, in the terms of his "doctor honoris causa" and the heading of the letter, honourably. He is someone who has caused "silent embarrassment" for French philosophers, rather like Hamlet who might be read to embarrass Queen Gertrude with his wordplay and "nightly colour" (1.2.68).[61] In a last dash attempt to ridicule Derrida, the letter suggested that his "[a]cademic status" was dubiously "based on ... semi-intelligible attacks upon the values of reason, truth, and scholarship".[62] However, Derrida does not aim for such attacks; rather, as Norris argues, Derrida's work "effectively challenges the traditional viewpoint that would treat philosophy as somehow belonging to a realm of thought ideally exempt from the vagaries of rhetoric, writing or so called 'literary' style."[63] If Derrida had indeed "stretch[ed] the normal forms of academic scholarship beyond recognition" as the letter argued, then this was not to defraud it, but to help give it a future.[64]

"There is [No Pun] Either Good or Bad But Thinking Makes It So" (*Hamlet,* 2.2.244–5)

"There is no such thing as a good pun" remarked Geoffrey H. Hartman while reading Derrida: "Puns are the only thing beyond good and evil".[65] All the same, as Hartman

---

[59]Derrida, "*Honoris Causa,*" 404.

[60]Smith et al., 420.

[61]Eagleton writes of Shakespeare's "deeply embarrassing dilemma" when "his belief in social stability is jeopardized by the very language in which it is articulated" (1).

[62]Derrida, "*Honoris Causa,*" 420.

[63]Norris, *Deconstruction*, 147

[64]On the question of writing "in a way that is accessible to the non-specialist reader," for example, Derrida remarks that "[e]verything possible must be done to come close to such accessibility, but on several conditions: I. *Never totally renounce* the demands proper to the discipline (whose complexity is never natural, nor definitively stabilized). ... What is essential here in my view is never to lose sight of the rigor of the discipline" ("*Honoris Causa,*" 414).

[65]Hartman, 46.

attests, "[e]very pun, in Derrida, is philosophically accountable".[66] One of the many ironies of the "Cambridge Affair", then, was that Derrida was already aware that being perceived as a punster could be punishing. Derrida responded to a certain reaction to his most playful book to date called *GLAS* with a nod to the perceived criminality of punning. The title of Derrida's introduction to a glossary of this book was "Proverb: 'He that would pun ...'", an allusion to the eighteenth-century proverb: "He that pun would pick a pocket". Derrida remarks that "contrary to the rumour and to what some would like you to believe, in that book there is not one single *pun.*"[67] Derrida qualifies this proposition to say that *GLAS* does not include puns if

> one persists in understanding by this word, as is often done in certain social-ideological situations and to defend certain norms, the free play, the complacent and slightly narcissistic relation to language, the exercise of virtuosity to no profit, without economy of sense or knowledge, without any necessity but that of enjoying one's mastery over one's language and the others.[68]

Derrida tries to cast off the idea that he is simply punning in his writing, apparently concerned that readers will then take his words to be merely playful or will lead them to feel distracted by some kind of trivial or redundant wordplay.

Nevertheless, when viewed within the larger context of his work, it can be seen that Derrida's wider argument is that wordplay is in a sense everywhere, not limited to a word or two. If Derrida acknowledges and announces his non-mastery over his texts, then, this is partly to leave them to the future: it is not so that he can expressly claim limited responsibility for them, but to acknowledge that this play is one of the "consequences of saying that whenever we use a word all of its possible significances come into play"—as Gordon C. F. Bearn attested when he considered inadvertent puns.[69] The term "pun" or, indeed, "wordplay" may be helpful to isolate what we read to be an intended moment of local verbal dexterity or allusion, but in the absolute this isolation is doomed to failure because any word might be read differently, whether through the word being read ironically, non-seriously, or with other definitions of the word calling to be signified: hence, also, the delight (or distrust) among some when other critics find a textual significance that they did not see at first. In this we can perhaps understand Derrida's will not to be seen as a writer who puns.

If Derrida's writing "borders on being unreadable", then, this is not because the philosopher is deliberately trying to misguide us. On the contrary, it is because he is working to show that all writing "borders on being unreadable". As Royle attests,

---

[66]Ibid., 22.

[67]Derrida, "Proverb: 'He that would pun...'," 17; "pun" is in English in Derrida's text.

[68]Ibid., 18.

[69]Bearn, 331. Gordon C. F. Bearn comments that, given the possibility of inadvertent puns, "I suppose it is no surprise to discover that if you begin with inadvertent significance, you will end by denying that anyone is master of the language they speak" (334).

Derrida's work consistently draws attention to a notion of the unreadable that is not opposed to readable. "Unreadability", he argues, "does not arrest reading, does not leave it paralyzed in the face of an opaque surface: rather, it starts reading and writing and translation moving again".[70]

His writing often takes the possibility of communication and his reader right to the border, but the risk is in order to point out that when it comes to the unreadability of language we are on the edge already: what makes the failure of communication possible is paradoxically also what makes communication possible. Far from being a nihilistic reading of communication, Derrida's work offers hope and possibility. If Derrida took his *double feeling* (of a nothing left/yet to come) ambivalence in regards to his writing, then, he had a fellow spirit in the hospitable Shakespeare who, despite having a character drown his book, still left enough play in his words and scenes so that his theatre could remain open for readings to come.

Coda: *Derrida and the Time of the Political*

After describing his political work to promote philosophy teaching in schools, Derrida responded to the question: "You seem to be saying that for the State, philosophy is a dangerous discourse that one must be wary of. What are the reasons for this wariness?" His response helps to reconsider the economies of wordplay in our own time. He answered:

> That depends on the state of the State. Political wariness (sometimes shared by a segment of the teaching faculty) toward this or that discourse is not always the essential obstruction. Whatever kind of regime they may have, industrial societies tend, out of concern for profitability, to reduce the share of discourses and formations that have a low productivity (a very difficult evaluation, often erroneous; this is the whole problem today with the "application" of research and the professionalization [we would now say commercialisation] of university education).[71]

My concern in this essay with the play of words—or what we might call alternatively the work of words—seems to tie in with this larger question of the productivity and the economy of certain academic research. So, we might see a relation between the notion of a pun as being an "ultimately pointless exhibition of playfulness"[72] or not doing the work of communication, and the accusation that Derrida's writing is either "false or trivial". No doubt this concern with the economy of words also leads to the frustrated impatience among some when Derrida tries to *coin* his own neologisms. Again, for humanities research, the pressure to deliver quick returns or definite yields might graph onto the notion that Shakespeare and theory is a waste of time or unprofitable.

---

[70]Royle, *Jacques Derrida*, 131, citing Derrida, "Living On," 116.

[71]Derrida, "Unsealing ('the old new language')," 126. See also Derrida, "This Strange Institution Called Literature," on the "economic evaluation" of play and his question: "Why, in wanting at all costs to avoid play, because it could be bad, do we also risk depriving ourselves of 'good' play …?" (64–5).

[72]Royle, *How to Read Shakespeare*, 13.

However, the resources that Derrida finds in Shakespeare's plays (his *Works*) suggests that, in turn, those working on Shakespeare should not be so hasty to dismiss Derrida's work. We might allow a little play or ghosting between Derrida and Shakespeare to work—not just to help us read Shakespeare, but to communicate to those outside the field(s) why reading Shakespeare and thinking with Shakespeare is resourceful, why we, like Derrida, "would like to read and write in the space or heritage of Shakespeare".[73] Hélène Cixous seems to be thinking through a Shakespearean legacy when she writes of Derrida:

> I said *let's play*, for he will have reminded us that everything is destined to *playing*, there is *some play*, it plays, like the earth on its axis, it is not frozen, fixed, stuck, it slides and this is right away already of the order of the political[,] it reminds us that one cannot *bank on, fix*, posit, stabilize, pose a thesis without a perhaps, an if, an as-if, and then a *but-if / but-yes*, a *mais-si*—that is a messiah, right away getting mixed up in it.
>
> …
>
> *Nota bene* right away: Warning. This vision of "we humans" as players played in no way lessens the measure of responsibility. It makes it more difficult to exercise responsibility, but it also makes it more desirable.[74]

Acknowledgements

I am grateful to Nicholas Royle for providing valuable comments on an earlier draft of my essay. Thanks also to Sophie Battell for trying to keep my language in order. I owe a special debt to Lucy Menon whose support during this project has been vital.

References

Bearn, Gordon C. F. "The Possibility of Puns: A Defence of Derrida." *Philosophy and Literature* 19, no. 2 (1995): 1–5.

Cixous, Hélène. "Jacques Derrida: Co-Responding Voix You." In *Derrida and the Time of the Political*, edited by Pheng Cheah and Suzanne Guerlac, and translated by Peggy Kamuf. Durham, NC: Duke University, 2009.

Czerniecki, Krystia. "The Jest Digested: Perspectives on History in *Henry V*." In *On Puns: The Foundations of Letters*, edited by Jonathan Culler. Oxford: Blackwell, 1988.

Davies, Sally. "The pun conundrum." 16 January 2013. [cited 16 January 2013]. Available from http://www.bbc.co.uk/news/magazine-21011778.

de Grazia, Margreta. *"Hamlet" without Hamlet*. Cambridge: Cambridge University Press, 2007.

Derrida, Jacques. "Différance." In *Speech and Phenomena: And Other Essays on Husserl's Theory of Signs*, translated by David Allison. Evanston, IL: Northwestern University Press, 1973.

———. *GLAS*. Translated by John P. Leavey Jr. and Richard Rand. Lincoln: University of Nebraska Press, 1986.

---

[73]Derrida, "This Strange Institution Called Literature," 67.
[74]Cixous, 48.

———. "*Honoris Causa*: 'This is *Also* Extremely Funny'." Translated by Marian Hobson and Christopher Johnson. In *Points …: Interviews, 1974–1994*, edited by Elisabeth Weber and translated by Peggy Kamuf et al. Stanford, CA: Stanford University Press, 1995. (First published in *Cambridge Review* 113, no. 2318 [October 1992]).

———. *Learning to Live Finally: The Last Interview*. Translated by Pascale-Anne Brault and Michael Naas. Basingstoke: Palgrave Macmillan, 2007, 131–8.

———. *Limited Inc*. Edited by Gerald Graff. Evanston, IL: Northwestern University Press, 1988.

———. "Living On." Translated by James Hulbert. In *Deconstruction and Criticism*, by Harold Bloom, Paul de Man, Jacques Derrida, Geoffrey Hartman and J. Hillis Miller. New York: Seabury Press, 1979.

———. *Of Grammatology*. Translated by Gayatri Chakravorty Spivak. Corrected ed. Baltimore, MD: Johns Hopkins University Press, 1997.

———. "Proverb: 'He That Would Pun …'." In *GLASsary*, by John Leavey Jr. Lincoln: University of Nebraska Press, 1986.

———. *Specters of Marx: The State of the Debt, the Work of Mourning, & the New International*. Translated by Peggy Kamuf. New York: Routledge, 1994.

———. "'This Strange Institution Called Literature': An Interview with Jacques Derrida." Translated by Geoffrey Bennington and Rachel Bowlby. In *Acts of Literature*, edited by Derek Attridge. London: Routledge, 1992.

———. "The Time is Out of Joint." Translated by Peggy Kamuf. In *Deconstruction is / in America: A New Sense of the Political*, edited by Anselm Haverkamp. New York: New York University Press, 1995.

———. "Unsealing ('The Old New Language')." In *Points …: Interviews, 1974–1994*, edited by Elisabeth Weber and translated by Peggy Kamuf et al. Stanford, CA: Stanford University Press, 1995.

Eagleton, Terry. *William Shakespeare*. Oxford: Blackwell, 1986.

Empson, William. *Seven Types of Ambiguity*. 3d ed. London: Chatto and Windus, 1970.

Garber, Marjorie. *Shakespeare's Ghost Writers: Literature as Uncanny Causality*. Rev. ed. New York: Routledge, 2010.

Greenblatt, Stephen. *Hamlet in Purgatory*. Princeton, NJ: Princeton University Press, 2001.

Harris, Jonathan Gil. *Shakespeare and Literary Theory: Oxford Shakespeare Topics*. Oxford: Oxford University Press, 2010.

Hartman, Geoffrey H. *Saving the Text: Literature/Derrida/Philosophy*. Baltimore, MD: Johns Hopkins University Press, 1981.

Herbrechter, Stefan, and Ivan Callus, eds. *Posthumanist Shakespeares*. Basingstoke: Palgrave Macmillan, 2012.

Johnson, Samuel. "Preface to the Plays of William Shakespeare." In *Dr Johnson on Shakespeare*, edited by W. K. Wimsatt. Harmondsworth: Penguin, 1969.

Lopez, Jeremy. "Meat, Magic, and Metamorphosis: On Puns and Wordplay." In *Theatrical Convention and Audience Response in Early Modern Drama*. Cambridge: Cambridge University Press, 2003.

Lupton, Julia Reinhard. *Thinking with Shakespeare: Essays on Politics and Life*. Chicago, IL: University of Chicago Press, 2012.

Mahood, Molly. *Shakespeare's Wordplay*. London: Methuen, 1957.

Montag, Warren. "Spirits Armed and Unarmed: Derrida's Specters of Marx." In *Ghostly Demarcations: A Symposium on Jacques Derrida's "Specters of Marx,"* edited by Michael Sprinker. London: Verso, 1999.

Müller, Chris. "Style and Arrogance: The Ethics of Heidegger's Style." In *Style in Theory: Between Literature and Philosophy*, edited by Ivan Callus, James Corby and Gloria Lauri-Lucente. London: Bloomsbury Academic, 2013.

Norris, Christopher. *Deconstruction: Theory and Practice*. Rev. ed. London: Routledge, 1991.

———. "Extraordinary Language: Why Wittgenstein Didn't Like Shakespeare." In *Fiction, Philosophy and Literary Theory: Will the Real Saul Kripke Please Stand Up?* London: Continuum Books, 2007.

———. "Provoking Philosophy: Shakespeare, Johnson, Wittgenstein, Derrida." In *Philosophy Outside-In: A Critique of Academic Reason*. Edinburgh: Edinburgh University Press, in press.

Orlet, Christopher. "Derrida's Bluff." *The American Spectator*, 15 October 2004. [cited 19 December 2012]. Available from http://spectator.org/archives/2004/10/15/derridas-bluff.

Parvini, Neema. *Shakespeare and Contemporary Theory: New Historicism and Cultural Materialism*. London: Bloomsbury Academic, 2012.

Peeters, Benoît. *Derrida: A Biography*. Translated by Andrew Brown. Cambridge: Polity, 2013.

Plain English Campaign Website. [cited 10 January 2012]. Available from http://www.plainenglish.co.uk/about-us.html.

Redfern, Walter. *Puns: More Senses than One*. 2d ed. London: Penguin Books, 2000.

Royle, Nicholas. *After Derrida*. Manchester: Manchester University Press, 1995.

———. *How To Read Shakespeare*. London: Granta Books, 2005.

———. *Jacques Derrida*. London: Routledge, 2003.

———. "Jacques Derrida's Language: (Bin Laden on the Telephone)." In *In Memory of Jacques Derrida*. Edinburgh: Edinburgh University Press, 2009.

———. "The Poet: *Julius Caesar* and the Democracy to Come." In "Angles on Derrida—Jacques Derrida and Anglophone Literature." Special issue, *Oxford Literary Review* 25 (2003): 39–62.

———. "Prologue." In "Shakespeare and Derrida." Special issue, *Oxford Literary Review* 34, no. 1 (2012): v–vi.

Shakespeare, William. *The Norton Shakespeare: Based on the Oxford Edition*. Edited by Stephen Greenblatt, Walter Cohen, Jean E. Howard and Katherine Eisaman Maus. New York: Norton, 1997.

Shakespeare and Derrida: An International Conference. [cited 18 December 2012]. Available from http://www.cardiff.ac.uk/encap/newsandevents/events/conferences/shakespeare.html.

Smith, Barry, Hans Albert, David Armstrong, Ruth Barcan Marcus, Keith Campbell, Richard Glauser, Rudolf Haller, Massiom Mugnai, Kevin Mulligan, Lorenzo Peña, Willard van Orman Quine, Wolfgang Röd, Edmund Ruggaldier, Karl Schumann, Daniel Schulthess, Peter Simons, René Thom, Dallas Willard, Jan Wolenski. "Derrida Degree a Question of Honour." In "Appendix" to Jacques Derrida, "*Honoris Causa*: 'This is Also Extremely Funny'." Translated by Marian Hobson and Christopher Johnson. In Points …: Interviews, 1974–1994, edited by Elisabeth Weber and translated by Peggy Kamuf et al. Stanford, CA: Stanford University Press, 1995. (First published in *The Times*, 9 May 1992.)

Tudeau-Clayton, Margaret. "Shakespeare's Extravagancy." In *Shakespeare et le jeu: Actes du Congrès organisé par la Société Française Shakespeare*, edited by Pierre Kapitaniak and Yves Peyré. Paris: SFS, 2005. [cited 10 December 2012]. Available from http://www.societefrancaiseshakespeare.org/document.php?id=711.

Vickers, Brian. *Appropriating Shakespeare: Contemporary Critical Quarrels*. New Haven, CT: Yale University Press, 1993.

Wilson, Richard. *Shakespeare in French Theory: King of Shadows*. London: Routledge, 2007.

Storm at Sea: *The Tempest*, Cultural Materialism and the Early Modern Political Aesthetic

Christopher Pye

Critical reception of The Tempest *has shifted over time from broadly aesthetic matters—the sublimating passage of matter into spirit, the work's self-conscious artfulness—to a concern with material context, particularly its status as colonial encounter. In fact, that division of critical attention has foreclosed engagement with the work's deepest political stakes. For it is precisely in its preoccupation with the problem of the aesthetic, and particularly with aesthetic autonomy, that the play encounters the most radical dimensions of its material and historical causation, this essay argues. In that sense,* The Tempest *is an important corrective to forms of cultural materialist analysis that have sought to historicize early modern works by bracketing the problem of the aesthetic altogether.*

The recent claims made for an outrightly empirical and statistical variant of cultural materialism in Shakespeare and Renaissance studies marks the distance the field has travelled from new historicism's more or less literary or hermeneutic worrying of the relationship between text and context. Still, what may give pause about such a wholesale empirical turn may not be purely a matter of nostalgic allegiance to literary-critical texture and complication. The modes of empirical analysis such as the "thin description" forwarded by Douglas Bruster assume persuasive force by virtue of a logic of adequation.[1] That is, the accretion of statistically categorizable instances has legitimacy insofar as it brings us closer to the presumed totality of the social or cultural field it describes—the more, the truer. To evoke that field as an "open unity" as Bruster does doesn't diminish the necessity of the relation between empiricism and totalization; the empirical procedure is founded on the unspoken positing of a horizon in order to constitute the field of "discovery" within which it stakes its claims.[2] Which doesn't mean that statistical analysis isn't persuasive. It is

---

[1] Bruster, 29–62.
[2] See Derrida, 128–35.

persuasive within the terms of a mode whose limits might nevertheless be of interest in the context of the era in which empiricism was first constituting itself as a procedure. The relation between symbolization, including fictionality, and empiricism in the early modern era remains a live question.

The problem of the relation between cultural materialism and historicization has become no less apparent at the level of the very matter of materialist analysis. As a number of critics, including Bruster, have rightly pointed out, while the attention to the object might imply a dethroning of the idealist subject,[3] to the extent that object studies has become just that—merely the study of objects—it bears no necessary relation to history.[4] To historicize the object, we would seem to need to understand it vis-à-vis the array of shifting social structures. And yet, that very process of historicization opens questions about materialism's object. Jonathan Gil Harris and Natasha Korda make a nuanced case for the temporality of the object. The "staged properties" referred to in the title of their collection alludes to material properties on stage but also to the historical stages of any given object. To temporalize the object thus is, however, to raise the question of what is being analyzed. If by "stages" we mean the varying inflection of an already given object over time, then the material object itself remains an unvarying and thus ahistorical ground. Even in those writings in which Harris explores the more complex polychronic untimeliness of the object—its containing multiple temporalities within itself—that object tends to amount to an already given materiality which then receives time's imprint: "the multiple traces of time [are] embedded in things"; "the objects of material culture are ... saturated with the ... imprints of many times."[5] If on the other hand by stages we mean a more radical claim concerning the active constitution or reconstitution of the object through its historic phases, then the focus of materialist analysis becomes not the object but the materiality of its inscription. In that sense, insofar as we associate materiality with historicity, which is to say with contingency, is the "object" necessarily the right object of materialist analysis at all?

The materiality forwarded by the recent, briskly self-proliferative "transversal theory" is in some regard committed to such an inscriptive account. Thus, the cultural materialism Bryan Reynolds and William N. West propose explicitly sets itself against a notion of materiality as recovered ground or reference.[6] Materialization is always rematerialization, the semiotic displacement of instantiated readings across the cultural and critical landscape.[7] Or it is and isn't that. For materialism is equally a matter of the

---

[3]Or might not, insofar as such attention reinforces the familiar subject/object binarism that has always underwritten the idealist subject. The symmetry of that supposed opposition is evident enough in accounts that seek to displace a subject orientation by reference to the quasi-biographical "life" or "career" of the object.
[4]Harris, "The New New Historicism's *Wunderkammer*"; Pye, *The Vanishing*, 2–4; Bruster, 198–203. Although I balk at his historical equation of contemporary materialism *tout court* with capitalist commodification, David Hawkes offers a deft summary of the materialist orientation in the long view and in early modern studies.
[5]Harris and Korda, 24; and Harris, *Untimely Matter*, 9, 7.
[6]Reynolds and West, 9, 15.
[7]See ibid., 9.

lived "affective presence" and positivity of those manifestations, what the authors describe as the sense of the "real" "here and now" of Shakespeare.[8] The reference here is to Deleuzian vitalism, but because that claim for the affective here and now is mustered in the service of a reaffirmation of the determining force of human agency, it becomes hard to distinguish from a variant of expressive humanism in which materiality becomes something secondary, the "objectified expression of humans".[9]

The tension between those strains in transversal theory—the inscriptive, the agential—bears on the largest stakes of the project. The force of transversalism lies in its capacity to prompt individuals and groups to "get ... outside themselves", to pass into the "antisubjective" subjunctive domain of transverse space.[10] And yet, because the model of the social the theory offers remains simply an "aggregate of individuals", we're left uncertain about just how decentring any tranverse effect can actually be.[11] Thus, when Reynolds writes that transversal territory is "where someone goes conceptually and emotionally when they venture, through what I call 'transversal movements,' beyond the boundaries of their own subjective territory", one wants to know who that "someone" is if not a subject, and whether, indeed, that someone who sustains herself across the space of its constituting territories isn't something like a transcendental subject.[12] The lingering ambiguity implicit in such accounts—does the subject determine material culture? Does materiality determine the subject?—bears on a larger question for cultural materialism. Is the language of causality right at all? While materialist criticism has been scrupulous about avoiding what it terms the "crude determinism" of, say, Marxist economic theory, it has been less worried about the discourse of causality. And yet, doesn't causal logic bring us well within the epistemological orbit of an already constituted idealist subject? What, then, does it mean to speak of the "causation" of that subject?

Where does all this leave us, vis-à-vis the relation between materiality and subjectivity, or between material inscription and the phenomenal consistency of that being? With, I'll suggest, a category that tends to fall decidedly out of view for politically oriented critique: the aesthetic. This will seem an odd recourse. Isn't aesthetics just what cultural materialist criticism seeks to move away from? Indeed, it's worth recalling how precisely that was the case, how expressly new historicism in its inaugural phase constituted itself as against the aesthetic, its commitment to porous contextualization and fragmentariness defined against the aesthetic's supposed investment in the autonomy and wholeness of the work. At another level, the sense of the strong and ongoing fit between early modern studies and cultural materialism, a fit that has often translated into a tendency to construe the work as a species of anthropological

---

[8]Ibid., 12–14.
[9]Ibid., 10.
[10]Reynolds, *Becoming Criminal*, 18.
[11]Ibid., 13.
[12]Ibid., 18.

artefact, is in good part underwritten by the claim that aesthetic considerations are ana-chronistic in relation to works produced prior to the philosophical elaboration of the category in the eighteenth century.

It's fair to ask whether the aesthetic is so easy to bracket. New historicist fragmenta-tion is, of course, an aesthetic effect, as is transverse theory's rapid-fire concatenation of terms. One can also argue the historical claim on empirical grounds. It's difficult to imagine an era in which the work is more reflective about its own status as work; think, broadly, about that emergent feeling for form in excess of content Clark Hulse has described as the distinguishing trait of the work of the era, the sense of "literariness" as such.[13] Insofar as it comprehended itself in terms of the return of a lost past, which is to say precisely as image, the Renaissance is itself an aesthetic conception, and before dismissing the term for just that reason it's important to acknowledge how directly such a conception bears on the emergence of modern conceptions of his-toricity and the political.[14]

But the relation between aesthetics and history is more complex. Precisely in its concern with the autonomy of the work, that is, with art insofar as it exceeds either an instrumental or referential account of its representational function, the aesthetic poses the most radical questions concerning the way in which non-referential language—the movement of inscription—assumes phenomenal form in the first place. In that sense, the aesthetic is directly bound up with the question how culture incarnates itself as an immanent form. One historical category among others, the aes-thetic is also the means through which difference—the sheer contingency of history—assumes a phenomenal condition and thus becomes cognizable.[15]

The ambiguity of the aesthetic's relation to history has particular force in relation to early modernity. On the one hand, I'll suggest that the emergence of something like an aesthetic subject is locatable within the era, affiliated with a historical shift in concepts of sovereignty and law. On the other, precisely because it is as yet unconsolidated, which is to say not yet bracketed off as a discrete philosophical category, the aesthetic remains directly bound up with the political at the most profound levels of historiciza-tion. The analysis that follows focuses on a single text—*The Tempest*—and makes no claims to the forms of contextualization appropriate to cultural analysis. At the same time, the stakes of the aesthetic extend beyond the literary work, and the relations among materiality, subjectivity and history engaged by the play have at least theoretical pertinence for some of the ground-level concerns of materialist criticism.

The Tempest is the right place to take up these questions about aesthetics and history, for they're at the heart of one of the play's central riddles. The most "aestheticizing" of Shakespeare's plays, the most preoccupied with its own formal autonomy, *The Tempest* is also the play most concerned with the "brave new world" of exogamous contact.

---

[13]Hulse, 31–5.

[14]On Renaissance *imitatio* and the construction of the modern political sphere, see Lacoue-Labarthe, 78; and Lefort, 270–1.

[15]See Redfield, 25.

Rather than taking up that apparent contradiction, critical reception of the play has tended simply to play it out over time, with the tide more or less shifting from a pre-occupation with, say, the neo-Platonic roots of Shakespeare's spiritualizing art to an understanding of the play as the *mis-en-scene* of colonial encounters. We'll see what's at stake in the failure of those traditions to engage each other, what that non-encounter protects against. But I'll say in advance that the intuitive solution to the play's riddle—the argument that the work's aspiration to aesthetic self-sufficiency buffers or ameliorates the alien encounter—is wrong. The relation between the aesthetic and historical causation is at once more complex and more direct.

The Tempest's concern with aestheticization is evident enough in its formal reflexivity, as well as its thematic concern with the magician as artful conjurer. But the relation between materiality and aesthetics is explicitly there in the preoccupation with sublimation both in the precise alchemical sense of the term—the metaphors drawn from that arcane transformative process run through the play—and more generally in the work's apparent etherealizing aims: the translation of—or declared failure to translate—gross matter into spirit. Such a movement into spirit is consistent with the play's dialectical place in Shakespeare's oeuvre. It's clunky but not wrong to read *The Tempest*, and indeed all the late "Romances", in terms of a Hegelian passage from comedy through tragedy to another form in which death is sublated—at once negated and inwardly retained—and thus redeemed. The reflexive, internalizing dimension of such a dialectical movement is consistent with the play's general preoccupation with memory and inwardness. The social/historical dimensions of the structure might then be apparent in the recursive movement of the play's opening, where we discover that the initiating storm scene, with it's thrilling class inversions—with death looming, the mariner/labourers freely command the courtiers—turns out to have been the work of the aristocratic humanist sorcerer all along; one might be tempted to see in that Shakespeare's revisionary account of the redeeming passage from artisanal stage into the illimitable space of authorial letters.

The aesthetic logic of the play is more complex, however, and what it implies of sovereign power is not of such a clinching sort. We can intuit that in the play's most striking formal trait. No Shakespeare drama is more tightly controlled, one of just two to observe the classical unities. And yet, no Shakespeare play is so dispersed, with its ambient voices, its projective relation between characters (Prospero imputes the usurping crimes of the father to the prospective son), its expansive web of specular correspondences in which, for instance, the "forward" and "backward" voices of a monster can figure the self-divisions of the master, and where characters eerily anticipate themselves—the hollow, bellowing voices Antonio concocts to cover his intended crime foretell the form his actual guilt will later take.[16]

---

[16]On the mixture of compression and pleonastic iteration in the play, see McDonald, 218–19. For a beautiful account of the lability of character and language in the play and its social implications, see Palfrey, 25–7, 144, 230.

In fact, those qualities of the play—its totalizing character, its dispersal—are of a piece. The autonomous character of the project is apparent in the play's attempted incorporation of its own limits precisely *as* constitutive limits: the storm scene, through which the play retroactively attempts to inscribe its own precipitating cause, the epilogue through which the fiction as fiction—Prospero stays in role—would include its reception and end. The play's knowingness about the contradiction of such a self-constituting gesture—the fact that it depends on a remainder simultaneously included and excluded—is evident from the curious formal status of the tempest itself, a founding, eponymous event that nonetheless remains ostentatiously marginal in relation to the play. Precisely because the play would establish itself as self-generative fiction, the division that constitutes that domain as such inhabits every element within it, producing the play's endlessly dissolutive, endlessly recuperative effects. The play secures itself, to the extent that it secures itself at all, not at the level of its mimetic or empirical particulars, but as an aesthetic field within which all tends toward a generalized and fluid allegoresis.

One can understand that formal trait in local literary terms—the dispersed character of the play, and of the romances generally, have been read as Shakespeare's response to the individuating tendencies of Jonsonian realism.[17] But the aesthetic logic of the drama can also be understood more ambitiously in relation to the political/representational logic of the era, the interval between theocratic institutions and fully formed absolutism. Provoked by the multiplication of post-Reformation belief structures, that interim is, in Walter Benjamin's account, characterized by a political-symbolic order without transcendental ground or recourse, a domain that is at once emptied out—a matter of pure theatricality—and illimitable. Such a radically immanent condition amounts, in Benjamin's turn on Carl Schmitt's analysis of the primordial dimension of the sovereign decision, to a permanent state of emergency, but one in which no decision is possible because no posture of externality from which such a decision could be made is available.[18] For English drama of the era, that symbolic condition is particularly manifest in the limitlessly reinscriptive mechanisms of the revenge cycle—*The Tempest*'s resolution, we should remember, is associated with an inward-turning forgiveness which seeks to arrest such a cycle. The aesthetic turn through which the work seeks to compass its own limits as limits and thus become, as it were, internal and external to itself enables that representational transformation, and the version of sovereignty—an explicitly aesthetic sovereignty—it implies.

The Tempest's preoccupation with autogenesis or self-constitution is most evident in the fantasy of patriarchal creation, and thus too in its demonization of the mother. It's not the only play to engage in that gesture. But the differences are telling. In *King Lear*, where sovereignty remains a thematic concern, the maternal is radically foreclosed and luridly returns, precisely in relation to the sovereign's madness: "O, how this mother

---

[17]Palfrey, 26.
[18]Benjamin, *Origin*, 66–71. See Weber, 187–90.

swells up toward my heart! / *Hysterica passio.*"[19] Founding demonization in *The Tempest* is virtually evoked as such—the witch, Sycorax, is represented as Prospero's mirror, the one's history directly and ironically mappable onto the other, the one conquest of the island repeating the other, one off-spring and heir for another. The maternal figure assumes the form of that included exclusion through which sovereign and play alike seek to constitute themselves as autonomous forms. When Prospero describes the crabbed woman "grown into a hoop", the strange image at once figures the woman as sheer negation—the familiar "naught" of the feminine—and as the very image of Prospero's own dream of self-completion.[20] The two meanings are consubstantial insofar as the hooped woman figures the negation and exclusion on which that possibility of auto-completion is founded.

Which is to say that the maternal is of a piece with the play's larger efforts to figure within itself its own inscribing grounds, positing that ground as a naturalized and thus legible continuum ranging from the gross matter upon which "any print of goodness wilt not take" to the "printless foot" of the ethereal spirits (1.2.351, 5.1.34). Along with the preoccupations with dynastic continuity, the play's extravagant investment in chastity should be understood in terms of the problem of grounds generally; the play stakes itself on Miranda's status as tabula rasa, a pure, groundless ground secured in the determinate interval between matter and spirit.[21] But it is also precisely around that question of inscription—the play's capacity to mark its own power to inscribe, to take—that one feels its greatest perturbations. "I pray thee, mark me", "Dost thou attend me?", "Pray thee, mark me", "Mark his condition": Prospero declaims (1.2.67, 78, 88, 117). "Do you mark me?", Gonzalo declares (2.1.169). Such moments have a psychological dimension. But the fact that the concern is reiterated across characters suggests its bearing on the way in which the radically incorporative and totalizing work, the absolute work, necessarily encounters the question of its own power to take.

The problem of inscription appears most vividly in the scenes where the play's creationist themes come to bear directly on the formation of subjectivities, including the moment that has received the most critical attention—Prospero's curiously overwrought response at the point where, recalling Caliban's plot, he dissolves the wedding masque. "Never till this day / Saw I him touched with anger so distempered", his daughter remarks (4.1.144–5). "I am vexed", Prospero says,

> ... my old brain is troubled.
> Be not disturbed with my infirmity.
>
> . . . .
>
> A turn or two I'll walk
> To still my beating mind. (4.1.158–63)

---

[19]Shakespeare, *King Lear*, 2.2.246–7.
[20]Shakespeare, *The Tempest*, 1.2.258. All further references in the text to *The Tempest* are to this edition.
[21]On imprinting as cultural, pedagogical and sexual reproduction in the play, see Goldberg, 124–8. Joan Pong Linton emphasizes the mimetological contradictions internal to the play's gendered forms of cultural imprinting (155–70).

Stephen Orgel is right to suggest that Prospero's reaction exceeds what can be explained by the recalled machinations of the hapless monster and his drunken co-conspirators. What disturbs the magician, Orgel observes, is more the fact of his own self-forgetfulness—it's that that brings thoughts of mortality.[22]

That forgetfulness amounts to the point where auto-creation threatens to become sheer repetition. Having restaged the entire history of his betrayal in order to rewrite its close, Prospero risks repeating the fall itself, the moment of his being lost to his books. He risks closing the hoop, as it were. Such forgetfulness can be psychologized; Prospero's uncharacteristic absorption in his own theatre is a stay against the paternal loss the wedding masque will inevitably bring with it for him. But there is something originary and irreducible in the moment. To have given oneself over thus is already to enact the mortal loss one fends against, a self-loss that by definition can only be known after the fact, at the point of coming to. We recall Caliban's earlier, equally ravishing, account of his own indeterminate coming to, his dream of a bereaved waking, and of waking to dream again. For the authorial master, as for the acculturated slave, consciousness is the consciousness of a recursive loss, neither absorption nor transcendence but the belated knowledge that one had already been inscribed.

"A turn or two I'll walk to still my beating mind." Prospero's phrase does in fact bring beginnings to mind, as well as ends: the opening tempest, or at least Miranda's response to that precipitating event. After the clamour of the shipboard scene, we shift to Prospero and his daughter on the island, and hear Miranda's cry:

> O, I have suffered
> With those that I saw suffer: a brave vessel—
> Who had, no doubt some noble creature, in her—
> Dashed all to pieces! (1.2.5–8)

Of course, what she has viewed is not a real event; her magician father has staged the storm, as she herself seems to know. Part of the ethical force of the scene derives from the audience's awareness of the discrepancy between its response to that stagy opening scene of drowning and Miranda's pure, absorptive sympathy. The distinction is not a matter of the status of the event—it's theatre for us, it's art for her—but of the condition of the subjectivity that apprehends it. If Miranda responds with absolute identification it's because, as yet unformed, she is, in a sense, everywhere. "Be collected", Prospero says, and, setting aside his robes, he proceeds to give her the means to be collected, the inclusive and to this point unspoken narrative of her life from her birth to the present moment (1.2.13).

It is Miranda herself, however, who completes the circuit of that narrative, drawing its thread back to the event Prospero set out to explain:

---

[22]Orgel, 50. Jeffrey Knapp considers distraction in the play more broadly as both the impediment to and the vehicle for the cultivation of a colonialism based on "temperate homebodiedness" (220–42).

> And now I pray you, sir,
> For still 'tis beating in my mind, your reason
> For raising this sea-storm. (1.2.175–7)

What beats in Miranda's mind is, of course, the tempest. But the status of that cause and end is hard to know. It is no longer the immediate impress of the event—the storm has past. Nor, however, is the beating mind a function of the recollective, narrativized self. Belonging neither to the mark of outward spectacle nor of inward narrative, distraction here suggests subjective causation—subjectivity's opening—precisely as what exceeds symbolic or cultural interpellation, a causeless cause.

A reverberation of the storm that went before, Prospero's beating mind is also the sound of something still to come. "Now my charms are all o'erthrown," Prospero announces as he turns outward to the audience at the close:

> And what strength I have's mine own,
>   Now 'tis true
> I must be here confined by you,
> Or sent to Naples. Let me not,
> .   .   .   .
>   ... dwell
> In this bare island by your spell
> But release me from my bands
> With the help of your good hands.
> Gentle breath of yours my sails
> Must fill, or else my project fails,
> Which was to please. ...
> .   .   .   .
>   ... my ending is despair
> Unless I be relieved by prayer,
> Which pierces so, that it assaults
> Mercy itself, and frees all faults.
> As you from crimes would pardoned be,
> Let your indulgence set me free. (5.1.319–38)

The tonal oddities of the Epilogue, the suggestions of force—of assaults and piercings —the freighted language of crime and punishment, is bound up with the unstable agonism of those moments where the Shakespearean spell-binder within—Puck, Prospero—addresses himself without, directly to the all-mastering audience. The audience might clap gently, graciously freeing the magician. Then again, given the perils of captivation figured throughout the drama but especially at the end in the circle of the spell-bound adversaries—image of our own absorbed relation to the stage—an audience would have more tendentious reasons to wish Prospero on his way, to clap with a spell-breaking vengeance, thus marking the play's limits, and its own mastering place beyond them.

But to claim one's power thus, to speed his ship on its way with something more violent than a gentle breath, is, of course, to repeat the tempest with which the play began, and thus to be back where one started, all the more bound-up. To release oneself from that double bind would be to applaud knowingly, precisely with the consciousness that one's response is already inscribed, and thus to hear it—one's own clapping—as something, again, at once inward and alien: to come to with the lingering, familiar and strange, sound of a beating in the mind. That state anticipates the *savoir faire*—the knowing that one doesn't know—of an emerging aesthetic subjectivity. But the effect equally recalls the traditional status of the sovereign as *major et minor se ipso*, above and below himself, beyond and within the law. Crucially, it is now the logic of the aesthetic that sustains that sovereign condition.

Groundless, reflexive, knowing: such an irresolute resolution embodies the play's version of aesthetic subjectivity in ideal form. And yet the beating mind remains disquieting. "Thou most lying slave, / Whom stripes may move, not kindness", Prospero says to Caliban (1.2.344–5). But if force lingers in the beating of the mind, it is unsettling precisely because it is intransitive and causeless—one thinks of the phantasmatic scene at the centre of Sigmund Freud's essay, "A Child is Being Beaten".[23] We might also hear Jacques Lacan's account of the drives where he recalls the butterfly that inspires in Freud's Wolfman "the phobic terror of recognizing that the beating of little wings is not so very far from the beating of causation, of the primal stripe marking his being for the first time with the grid of desire."[24] What pulses in the drives is the workings of a negation indistinguishable from the foundations of being: "Ban, ban, Ca-Caliban", the monster reverberates (2.2.179).

That prospect of a purely reiterative negation troubles the play's larger, salvific project of dialectical internalization. The beating mind bears the mark of fatality insofar as it suggests that the blind, inscribing recoils of revenge may not, finally, be distinct from the reflexive, inward turn of conscience and reflective consciousness, the outward law of the one ultimately indistinguishable from the spirit of the other.[25] Which is also to say that it exposes the arbitrary, forcibly posited character

---

[23]Freud. For the classic analysis of the intransitive scene, see Laplanche.

[24]Lacan, 76.

[25]The structural relation between reflexive reason and revenge is apparent in the passage from Michael Montaigne whose phrases echo through Prospero's articulation of forgiveness. Montaigne speaks of the distinction between goodness and the higher order of virtue:

> He that through a natural facility and genuine mildness should neglect or condemn injuries received, should no doubt perform a rare action and worthy commendation; but he who being stung to the quick with any wrong or offence received, should arm himself with reason against this furiously blind desire of revenge, and in the end after a great conflict yield himself master over it, should doubtless do much more. (211)

The difference involves more than the intensity of the affront; it's a distinction between goodness as natural inclination and a virtue founded on the capacity to reflexively recognize one's blind, reiterative inclination. On the relation between the passage and *The Tempest*, see Yachnin, 169–70; and Prosser.

of the political-theological translation the aesthetic seeks to oversee—recall the play ends with reference to the violence of prayer. Consciousness itself redounds like something poisonously extrinsic—"Do not infest your mind with beating on / the strangeness of this business", Prospero says to his spell-bound adversaries in their coming to (5.1.246–7). Aesthetic internalization—sublimation—turns out to be indistinguishable from the incorporative atavism of the drives. "A grace it had, devouring", Prospero says of the apparitional banquet Ariel conjures for the conscience-stricken courtiers (3.3.84). We devour it, it devours us, and what is devoured is nothing, death: "What, must our mouths be cold?" says the storm-tossed mariner (1.1.52). And that consumption is reflexive consciousness: "they devour their reason", Prospero says of his wide-eyed audience within the play (5.1.155). The line suggests the prophylactic dimension of a latter era's categorical distinction between aesthetic judgement and pure reason.

Understood in these terms, the political-aesthetic conjunction most directly manifests itself at the level of the creature. The riddle of Caliban's anagrammatical name is bound up with the reverting consumption the play intimates at its close. The cannibal who eats his own kind is for Shakespeare always a figure for a self-devouring, as if the fascinating, illegible "primitive" in fact offered back nothing but the consuming figure of our own aesthetic consumption, a truth that returns upon us exactly in proportion to the super-subtle interpretive force through which we claim the power to know him for the cannibal he is.[26]

Such a reversionary understanding of the creatural at once bears out and complicates recent accounts of the politics of "bare life". It wouldn't be wrong to hear in Caliban's self-referring chant what Giorgio Agamben describes as the logic of the sovereign ban, that auto-exclusion through which the sovereign would establish itself as "self-constituting self-relation".[27] At the same time, insofar as the monster figures itself as nothing but the abyssal reduplication of that structure, he also implies a critique of Agamben's project by suggesting the way that project wavers between an account of the sovereign ban as what problematizes "the structure of reference in general" and his account of bare life—the domain of the creatural—as the object, the correlate, or, precisely, "the first and immediate referent" of such a ban.[28] For Agamben, much hangs on that surreptitious slide: the entire ligature between the dialectal and the Foucauldian, bio-political dimensions of the undertaking. To hypostatize the creature thus, to use the creatural to give objectified form to the contradiction of sovereign constitution—to resort to the category of "bare life" as a substantive term at all—is at once to forget and blindly reiterate that self-banning movement. For Agamben, that means repeating the "materialization of the state of

---

[26]On the relation between cannibalism and humanism's "threatened ideal of incorporative reading"—a matter of European readers' relation to "their own kind," see Yachnin, 164. On the reflexivity of the European preoccupation with the cannibal generally, see Greene, 121; and Pye, "To throw out our eyes," 434.

[27]Agamben, 38.

[28]Ibid., 29, 107.

exception" that marks, in his account, the most egregious moments in the epochal history he narrates.[29]

I've been arguing that political aestheticization, that historical process by which sovereignty is recouped through a mechanism that might seem to be ameliorative—a sublimation of power—in fact brings to view something dire at the ontological core of the political, something more troubling than the death of kings. But the nature of *The Tempest*'s engagement with the aesthetic as we've traced it also bears on the riddle with which we began. It is precisely because *The Tempest* is the most aestheticizing of Shakespeare's plays that it's the play most preoccupied with radically extrinsic causes, with history as such, which is to say history as sheer contingency.

If the beating mind suggests causation, it does so as the returning trace of a missed encounter, in Lacan's formulation, an encounter "forever missed"—it is that status as missed encounter that gives material causation its traumatic, inassimilable character. The beating mind marks the point where the play encounters its own best known cause in just such a form. In 1610, William Strachey, the Secretary and one of the stockholders of the Virginia Company's colony in Jamestown, wrote a letter back describing the storm that left their ship wrecked on the Island of Bermuda, suspending the expedition intended to reimpose government on the dissolving colony. Anticipating the play's opening moments, Strachey describes the scene in which the tempest, striking all with "amazement" and "distraction", seems to unhinge all human government. The sea "beat [the governor] from his hold. … [and] struck him from the place where he sate, and grovelled him, and all us about him on our faces, beating together with our breathes all thoughts from our bosoms else than that we were now sinking."[30]

The mingling of the beating of the storm and "our breaths" recalls the opening of *The Tempest*—"you do assist the storm", the Boatswain tells the bellowing courtiers —and the Epilogue, where we are made conscious of our own breaths; one can imagine the description of the encounter with watery death as something like the imaginative kernel of the play—the revolutionary kernel, even, given its relation to the undoing of sovereign governance. But to recognize that relation to the limits of sovereignty, it's important to hold off on the overhasty referential claim. The force of the

---

[29]More broadly, Caliban reformulates the question of sovereignty, focusing it not on what lies beyond the structure of the sovereign ban—Giorgio Agamben's antinomian preoccupation—but on whether the movement of the ban does or doesn't belong to the sovereign. The continuation of Caliban's ditty—"Ban, ban, Cacaliban / Has a new master—get a new man"—seems to offer the promise of an entire miniature political genealogy from the originative self-banning ban to mastery to the getting of a man indistinguishable from that new subjection. But the question is precisely the genealogical one, how one passes from the reiterative, backward and forward, doing and undoing of the first line—the figuration in small of all those dispersive voices that may or may not have inhabited the island before the magician's arrival—and the conversion of that into a developmental form. The political aesthetic instance, and the instance of sovereignty, is the force that manages that conversion. Insofar as such force amounts to an ambiguously reiterative banning of banning, it will always be an uncertain gesture, a force that calls for no end of force. My account here contrasts with Julia Lupton's suggestive Agambenian analysis of Caliban as protosymbolic creaturely ground (161–80).

[30]"A true repertory of the wreck and redemption of Sir Thomas Gates," cited in Orgel, Appendix B; in Shakespeare, *The Tempest*, 209, 211.

account, and its status as source, is less a function of the dramatic fact of death's approach than of the rhetorical slippage that marks that approach. "Beating together with our breaths all thoughts from our bosoms." Does the storm knock from the mariners both their breaths and all thoughts save of death? Or does breath join with storm to beat away all thoughts except of death? Mingled indistinguishably with the storm as it is at the play's close, breath figures at once as effect and cause, an ellipsis equivalent to the impossible act of thinking one's own death. The disaster that turns the entire colonial enterprise into a missed encounter—Bermuda, not Jamestown—is the disaster of the irreducibly missed encounter, a reaction that is also its cause.

That beating amounts to Shakespeare's brush with historical cause insofar as we imagine him hearing in it the echo of an enterprise that's still to come and already past. In that sense, it resonates with Benjamin's account of the revolutionary, elliptical instance that breaks the narrative continuums of historicist history.[31] What Strachey's and Shakespeare's (and for that matter Benjamin's) storms evoke of the limits of the political imaginary in the undoing of human governance and state should be understood in relation to that opening of historical causation. It would be a mistake to imagine such vexations as a function of the aesthetic's encounter with history in any simple sense, as if history breached art from some space beyond. This is a textual encounter, of course. More to the point, precisely in its totalizing movement, the aesthetic solicits and provokes history as the trace of an inassimilable cause, an infraction that occurs neither exactly from within nor from without.

Such an account of the relation between aesthetics and history brings us back to cultural materialism, and particularly to one of its mantras: the insistence that the work must be understood as "embedded" in culture, and thus, a fortiori, as embedded in history. Such a model, which casts the work as an apartment in the mansion of culture, fails to allow for what the aesthetic might suggest about the limits and thus the conditions for the possibility of culture and history as consolidating forms. In bringing those limits to account, the aesthetic can reorient cultural analysis in its particulars, suggesting, for example, that the colonial project may be staked less on the empirical instance of the disciplinary encounter than on the forcible conversion of the missed encounter into just such a familiar and manageable scene of first encounters, and the translation of the intractable beating of causation into a drama of disciplinary force. It might also suggest that the versions of cultural criticism that remain wedded to empirical cause as an explanatory limit may not sufficiently separate themselves from that project.

References

Agamben, Giorgio. *Homo Sacer: Sovereign Power and Bare Life*. Translated by Daniel Heller-Roazen. Stanford, CA: Stanford University Press, 1998.

Benjamin, Walter. *Origin of the German Tragic Drama*. Translated by John Osborne. London: Verso, 1998.

---

[31]Benjamin, "Theses on the Philosophy of History," 253–64.

———. "Theses on the Philosophy of History." In *Illuminations*, edited by Hannah Arendt. New York: Schocken, 1969.

Bruster, Douglas. *Shakespeare and the Question of Culture: Early Modern Literature and the Cultural Turn*. New York: Palgrave, 2003.

Derrida, Jacques. *Rogues: Two Essays on Reason*. Translated by Pascale-Anne Brault and Michael Naas. Stanford, CA: Stanford University Press, 2005.

Freud, Sigmund. "A Child is Being Beaten." In *On Freud's "A Child is Being Beaten,"* edited by Ethel Person. New Haven, CT: Yale University Press, 1997.

Goldberg, Jonathan. *Tempest in the Caribbean*. Minneapolis: University of Minnesota Press, 2004.

Greene, Roland. *Unrequited Conquests: Love and Empire in the Colonial Americas* Chicago, IL: University of Chicago Press, 1999.

Harris, Jonathan Gil. "The New New Historicism's *Wunderkammer* of Objects." *European Journal of English Studies* 4, no. 2 (2000): 1–23.

———. *Untimely Matter in the Time of Shakespeare*. Philadelphia: University of Pennsylvania Press, 2009.

Harris, Jonathan Gil, and Natasha Korda. *Staged Properties in Early Modern English Drama*. Cambridge: Cambridge University Press, 2002.

Hawkes, David. "Against Materialism in Literary Theory." In *The Return of Theory in Early Modern Studies*, edited by Paul Cefalu and Bryan Reynolds. New York: Palgrave, 2011.

Hulse, Clark. "Tudor Aesthetics." In *The Cambridge Companion to English Literature 1500–1600*, edited by Arthur Kinney. Cambridge: Cambridge University Press, 2000.

Knapp, Jeffrey. *An Empire Nowhere: England, America, and Literature from "Utopia" to "The Tempest"*. Berkeley: University of California Press, 1992.

Lacan, Jacques. *The Four Fundamental Concepts of Psychoanalysis*. Edited by Jacques-Alain Miller, translated by Alan Sheridan. New York: Norton, 1981.

Lacoue-Labarthe, Philippe. *Heidegger, Art, and Politics: The Fiction of the Political*. London: Blackwell, 1990.

Laplanche, Jean. *Life and Death in Psychoanalysis*. Translated by Jeffrey Mehlman. Baltimore, MD: Johns Hopkins University Press, 1976.

Lefort, Claude. *Democracy and Political Theory*. Translated by David Macey. New York: Polity, 1991.

Linton, Joan Pong. *The Romance of the New World: Gender and the Literary Formations of English Colonialism*. Cambridge: Cambridge University Press, 1998.

Lupton, Julia Reinhard. *Citizen-Saints: Shakespeare and Political Theology*. Chicago, IL: University of Chicago Press, 2005.

McDonald, Russ. "Reading *The Tempest*." In *Critical Essays on Shakespeare's "The Tempest"*, edited by Virginia Vaughan and Alden Vaughan. London: Twayne, 1998.

Montaigne, Michael. *The Essayes of Michael Lord of Montaigne*. Edited by Henry Morley, translated by John Florio. London: Routledge, 1893.

Orgel, Stephen. "Introduction." In *The Tempest*, edited by Stephen Orgel. Oxford: Clarendon Press, 1987.

Palfrey, Simon. *Late Shakespeare: A New World of Words*. Oxford: Oxford University Press, 1997.

Prosser, Eleanor. "Shakespeare, Montaigne, and the 'Rarer Action'." *Shakespeare Studies* 1 (1965): 261–4.

Pye, Christopher. "'To Throw Out Our Eyes For Brave Othello': Shakespeare and Aesthetic Ideology." *Shakespeare Quarterly* 60, no. 4 (winter 2009): 423–47.

———. *The Vanishing: Shakespeare, the Subject, and Early Modern Culture*. Durham, NC: Duke University Press, 2000.

Redfield, Marc. *The Politics of Aesthetics: Nationalism, Gender, Romanticism*. Stanford, CA: Stanford University Press, 2003.

Reynolds, Bryan. *Becoming Criminal: Transversal Performance and Cultural Dissidence in Early Modern England*. Baltimore, MD: Johns Hopkins University Press, 2002.

Reynolds, Bryan, and William N. West. "Introduction: Shakespearean Emergences: Back from Materialisms to Tranversalisms and Beyond." In *Rematerializing Shakespeare: Authority and Representation on the Early Modern Stage*, edited by Bryan Reynolds and William N. West. Houndmills: Palgrave, 2005.

Shakespeare, William. *King Lear: Arden Shakespeare*. Edited by R. A. Foakes. London: Thompson, 2001.

———. *The Tempest*. Edited by Stephen Orgel. Oxford: Clarendon Press, 1987.

Weber, Samuel. *Benjamin's –abilities*. Cambridge, MA: Harvard University Press, 2008.

Yachnin, Paul. "Eating Montaigne." In *Reading Renaissance Ethics*, edited by Marshall Grossman. London: Routledge, 2007.

Listening to the Body ...: Transitioning to Shakespeare and Theory

François-Xavier Gleyzon and Johann Gregory

Hoc Est Enim Corpus Meum

In tormentis ...

And yet these beings from the past live
within us at the bottom of our leanings,
in the *beat* of our blood. They weigh
upon our destiny. They are that gesture
that comes back to the surface in this
way *from the depths of time.*

Rainer Maria Rilke[1]

A frail and anxious being comes towards you. At a lively and determined pace never-theless, its face tense, sharp and alienated, this strange being halts its forward move-ment, contorts itself and addresses itself to you. In angst, it cries out in a tremulous and panting breath: "Katastrophal." (Catastrophic). "Hilfe!" (Help!).[2] How does one listen to the body? How does one embrace the deep forces and bodily forms of the past buried in the body now, in our bodies?

Catching its breath it then enunciates a coherent passage interspersed with frag-ments and torments that afterwards make way for total schizophrenic collapse:

At the end of an investigation by a historian comparable to that of a detective, the materials we have at our disposal are first of all spread out in front of us like an

---

[1] Rilke, 43.
[2] Warburg, *Gesammelte Schriften*, 29:2854.

inert dead mass; in the course of these archaeological exhumations, nothing more has been brought to light apparently than milestones lining roads abandoned long ago, bearing figures half worn away. But in our search for indirect methods to bring the past back to life, historical nominalism is set long term to reassert itself: an external datum like knowledge [of a figure, of a person] revives it like a person *of flesh and blood.*[3]

Katastrophal.[4]

What I have seen and lived through only scratches the surface of the things I now have the right to talk about. Let me start by saying that the insoluble problem that they pose has weighed on my soul so oppressively that I would never have dared to express myself scientifically on this subject during the period when I was in good health. But at present ... in a closed institution ... I have the impression of *being a seismograph. ... I am letting out of me the signs I have received.*[5]

MEINE SATANISCHE FRESSLUST (MY SATANIC DESIRE TO DEVOUR)[6]

What can one say about these lines? What is this desire to listen to the body so as to better understand, to grasp, to incorporate, even to devour it? From where does this strange and enigmatic thought come to us, this delirious thought, which nevertheless expresses what no historian would dare to formulate perhaps: to appropriate and incorporate the body of the past, its flesh and blood, in order to let out and retransmit the signs into the present. It was during his research seminar in the summer of 1927 at the University of Hamburg—three years to the day after his internment in the psychiatric clinic of Kreuzlingen directed by the famous Ludwig Binswanger—that Aby Warburg suggested "penetrating" the corpus of the past by means of an instrument whose specific design and function are exactly tailored to listening, harnessing and recording: *the seismograph.*

Right from the outset of his seminar, Warburg concentrated on describing and making visible the activities of Burckhardt and Nietzsche as philosophers and historians inasmuch as they were true "receptors", "captors" (*Auffänger*) or even "mnemic waves" (*mnemischen Wellen*) of history, of historicity (*geschichtliches*), and concluded that "both of them [were] highly sensitive *seismographs*" (*sehr empfindliche Seismographen*).[7] For Warburg, the historian, the historian-seismograph, must always stay in contact with and listen to this *geschichtliches*. His task consists in harnessing invisible underground sound waves, agitations—shocks, counter-shocks and tremors—of the crust of the terrestrial body which *survive* still buried in the depths of time, in the

---

[3]Warburg, "Bildniskunst und florentinisches Bürgertum," 112.
[4]Warburg, *Gesammelte Schriften*, 29:2854.
[5]Warburg, *Reise-Erinnerungen aus dem Gebiet*, 254.
[6]Warburg, *Gesammelte Schriften*, 47:4168.
[7]Warburg, "Seminarum über Jacob Burckhardt," 21. See also the brilliant study by Georges Didi-Huberman, 117–25, which one should read in conjunction with that of Philippe-Alain Michaud's *Aby Warburg et l'image en mouvement*.

depths of the past (both geological and organic), and which he afterwards transmits visually to the gaze. He sensitively records and then transmits *to the present* the movement of past layers/strata, past memories which still survive under our soil so as to seize on a possible becoming, a becoming waiting to manifest itself.[8] The recording of the seismograph—by its traces, inscriptions and revelatory graphs—bears witness to a whole *episteme* of time, of secret and buried movements, rhythms and phenomena. It is indeed all this dynamism as much as that underground intensity of forms of energy (*energia*) that flows/circulates at the heart of the body/corpus of history that Warburg will not cease to seize/harness with the scientific, even empirical method, of recording.

In stating and announcing this new methodology or technology of working—this veritable seism we might say with regard to the "traditional" activities of the historian—Warburg both invents and demonstrates the radical need for an extension of the seismological discipline, in other words of the graphic recording field of the life of the *terrestrial* body, so as to apply it *ipso facto* to the body itself of "historicity" (*geschichtliches*); the place where, most precisely, the most subtle forms and forces of the past subsist and survive. We know that this *organic* seismology advanced by Warburg finds its origin in the works, as notable as they were noted, of Étienne-Jules Marey, who as early as 1878 in his celebrated *méthode graphique* concentrated on revealing and on (re)transmitting "the recording of the state of the body (organic/human) at each instant of its change of state."[9] Marey also, driven by an unshakeable *audio-scopic* will and eagerness "to listen and see more and more", works away at rendering the body's energy visible in the subtlest and least noticeable of its movements, even its spasms, its crises, its underground disturbances—in short its veritable seisms or even its *aura hysterica* or *passio hysterica*.

What relevance does this have to the Shakespearean *corpus*? How does this relate to the moment when our gaze finally opens the volume, "the folding of the paper and the depth within that it establishes, the shadows disseminated in black characters," which finally offers itself to us?[10] Just as much as Burckhardt and Nietzsche were for Warburg, Shakespeare is our seismograph—he is that "worthy pionner" (1.5.165) like the "mole" in *Hamlet* (1.5.164), who does not cease from working underground and whose earth-shattering revelations—*veritable shock waves*—come both to shake the basis and the foundations of the kingdom of Elsinore and to strike with force its hereditary prince, Hamlet.[11] *A seismic phenomenon*, the Shakespeare corpus should not be construed as conceivable but as *perceivable* even *receivable* as so many vibrations, waves and rhythmical modulations which suddenly loom up from the past in our

---

[8]For a detailed study demonstrating the relevance of the Warburgian seismographic device as a methodological/hermeneutic key in the work of William Shakespeare, see Gleyzon, xviii.

[9]Marey, 12.

[10]Mallarmé, 379.

[11]Shakespeare. Line numbers for the plays are taken from *The Norton Shakespeare: Based on the Oxford Edition*, and citations are given in the text.

present. Thus Shakespeare, as Hugo von Hofmannsthal so admirably puts it with regard to the poet and the artist in general:

> is like a seismograph that vibrates from every quake, even if it is thousands of miles away. It's not that he thinks incessantly of all things in the world. But they think of him. They are in him and thus do they rule over him. Even his dull hours, his depressions, his confusions are impersonal states; they are like the spasms of the seismograph, and a deep enough gaze could read more mysterious things in them than in his [work].[12]

The articles that follow will need to be read as so many lines on a seismograph. Each of their traces bears witness to their own unique will to retransmit the forms and dynamic forces for listening to the body/the corpus in/of Shakespeare. The first line in Katherine Schaap Williams's article, "Performing Disability and Theorizing Deformity", has as its purpose to read/visualize the body of Richard III "in his ever changing deformations" so as to argue, using disability theory, that not only the "deform'd, unfinish'd" (1.1.20) and twisted hunchback with a shrivelled arm eludes and resists any fixed "aesthetic" categorization, but also that this performative indeterminacy inherent in his body reveals a political strategy which Richard uses to his advantage. "A political monster", *Richard II* seems in the same way to bring back to life the close and organic link between the Sovereign and the Beast. Through a rereading if not a rehabilitation of the work of Michel Foucault at the heart of Shakespeare studies, Richard Wilson in "Ship of Fools: Foucault and the Shakespeareans" concentrates on re-emphasizing the relevance of Foucault's works with regard to Shakespeare, that "pre-modern playwright" whose writings still record and in a compelling way "a kind of madness that is in the process of disappearing".[13] In the third article entitled "'Untimely ripp'd': On Natality, Sovereignty and Unbearable Life", Arthur Bradley concentrates on demonstrating how *Macbeth* is first and foremost organized around the bodies of child birth—"naked new born babes, birth-strangled babes, a bloody child, a child crowned with a tree in his hand, and a child untimely ripped from his mother's womb." Through a politico-theological rereading of the concept of "unbearable life" elaborated by Giorgio Agamben, Bradley argues that the body that comes into the world, the body of the "naked new-born babe" (1.7.23), does not stop constituting a threat, even a veritable challenge to the sovereign's rule. In this way "the challenge of rule becomes to foreclose the birth of species of life, which, by the bare fact of their coming into the world, would constitute a challenge to the sovereign bio-political command over what constitutes life and death."

Drew Daniel's essay, "Syllogisms and Tears in Timon of Athens", concentrates on deconstructing two distinct social entities, Master and Servant, Timon and Flavius,

---

[12]Hofmannsthal, 54.

[13]The expression "pre-modern playwright" is attributed to Shakespeare by Richard Wilson (76). The citation from the end of the sentence is from Foucault, 37.

whose relationships are defined and mutually determined by a system of monetary transaction, that is "through bonds, which are at once financially determined and emotionally expressive." If the play is based on a structure of economic exchange "in which the end of fortune is the end of service and the end of love", Shakespeare, as Daniel demonstrates, inserts a counterpoint in the figure of the loyal Flavius who, "with tears in his eyes", "visits Timon in his misanthropic isolation in Act Four, Scene Three and attempts unsuccessfully to serve his former master even after the money has run out." There is here a link almost polycentric, even polyorganic between the monetary sign of Timon's debt (gold coins) and the tears of Flavius. The syllogistic rhetoric, however, of denial/incredulity, of resistance, which Timon deploys against Flavius's tears, seems to manifest a singular tension, a dynamic of conflict, between an affective investment and an economic determination. Formulated alternatively, and as Daniel posits, "Specifically, in what sense do Timon's syllogisms constitute a response to, if not a repayment for, Flavius' tears?"

"Opening the Sacred Body or the Profaned Host in *The Merchant of Venice*" by François-Xavier Gleyzon is the last essay in this volume. It aims at rethinking the Eucharistic utterance "This is my body. ... This is my blood" not merely as the key formulation of representation, but first and foremost as a decisive role in the attempt to write the body as a site/sight of terror and torture. The inherent sacrificial violence of the Eucharist in the Cenacle seems to be confirmed by the startling phrase of Saint Ephrem's prayers, in which he refers to the body and blood of Christ as "Your all-pure and terrifying Mysteries."[14] Focusing upon Shakespeare's drama along with specific artworks by Crivelli, Hans Sebald Beham and Paolo Uccello, the essay records and traces the phenomena and events of opening and cutting that leave their ekphrastic imprints upon the textual landscape of *The Merchant of Venice*. As Gleyzon points out, it will not be a matter here of "repeating or returning to the paradigm of the circumcision", but of revealing that the *scene/cène* (*s/cène*) of the trial highlights a murderous "Eucharistic attempt" conceived by Shylock on Antonio's life.

Thus begins the second issue of "Shakespeare and Theory", bringing to a close the first. All these essays bear witness to a unified will and a unified plan. All act as listening posts for Shakespeare. Attentive and sensitive, they endeavour to penetrate "that secret point" buried deep (*geheimer Punkt*), "that within which passeth show" (*Hamlet*, 1.2.85) which, as the admirable funerary tribute from Ernst Cassirer testifies, was also the whole of Aby Warburg's endeavour:

> In his discourse on Shakespeare, the young Goethe affirms that Shakespeare's plots, to use the language of everyday, are not plots as his plays all revolve around that secret point that no philosopher has yet perceived and determined, wherein are conjoined the specialness of our "I," the so-called freedom of our will and the necessary functioning of all these things. Warburg's research too was permanently orientated

---

[14]Clément, 87.

towards this "secret point" (*geheimer Punkt*) and, as if under its spell, his gaze was attached to it.[15]

Acknowledgements

The guest editors would like to thank again the contributors to these two special issues on Shakespeare and theory for their generous offerings. Thanks are also due to Katherine Williams at Taylor & Francis for her help with the production editing, to Astrid van Hoek for co-ordinating the publication process at *English Studies*, and to Odin Dekkers for responding hospitably to our initial proposal.

References

Cassirer, Ernst. "Éloge funèbre du professeur Aby M. Warburg" ("Funeral oration for Professor Aby M. Warburg"). In *Œuvres, XII. Écrits sur l'art*. Paris: Le Cerf, 1995.

Clément, Olivier. *Three Prayers: The Lord's Prayer, O Heavenly King, Prayer of St Ephrem*. Translated by Michael Breck. Crestwood, NY: St Vladimir's Seminary Press, 2000.

Didi-Huberman, Georges. "Sismographie des temps mouvants." In *L'Image survivante: histoire de l'art et temps des fantômes selon Aby Warburg*. Paris: Ed. de Minuit, 2002.

Foucault, Michel. *The History of Madness*. Translated by Jonathan Murphy and Jean Khalfa. London: Routledge, 2006.

Gleyzon, François-Xavier. *Shakespeare's Spiral: Tracing the Snail in* King Lear *and Renaissance Painting*. Lanham, MD: University Press of America, 2010.

Hofmannsthal, Hugo von. *The Poet and the Present Time*. Vol. I. Frankfurt am Main: Fischer, 1979.

Mallarmé, Stéphane. "Quant au livre." In *Œuvres complètes*, edited by H. Mondor and G.-Jean Aubry. Paris: Gallimard, 1945.

Marey, Étienne-Jules. *La méthode graphique dans les sciences expérimentales et principalement en physiologie et en médecine*. Paris: Masson, 1878.

Michaud, Philippe-Alain. *Aby Warburg et l'image en mouvement*. Paris: Macula, 1998.

Rilke, Rainer Maria. *Lettre à un jeune poète: Sur le jeune poète—Sur le poète. Classiques du 20ième siècle*. Vol. 8, no. 1. Québec: La Bibliothèque du Québec, 1988.

Shakespeare, William. *The Norton Shakespeare: Based on the Oxford Edition*. Edited by Stephen Greenblatt, Walter Cohen, Jean E. Howard and Katherine Eisaman Maus. New York: Norton, 1997.

Warburg, Aby. "Bildniskunst und florentinisches Bürgertum." In *Ausgewählte Schriften und Würdigungen*, edited by D. Wuttke. Baden-Baden: Koerner-Verlag, 1980.

———. *Gesammelte Schriften*. Bd. 29. Berlin: Tagebuch der Kulturwissenschaftlichen Bibliotek Warburg, 2001.

———.*Gesammelte Schriften*. Bd. 47. Berlin: Tagebuch der Kulturwissenschaftlichen Bibliotek Warburg, 2001.

———. *Reise-Erinnerungen aus dem Gebiet der Pueblos*. 1923. London: Warburg Institute Archive, III.

———. "Seminarum über Jacob Burckhardt." 1927. Reprint "Aby Warburgs Seminarübungen über Jacob Burckhardt im Sommersemester 1927." In *Idea: Jahrbuch der Hamburger Kunsthalle*. Vol. 10. München: Prestel, 1991.

Wilson, Richard. *Shakespeare in French Theory: King of Shadows*. London: Routledge, 2007.

---

[15]Cassirer, 55–6.

Performing Disability and Theorizing Deformity

Katherine Schaap Williams

William Shakespeare's Richard III *has been the key text for thinking about disability in the early modern period. While critics have taken Richard's "deformed" body as legible and morally emblematic, this essay traces how Shakespeare's character resists specificity about his shape. Refusing to describe the expected hunchback in his famous opening speech, seducing Anne and suddenly producing a withered arm, Richard recruits his audience to observe his ever-changing deformations. This essay accounts for deformity as an unfixed, performative force that Richard uses to his political advantage, arguing that the play produces disability as indistinction. Bringing disability theory to bear on the spectacle of Richard's deformed body—and using Shakespeare's play to rethink early modern disability—I show how the play highlights the indeterminacy of deformity as a resource for theatrical statecraft.*

1. Seeing Richard's Body

The 1606 play *The Returne from Parnassus* stages a curious moment that compresses stage history and calibrates dramatic character through the actor's body. Richard Burbage, the famous actor, appears briefly in the play as he evaluates prospective actors with Will Kempe, another luminary of the early modern stage. When they see Philomusus, one of the main characters in *Returne*, Kempe suggests that Philomusus would excel as "a foolish Mayre or a foolish Justice" (4.3.55–6), but Burbage disagrees, summoning Philomusus with another request:

> Bur. I like your face, and the proportion of your body for Richard the 3. I pray, M. Phil. Let me see you act a little of it.
>
> Phil. Now is the winter of our discontent,
>   Made glorious summer by the sonne of Yorke,
>
> Bur. Very well I assure you. (4.3.80–4)[1]

This exchange—less than fifteen years after the first performances of William Shakespeare's *The Tragedy of King Richard III*, in which Burbage starred—suggests

---

[1]All quotations from *Returne* cited parenthetically by act, scene and line number.

This article was originally published with errors. This version has been corrected. Please see Erratum (http://dx.doi.org/10.1080/0013838X.2013.866798).

the popularity, conventionality and iterability of Richard's role. Invited to "act", Philomusus promptly strikes a pose and begins the opening soliloquy of *Richard III*. Burbage cuts him off after these two lines (when it turns out that Philomusus would not be a good actor). The invitation seems to mock Philomusus, not immediately for a lack of acting ability, but for his features: a "face" and bodily "proportion" that instantly suggest Richard III might not be a compliment, even as the figure Philomusus cuts appears to offer an advantage for this role. However, the relation between actor's body and character's body becomes less clear when Burbage sizes up Philomusus: the doubling introduces a fundamental uncertainty into the exchange when the invitation to act Richard suggests that Philomusus resembles, in a sense, Burbage himself.

This scene in *Returne* glances back at Shakespeare's *Richard III*, probably performed in 1593 or 1594 and reprinted in quarto versions six times before the 1623 Folio. It is, of course, a commonplace that Richard's distinctive body is the emblem of the play's didactic preoccupations. The play foregrounds Richard's body from the opening scene, and scholars have argued astutely for the political, theological and moral lessons his figure provides, suggesting that the play's early modern audience "would immediately have recognized Richard's physical deformity and moral depravity as a synecdoche for the state"[2] and understood Richard as the "vehicle for the doctrine that villainy in the soul was predicated by a correspondent deformity in the body".[3] Given this emphasis on the legibility of Richard's body in the critical history, I want to ask: what exactly does Richard's body look like on the stage? Critics have been quick to describe the Richard of Shakespeare's play: "A twisted mind in a twisted shape, Richard, the crippled figure, has an unbalanced and unfinished body, a hump, a limp, and perhaps … even acquires a withered or shortened arm by the middle of the play."[4] This body becomes the shorthand to his character's deeper purposes: "In acting the body—hunched, limping, and creeping in the margins—the actor will automatically enact mind, manner, and motive."[5] Indeed, the "deformed Richard Crookback" becomes one example of a whole class of characters whose "sheer physique is so extraordinary that their very bodies make a continuous implicit contribution on their own account, as powerful cultural signs, to the dramatic narrative".[6] What interests me in these familiar interpretations is how easily we—a long line of critics, actors and audiences—come to assume that we know what Richard's "deformity" looks like and what this deformed body means in the dramatic fiction.

Richard's appearance is also crucial for critics in disability theory, who have turned to him as a key figure for a historical narrative of disabled identity. Richard often comes to stand in for Shakespeare and, by extension, for sixteenth- and seventeenth-century

---

[2]Charnes, 30.
[3]Wilks, 19.
[4]Besnault and Bitot, 110.
[5]Palfrey and Stern, 359.
[6]Gibbons, 62.

ideas about disability. In the most fully explicated reading of *Richard III* in disability studies, David Mitchell and Sharon Snyder argue that the play reflects a "late Renaissance perspective on the narrative mutability of disability" that incorporates "medieval interpretations of disability as a sign for misfortune".[7] Reading the "mutability" of Richard's character begins to approach the contemporary "social" model of disability, which separates impairment from disability. In this framework, disability happens through the interaction between an impaired body and the social and cultural environments that disable that body. A reading of Richard that emphasizes the disabling effects of negative social attitudes allows disability critics to posit a continuum between bodies of the past and the contemporary moment, so that "the wondrous monsters of antiquity, who became the fascinating freaks of the nineteenth century, transformed into the disabled people of the later twentieth century".[8] As part of a lineage of disabled identity, Richard's distinctive body—especially the hunchback formation—might be recognizably "disabled" in contemporary terms.

However, critics have also read Richard as, crucially, *not* an example of disabled identity, arguing that what we call disability comes later, after historical changes that produce post-industrial medicalized bodies through techniques of biopower.[9] This genealogy of disability historicizes the emergence of the "normal" body through standards of quantification, in order to highlight and critique how "abnormal" bodies become subject to cultural exclusion and institutional control. Within this narrative, Lennard Davis points out that "rather than disability, what is called to readers' attention before the eighteenth century is *deformity*" as a category of somatic difference rather than stigmatized identity.[10] This notion of deformity remains firmly on the side of impairment, before a social construction of disability, and Richard stands out as a pre-modern example of a prior historical moment from which modes of interpretation have shifted. Yet, as Christopher Baswell argues, even if the term "disability" does not come to describe bodily experience until the end of the eighteenth century, we can still examine what "kinds of social and intellectual encounters with eccentric bodies and eccentric minds preced[e] that concept".[11] In this essay, I ask: if Richard's distinctive body can work as evidence both for the development of disability as an identity category and for Renaissance cultural attitudes toward anomalous bodies, then what exactly does Shakespeare's play reveal about a concept of disability still inchoate in the early modern period?

Here, I consider how a richer concept of "deformity", the term that Shakespeare's Richard uses to describe his figure, reworks early modern "disability" from fixity to

---

[7]Mitchell and Snyder, 103. Similarly, Comber observes, "Shakespeare's original audience would have viewed Richard's impairment as a marker of his evil because that is what lingering medieval perceptions of disability had trained them to do" (192).

[8]Garland-Thomson, 58.

[9]See Turner, and Deutsch and Nussbaum for discussion of the beginnings of this shift in England in the late seventeenth century and throughout the eighteenth century.

[10]Davis, 52.

[11]Baswell, unpaginated. Recent work pursues this possibility; see the introductory essays by Hobgood and Wood, and Singer, in collections devoted to medieval and early modern bodies and disability theory.

indeterminacy to reveal disability as a theatrical asset.[12] While critics have imagined a specific body for Richard, one with unambiguous moral meaning, I argue that disability—as an interaction between the deformed body and the world that constrains this body—first emerges in *Richard III* as indistinction, the inability to categorize Richard's body clearly. Richard uses this indistinction to his advantage to enable his rise to kingship. I begin showing how Shakespeare's play differs from other texts in refusing to specify the exact details of Richard's form. Along with his own pronouncement of deformity, Richard's body becomes rhetorically identified with oozy contagion, social corruption, bestiality, divine judgment and prophetic ciphers of English history. The play, however, is at pains to muddle these interpretive categories into conflated and competing discourses. Shakespeare's Richard recognizes the possibilities for manipulating these competing interpretations because they presume legible impairment and a static model of deformity signified by the expected hump. Richard's performance of disability confounds the desire for interpretive certainty that other characters express when they call attention to his bodily features. To construct a more complex model of early modern disability, I argue, we must rethink disability around the slipperiness and incoherence—rather than fixity—of the concept of deformity.

2. Re-reading *Richard III*

The chief historical source for Shakespeare's play, Thomas More's *The History of King Richard the Third* (ca.1513), which influenced Edward Hall and Raphael Holinshed in their sixteenth-century histories, describes Richard's body in a brief digression at the outset of the narrative:

> Richard, the third son ... was in wit and courage equal with either of them [his brothers], in body and prowess far under them both: little of stature, ill-featured of limbs, crook-backed, his left shoulder much higher than his right, hard-favored of visage ... He was malicious, wrathful, envious, and from afore his birth, ever froward.[13]

More's account dissociates "wit and courage" from "body and prowess", but the terms introduced for Richard's body become the keywords for later representations: "crook-backed", "ill-featured" and "hard-favored". The description suggests that Richard is short, his shoulders are of different heights and his back is bent into a hunchback formation. While More describes Richard's talent for dissimulation and his cruelty, this excursus on Richard's body and disposition is only a small portion of the narrative, which concentrates instead on the multiple occasions of public performance that

---

[12]I have argued elsewhere (Williams, "Enabling Richard") that to conflate "deformity" with "disability" in the play is to miss how Richard employs his visible difference to his own ends; here I depart from this argument to consider the stakes of deformity as a theatrical strategy.
[13]More, 9–10.

test and subtend Richard's political machinations. More considers what his audience can learn, not so much from Richard's body, but from his mastery of cunning in the steady consolidation of tyrannical power.

Yet the dramatic representations that precede *Richard III* seize upon the form of "Richard, the third son". The unattributed play *The True Tragedie of Richard III* (1594) opens with a dialogue between the characters of "Poetrie" and "Truth", who introduce "Richard Duke of Gloster" through description. Poetrie asks: "What maner of man was this Richard Duke of Gloster?" and Truth replies: "A man ill shaped, crooked backed, lame armed, withal, / Valiantly minded, but tyrannous in authoritie."[14] Truth's summation reads like an excerpt from More's history, setting out the essential features of his body, and adding the "lame armed" to Richard. Truth's account conjures an image and delivers the didactic takeaway ("Valiantly minded, but tyrannous") before Richard himself appears on the stage. Richard, then, enters the dramatic action of the play within a moral framework: Truth and Poetrie explicate his character's appearance and heighten audience expectations for the emblematic figure of tyranny they will see.

The play that precedes *Richard III* in Shakespeare's history cycle has the most extensive discussion of the character's body. In *3 Henry VI* (ca.1591–92), Richard is called "scolding crookback" (5.5.30), "misshapen Dick" (5.5.35), "Hard-favoured Richard" (5.5.77) and "an indigested and deformed lump" (5.6.51).[15] Repeating More's epithets and adding new descriptions, the other characters in the play do not hesitate to explicate the meaning of these details. When Richard comes to kill King Henry, Henry claims that Richard's pre-natal teeth were "To signify thou cam'st to bite the world; / And if the rest be true which I have heard / Thou cam'st—" (5.6.54–6), and breaks off as Richard, calling him a "prophet", kills him. However, it is not just the other characters that proclaim the significance of his features: Richard himself adopts a prophetic framework that aligns his body as the cause of his disposition and future actions. After killing Henry, Richard returns to the question of his portentous birth with a belated answer:

> And so I was, which plainly signified
> That I should snarl and bite and play the dog.
> Then, since the heavens have shaped my body so,
> Let hell make crooked my mind to answer it. (5.6.76–9)

Like Henry, the Richard of *3 Henry VI* claims that his body should "signify", wresting his "misshapen" form into "plainly" visible providential history.[16] These brief

---

[14]*True Tragedie*, sig. A3v, 50–2. While the only extant quarto of the play was printed in 1594, the play was performed by the Queen's Men, probably in the late 1580s or early 1590s.

[15]I refer to the play with the short title; this and all further quotations from *3 Henry VI* cited parenthetically by act, scene and line.

[16]Productions of *Richard III* regularly import these lines into the play as an additional explanatory mechanism for his character.

examples suggest that by *Richard III*, the "crookback" character is associated with a set of physical features—the hump, the uneven shoulders, the limp, the shortened arm—that come to be expected at the outset as a site of explication when Richard shows up in a play.

Shakespeare's Richard in *Richard III*, however, refuses to spell out the features of his body in the opening lines. His soliloquy begins with a decisive and repeated "Now" to commence the play and in the middle section Richard theorizes his form as a decisive rejection of the sociality of the present moment. He is "not shaped for sportive tricks / Nor made to court an amorous looking-glass" (1.1.14–15); he is "rudely stamped" (1.1.16) and "curtailed of this fair proportion" (1.1.18) and "cheated of feature" (1.1.19). He is, he claims:

> Deformed, unfinished, sent before my time
> Into this breathing world scarce half made up—
> And that so lamely and unfashionable
> That dogs bark at me as I halt by them—
> Why, I in this weak piping time of peace
> Have no delight to pass away the time,
> Unless to spy my shadow in the sun
> And descant on mine own deformity. (1.1.20–27)[17]

Richard's vocabulary of scorn—"unfinished", "cheated of feature", "unfashionable"—catalogue his body's social defects under the rubric of "deformity". However, this description refuses the specificity of the source texts, and even Shakespeare's earlier plays: the terms that describe his body rely on negation or abstraction ("not shaped", "curtailed") instead of the bodily attributes the other plays offer. Even Richard's "halt" calls attention to the motion of his body rather than naming an offending feature. Where, for this Richard, is the "crookback"? Richard begins the play by calling attention to a theatrical body that he displays to the audience, a body laden with expectations, but he does not tell the audience exactly what they see. Instead of describing how his body looks, Richard draws out what his body can—or cannot—do through movement. In his opening speech, Richard wants his audience to believe that his deformed body is his identity, and that this body is disabling within his social setting.

Never explicit about his appearance, Richard goes on to emphasize his body's features as he pleases. After claiming he cannot "court", Richard's success in wooing Anne in the very next scene confirms that he is quite capable of performing the role of lover. Anne begins by lamenting her husband's death at the hands of the "lump of foul deformity" (1.2.55), Richard: "Villain, thou know'st no law of God nor man. / No beast so fierce but knows some touch of pity" (1.2.70–1). Richard's response

---

[17]This and all further quotations from the Norton edition of *Richard III* and cited parenthetically by act, scene and line.

selectively engages her interpretive structure only to distort it: "But I know none—and therefore am no beast" (1.2.72). This verbal pattern continues, as Anne enumerates Richard's crimes to his stichomythic response. The rhetorical intensity increases until, just as in the first scene, Richard highlights bodily insufficiency, here as a sign of lack finally enabled by love. He "confesses" to Anne: "Those eyes of thine from mine have drawn salt tears, / Shamed their aspect with store of childish drops" (1.2.153–4) and claims, "My tongue could never learn sweet smoothing word; / But now thy beauty is proposed my fee, / My proud heart sues and prompts my tongue to speak" (1.2.156–8). With words of "suit" and "smoothing", the script cues gesture and action: proffering his sword and kneeling, Richard exposes his body and tells Anne "Take up the sword again, or take up me" (1.2.171), arguing that his gestural display shows the signs of a "far truer love" (1.2.176) that he feels.

When he is successful in courtship, Richard appreciates the particular malleability of his form, even to the point of occupying the very spaces he rejected in his opening soliloquy. Once Anne concedes and Richard is alone again on the stage, he exults in his performative triumph, marvelling that Anne will "abase her eyes" (1.2.233) on him, "that halts and am misshapen thus" (1.3.237). He exclaims:

> I do mistake my person all this while.
> Upon my life she finds, although I cannot,
> Myself to be a marv'lous proper man.
> I'll be at charges for a looking-glass
> And entertain a score or two of tailors
> To study fashions to adorn my body. (1.2.239–44)

Richard uses Anne's acquiescence to shape his future interpretations, revaluing his own ability to present himself as "marv'lous proper". Invoking an implicit sense of ideal attributes, Richard suggests that he can perform this persona, and his plan to engage tailors and "study fashions" articulates the body that—just the scene before—he imagined as "lamely and unfashionable" (1.1.22). Richard's "favour" for himself produces an exultant appraisal of his shape: proclaiming, "Shine out, fair sun, till I have bought a glass, / That I may see my shadow as I pass" (1.2.249–50), he imagines himself seeing his form not only to "descant", but to appreciate his newfound capacity to act in the world.

By contrast, Richard also produces his deformity as exaggerated recognition, assuring others that there is nothing more to know about this body than its limitations. When he enters the conference with Queen Elizabeth and the nobles, Richard decries his inability to engage in rituals of courtly sociability. He claims:

> Because I cannot flatter and look fair,
> Smile in men's faces, smooth, deceive, and cog,
> Duck with French nods and apish courtesy.
> I must be held a rancorous enemy.
> Cannot a plain man live and think no harm,

But this his simple truth must be abused
With silken, sly, insinuating jacks? (1.3.47–53)

Richard equates his anomalous body with the "plain" and "simple truth", unlike the "silken, sly, insinuating jacks" who surround him, whose bodies never reveal their true selves. Deformity becomes a claim to honesty, in that excessive scrutiny of his body would demonstrate that he cannot dissemble or counterfeit. Richard aligns a talent for courtesy with the fraudulent ("apish") and the foreign ("French nods"), against which his body's deformity—a seeming inability to become anything other than what it is—appears virtuously resistant. Reversing his earlier disparagement of his body as "unnatural", he claims that his bodily inability to "flatter and look fair" or "smooth, deceive, and cog" makes his sincerity self-evident, even though the audience in the theatre, having watched Richard pursue Clarence's death by this point in the play, is well aware of Richard's capacity for deception.

Thus Richard himself multiplies the possible interpretations of his body—as unfit for court, as skilful lover, as evidently honest—even as he decodes this body for different audiences. Richard's incessant revelation shifts his appearance with each description. Of course, Richard's audience within the dramatic fiction does not accept his interpretations without resistance: Anne rejects him at first as a "foul devil" (1.2.50), "diffused infection of a man" (1.2.78) and "hedgehog" (1.2.102); Margaret curses him as "elvish-marked, abortive, rooting hog" (1.3.225), the "slave of nature and the son of hell" (1.3.227), and calls him a "bottled spider" (1.3.240), "poisonous bunch-backed toad" (1.3.244) and "yonder dog" (1.3.287). Cursing Richard within a providential structure, the women's epithets—like the association with the "beasts" that Richard rejects—move down the scale of being in the search for fitting invective. However, Richard evades these epithets, interrupting Margaret's curse to "make the period" (1.3.236) with her name rather than his own, so that her curse is "done" by Richard and "ends in 'Margaret'" (1.3.237). As the play progresses this language is revealed as strikingly ineffective, either to describe Richard's body accurately or to resist his political actions. The women's interpretations of his figure as providential curse and singular evil are too limited to account for the mobility with which Richard himself changes the interpretive structure in which his body appears.

In fact, the play repeatedly stages acts of misinterpretation that highlight not the clarity of Richard's body—as a sign of evil—but its illegibility. Read in reference to early modern beliefs about physiognomy, the expected shape of Richard's body could easily suggest inner evil. Practices of physiognomy in the period depend upon what Roy Porter calls the "hermeneutic process" of detecting the body's signs in order to determine natural tendencies and useful predictors of social and moral behaviour.[18] *Richard III*, however, seems interested in moments in which physiognomic interpretation is

---

[18]Porter, 190.

undermined or mistaken.[19] The play never makes explicit a causative relation between Richard's mind and body, and the interpretive problem his body poses intensifies when the play announces "monstrous" actions, which we might expect to locate with Richard. While acknowledging that Richard is never *actually* called a monster in the play, critics repeatedly identify him as monstrous in the sense that he is "simply a composite of 'monstrous' markers and behaviours".[20] This assumption derives in part from the common juxtaposition of deformity and monstrosity in early modern texts—as when, for example, Ambroise Paré repeatedly describes anomalous births as "monstrous and deformed"—but here, I want to suggest, the play resists putting the two terms in proximity to describe Richard.[21] Although Richard cites his "deformity" from the beginning, his characterization of a time-bound relation to nature is as close as he comes to the boundaries of the human that monsters trouble. Richard's body, with its multiplication of indistinction, never becomes a clearly interpretable portent—to follow one etymology of the monstrous—because his body never stays the same.

Instead, in the play, "monstrous" registers acts of bad political interpretation, demonstrating not the interpretability of a bodily sign, but the effective display of political power. In the curious timing of Act Three, Scene 4, Richard enters belatedly for the conference of nobles, requests the Bishop of Ely to send for some strawberries, withdraws with Buckingham and then re-enters in a fit of energetic passion to ask "what they deserve / That do conspire my death with devilish plots / Of damned witchcraft" (3.4.59–61). When Hastings volunteers "deserved death" (3.4.66) as sufficient punishment, Richard brandishes evidence of the "hellish charms" (3.4.62):

> Then be your eyes the witness of their evil:
> See how I am bewitched. Behold, mine arm
> Is like a blasted sapling withered up.
> And this is Edward's wife, that monstrous witch,
> Consorted with that harlot, strumpet Shore,
> That by their witchcraft thus have marked me. (3.4.67–72)

Richard's "Behold" directs the attention of his onstage (and offstage) audience to his body once more to claim his "withered up" arm as evidence of "ill"—but not his own evil. Richard directs the force of the "monstrous" accusation against the women and their supposed witchcraft. The staging possibilities could include a prosthesis that the actor adopts offstage before he re-enters, so that he displays an arm that does, in fact, look different. However, this theatrical accommodation to one textual cue forecloses on the real power dynamic of the scene: Richard's arm looks exactly the same as it has throughout the play. This is a test to see whether his audience is

---

[19]I am thinking here, for example, of Hastings' assessment—which turns out to be utterly wrong—of Richard's inability to hide his "love or hate" (3.4.57). See Torrey's extensive discussion of physiognomy and *Richard III*.
[20]Burnett, 93; see also Moulton's incisive reading of "monstrosity" within the play.
[21]Paré, 42. See also Stagg's discussion of characteristic deformities of the monstrous body.

willing to participate in his fantasy of political power. If nothing about Richard's body has changed, the point of the display is not to confirm his body in a "monstrous" sign, but to reveal those who resist his interpretation. Hastings begins to respond, "If they have done this deed, my gracious lord—" (3.4.73), and Richard interrupts: "'If? Thou protector of this damned strumpet, / Talk'st thou to me of 'ifs? Thou art a traitor.— / Off with his head" (3.4.74–6). Richard again produces a deformed body in front of an audience, not to highlight the limitation of his shape but to index the frightening consolidation of his power.

Because the theatrical effectiveness of Richard's deformity inheres in its indistinction and multiple interpretations, his body falls out of focus intermittently. There are moments in which his body sounds, contradictorily, as if it is not deformed at all. Buckingham, Richard's collaborator in staging public support for his reign, appeals to corporate imagery in a bid for Richard's kingship: "Withal, I did infer your lineaments— / Being the right idea of your father / Both in your face and nobleness of mind" (3.7.12–14). Although his first attempt fails, Buckingham returns to this preoccupation with Richard's body a second time, staging the barely successful plea before the crowd. Buckingham exhorts Richard: "Know then, it is your fault that you resign … The lineal glory of your royal house / To the corruption of a blemished stock" (3.7.117, 121–2), and then urges him to mend the "body" of the nation: "The noble isle doth want her proper limbs: / Her face defaced with scars of infamy" (3.7.125–6), contrasting a corporate figure with a corporeal enactment. Conjured through public speech-acts, the images allow Richard's body to shift into visibility through rhetoric, not to show his deformity but to emphasize his fitness for the task of being king.

Within the play, however, Richard has produced his deformity as a sign of many things, from his lack of fitness to court to his status as victim. The play thus marks a transition in its final acts, when disability as indistinction resolves into disability as limitation. Tobin Siebers has argued that "when a disabled body moves into a social space, the lack of fit exposes the shape of the normative body for which the space was originally designed".[22] As Richard transforms himself into "King Richard"—a shift in character borne out by the speech prefixes in the play's printed text—and seeks to preserve the kingship he then holds, the body that he pronounces "deformed" drops out of language completely, and all that remains is spectacle. Certainly, as Linda Charnes has argued, Richard appropriates the notion of the "King's Two Bodies" in order to "transform 'handicaps' of his own" by "sublat[ing] his deformed body to the perfect 'Body' of the king".[23] Yet the body that Richard performs in order to achieve kingship is laden with the risk of its own visibility and he cannot easily jettison this body even after he becomes King Richard; the audience continues to see the spectacle that Richard presents. The "normative" ideal, to

---

[22]Siebers, 105.
[23]Charnes, 32.

follow Siebers, of the king's body is "fair", the word used previously to describe Richmond, who triumphs at the end of the play. The deformed and deforming body that Richard Gloucester has employed until this point becomes a liability for the fixed body of King Richard.

3. Re-imagining Deformity

In Richard's resounding proclamation of his "deformity", Shakespeare stages a term already marked by interpretive complexity. The designation "deformed" collates a broad range of examples in the sixteenth and seventeenth centuries, many of them entirely negative. George Puttenham's treatise on poetry, *The Art of English Poesy* (1589), defines "deformities" as "excesses or defects or confusions and disorders in the sensible objects";[24] Philip Sidney's *Defence of Poesie* (1595) claims that "we laugh at deformed creatures, wherein certainly we cannot delight";[25] and the pamphlet *Hic Mulier* (1620) conceptualizes deformity as one effect of cross-dressing women who "mould their bodies to every deformed fashion, their tongues to vile and horrible profanations".[26] However, deformity is also a vexed ontological category, in which a lack of uniformity provokes a range of interpretations. Edward Reynolds identifies deformity as an example of the "aberrations and irregularities of Nature"; a problem of ungovernable resistance to form, deformity may serve one of two functions, either "divine malediction" for human sin or a foil to "set forth the beautie of regular operations, (which by deformitie and confusion will appear more beautifull)".[27] The precarious distinction between the two functions of deformity is especially unstable with reference to the human body, for, as William Vaughan notes: "he that is deformed in his body, may conceal a generous spirit within, like unto a tottered ship, which containes within it more goods then tenne such ships are worth".[28] These examples take "deformity" as a disruption of "form", a general principle of that which is apt, suitable and measured. The contours of deformity are never quite defined, only denounced through negative designation, as the prefix suggests. The concept of deformity thus presumes a recognizably—on some intuitive, if not exactly quantifiable, level—irregular form that prompts affective response and requires an interpretive judgment about aesthetic and ethical value.

As a verb, however, "deforming" is also a way to think about the act of playing, one of the early modern terms for dramatic performance. "Deforming" action is a defining characteristic of the Vice, one of the most popular characters from medieval morality

---

[24]Puttenham, 347.
[25]Sidney, 68.
[26]*Hic Mulier*, 269.
[27]Reynolds, 33. Quoted in Baker, who emphasizes the gendered dimensions of "deformity" in the early modern period. See also Torrey's insightful account.
[28]Vaughan, 343.

plays, who takes "sportive tricks" as his specialty.[29] Tracing an older lineage of performance back to practices of playing that aimed at "deformity, rather than form, *disfigurement rather than pure figuration*", Robert Weimann has shown how the Vice character occupies a structural position marked by spatial proximity to the audience.[30] Richard explicitly alludes to himself as a Vice figure, but more than this, his "rhetoric of deformation"[31] is matched by his delight in manipulating his deformity into as many shapes as possible. This mobile relation to form, William West suggests, is fundamental to the theatre: "the reforming, or deforming, or performing, of the player's substance into a series of new forms while maintaining a material sameness".[32]

Deformity, then, illuminates the complexity of the relationship between the body of the actor and the body of the character he projects. The theatre employs the powerfully affective device of the actor's body beneath the character's theatrical body, and this overlapping presentation complicates the dramatic fiction's descriptions of the character the actor personates. Theatrical performance thus trades a kind of clarity produced by the written word for the thrill of the human actor; as Bert States observes, "[w]hat the text loses in significative power in the theater it gains in corporeal presence, in which there is extraordinary perceptual satisfaction".[33] The conceptual richness of "deforming" acts in the theatre, oscillating between presentation and representation, amplifies the "corporeal presence" of the actor on which the theatre depends. Following Robert McRuer's point that Richard demonstrates a "crip perspective", which is "not as invested in substance or authenticity as in processes that unsettle, unravel, and unmake straightness" (296), I would note that Richard's "unmaking" occurs through theatrical playing—and playing with expectations about the character's body as Richard's deformations shift from scene to scene. In *Richard III*, the putatively disabled body is also the most extreme example of the performative body.

In assigning to Richard's character the representational indeterminacy and the presentational visibility of deformity, Shakespeare's play sets up a particular challenge for actors. The stage history of *Richard III* records how actors—from Colley Cibber, David Garrick and Edmund Kean, to Laurence Olivier, Antony Sher and Ian McKellen—identify in Richard's distinctive theatrical body an invitation, if daunting, for idiosyncratic interpretation.[34] Although Richard's body is a lacuna in the text, actors have experimented with filling the physicality of the role in different ways; a robust theatrical tradition has taken Richard's "descant" as an invitation to stage extraordinary bodily features, playing up the possibilities of the hunched back, exaggerating the limp and crooked gait, and brandishing a "withered" arm. Richard appears in nearly

---

[29]Alan Dessen notes that "If allusions from the 1580s through the 1600s are to be trusted, the best remembered figure from late Tudor and early Elizabethan drama was not Everyman, Mankind, or Wit but the Vice" (110).
[30]Weimann, *Author's Pen*, 81. See also Weimann, *Shakespeare*, 42–56.
[31]Garber, 43.
[32]West, 113. My thinking here is indebted to West's discussion of *Richard III*.
[33]States, 29.
[34]See Colley and Wood for extensive accounts of production history of the play.

every scene in the lengthy play, and the production history of *Richard III* is rife with mythologies of harm caused by the contortions and vulnerabilities the act of perform-ance imposes. Theatrical disability poses a risk of "real" disability to the actor and the disjunct between the acting body and a character's deformity must be effaced for a suc-cessful performance of disability and maintained for a safe performance.

Yet this challenge to the actor's body is also part of the delight: Richard's character offers an actor the chance to become absorbed by a physically demanding role. Carrie Sandhal has argued more generally that a notion of acting that begins from a "neutral" stance means that the "appropriate actor's body for any character, even a char-acter that is literally disabled or symbolically struggling, is not only the able body, but also the extraordinarily able body".[35] This is the paradox of taking Richard as the key example of early modern disability: Richard's role depends upon the actor's body that is especially capable. To read the play's production history as built around the difficulty of perform-ing a deformed body is to begin to see how Richard's double-facing presence in the narrative of disability theory reproduces the uniqueness inscribed within the role itself. While the actor's performance calls attention to Richard's deformity, however con-ceived, the character's distinctive body calls attention to the physical ability of the actor—and the actor's instantiation changes the shape of Richard himself.

One of the prominent anecdotes to which early modern critics turn to think about the reception of *Richard III* emphasizes the extent to which the Richards—Burbage and Gloucester—become indistinguishable through impersonation. John Manningham's diary entry, dated 13 March 1602, records a theatre-driven tryst that depends upon confusing actor and character: "Upon a tyme when Burbidge played Rich 3, there was a Citizen grewe soe farre in liking with him, that before shee went from the play shee appointed him to come that night unto hir by the name of Ri the 3."[36] Jean Howard asks, "In the anecdote, who is attractive: Richard III or the Burbage who impersonated him?"[37] The undecidability of the referent—which Richard?—recalls the opening of this essay, in which Burbage's character identifies the "face and body" of the Richard he popularized in another actor. Richard's body seems both to exist as a form to be identified elsewhere and to draw upon Burbage's own iterative participation in the act of playing. However, to read the Richard/Richard overlap in the Citizen's reported request is also to draw out the irresistibility of Richard's character: after watching Burbage play Richard, the Citizen wants to play Anne.[38] She asks to be seduced by Richard's compelling presence, by the arresting spec-tacle of his deformed body. She wants not simply Burbage, but Burbage as the character

---

[35]Sandhal, 262.

[36]Manningham, 75.

[37]Howard, 210.

[38]Compare Berger, who describes the scene between Anne and Richard succinctly: "She *gets* herself seduced" (404) and Hodgdon, who speculates on the Citizen's request as a moment in which "the spectator can reperform the performance" (212).

he personates. Making the appointment, the Citizen insists on having Richard III played offstage, desirable in his disability.

If we read early modern drama to theorize disability in the period, then *Richard III* is one of the right plays to read but the wrong play to take as exemplary: Richard's "deformity" is not static, nor is it easily parsed. While the legacy of Richard's body is one that reduces his character to a particular bodily stereotype, Shakespeare's *Richard III* associates deformity with sexual and political power. In doing so, the play upends the critical and cultural impulses to codify Richard's form into a specific, legible, bodily formation. Richard mobilizes deformity as the object of interpretive fervour and leverages this attention to his shape for seductive power. What does it mean that the dramatic character taken as the most emblematic of disability on the early modern stage is the one who presents the most challenging physical role for the actor? Richard's dramatic character offers the chance for virtuosic acting as the play invokes a long history of speculation about his over-determined body and incites the desire of his onstage and offstage audiences to see this body. Refusing to make this body explicit except through the actor's gestures and movement, the play reveals disability—here, as the bodily indistinction that Richard performs—as a powerful theatrical resource for the early modern stage.

Acknowledgements

I am grateful to Emily Bartels, Henry Turner, Elin Diamond, Colleen Rosenfeld and Debapriya Sarkar for offering valuable comments on this essay.

References

Baker, Naomi. *Plain Ugly: The Unattractive Body in Early Modern Culture*. Manchester: Manchester University Press, 2010.

Baswell, Christopher. "It's Only at the Bodleian that I am a Cripple." *Times Higher Education*, 6 December 2006, unpaginated. Available from http://www.timeshighereducation.co.uk/207192.article

Berger, Harry. "Conscience and Complicity in *Richard III*." In *Richard III*, edited by Thomas Cartelli. New York: Norton, 2009.

Besnault, Marie-Helene, and Michel Bitot. "Historical Legacy and Fiction: The Poetical Reinvention of King Richard III." In *The Cambridge Companion to Shakespeare's History Plays*, edited by Michael Hattaway. Cambridge: Cambridge University Press, 2002.

Burnett, Mark Thornton. *Constructing "Monsters" in Shakespearean Drama and Early Modern Culture*. New York: Palgrave Macmillan, 2002.

Charnes, Linda. *Notorious Identity: Materializing the Subject in Shakespeare*. Cambridge, MA: Harvard University Press, 1993.

Colley, Scott. *Richard's Himself Again: A Stage History of Richard III*. Westport, CT: Greenwood Press, 1992.

Comber, Abigail Elizabeth. "A Medieval King 'Disabled' by an Early Modern Construct: A Contextual Examination of *Richard III*." In *Disability in the Middle Ages: Reconsiderations and Reverberations*, edited by Joshua R. Eyler. New York: Ashgate, 2010.

Davis, Lennard J. *Bending Over Backward: Disability, Dismodernism, and other Difficult Positions.* New York: New York University Press, 2002.

Dessen, Alan. *Recovering Shakespeare's Theatrical Vocabulary.* Cambridge: Cambridge University Press, 2006.

Deutsch, Helen, and Felicity Nussbaum, eds. *"Defects": Engendering the Modern Body.* Ann Arbor: University of Michigan Press, 2000.

Garber, Marjorie. *Shakespeare's Ghost Writers: Literature as Uncanny Causality.* New York: Methuen, 1987.

Garland-Thomson, Rosemarie. *Extraordinary Bodies: Figuring Physical Disability in American Culture and Literature.* New York: Columbia University Press, 1997.

Gibbons, Brian. *Shakespeare and Multiplicity.* Cambridge: Cambridge University Press, 1995.

Hic Mulier. In *Half Humankind: Contexts and Texts of the Controversy about Women in England, 1540–1640*, edited by Katherine Henderson and Barbara F. McManus. Chicago: University of Illinois Press, 1985.

Hobgood, Allison P., and David Houston Wood. "Ethical Staring: Disabling the English Renaissance." In *Rediscovering Disability in Early Modern England*, edited by Allison P. Hobgood and David Houston Wood. Columbus: Ohio State University Press, 2013.

Hodgdon, Barbara. "Replicating Richard: Body Doubles, Body Politics." *Theatre Journal* 50, no. 2 (1998): 207–25.

Howard, Jean. "Stage Masculinities, National History, and the Making of London Theatrical Culture." In *Center or Margin*, edited by Lena Cowen Orlin. Cranmont, NJ: Associated University Press, 2006.

Manningham, John. *The Diary of John Manningham.* Edited by John Bruce. London: Camden Society, 1868.

McRuer, Robert. "Fuck the Disabled: The Prequel." In *Shakesqueer: A Queer Companion to the Complete Works of Shakespeare*, edited by Madhavi Menon. Durham, NC: Duke University Press, 2011.

Mitchell, David, and Sharon L. Snyder. *Narrative Prosthesis: Disability and the Dependencies of Discourse.* Ann Arbor: University of Michigan Press, 2000.

More, Thomas. *The History of King Richard the Third.* Edited by George M. Logan. Bloomington: Indiana University Press, 2005.

Moulton, Ian Frederick. "'A Monster Great Deformed': The Unruly Masculinity of *Richard III*." *Shakespeare Quarterly* 47, no. 3 (1996): 251–68.

Palfrey, Simon, and Tiffany Stern. *Shakespeare in Parts.* Oxford: Oxford University Press, 2007.

Paré, Ambroise. *Of Monsters and Marvels.* Translated and edited by Janis L. Pallister. Chicago: University of Chicago Press, 1982.

Porter, Roy. *Windows of the Soul: Physiognomy in European Culture 1470–1780.* Oxford: Clarendon Press, 2005.

Puttenham, George. *The Arte of English Poesie.* Edited by Frank Whigham and Wayne A. Rebhorn. Ithaca, NJ: Cornell University Press, 2007.

The Returne from Parnassus: Or The Scourge of Simony. London, 1606.

Reynolds, Edward. *A Treatise of the Passions and Faculties of the Soul of Man; With the Several Dignities and Corruptions thereunto Belonging.* London, 1640.

Sandhal, Carrie. "The Tyranny of Neutral." In *Bodies in Commotion: Disability and Performance*, edited by Carrie Sandhal and Philip Auslander. Ann Arbor: University of Michigan Press, 2005.

Shakespeare, William. *The Tragedy of King Richard the Third.* Edited by Stephen Greenblatt. *The Norton Shakespeare.* Edited by Stephen Greenblatt, Walter Cohen, Jean E. Howard and Katharine Eisaman Maus. New York: Norton, 1997.

————. *The True Tragedy of Richard Duke of York and the Good King Henry the Sixth (3 Henry VI)*. Edited by Jean E. Howard. *The Norton Shakespeare*. Edited by Stephen Greenblatt, Walter Cohen, Jean E. Howard and Katharine Eisaman Maus. New York: Norton, 1997.

Sidney, Philip. *A Defence of Poetry*. Edited by J. A. Van Dorst. Oxford: Oxford University Press, 1966.

Siebers, Tobin. *Disability Theory*. Ann Arbor: University of Michigan Press, 2008.

Singer, Julie. "Disability and the Social Body." *Postmedieval: A Journal of Medieval Cultural Studies* 3, no. 2 (2012): 135–41.

Stagg, Kevin. "Representing Physical Difference: The Materiality of the Monstrous." In *Social Histories of Disability and Deformity*, edited by David M. Turner and Kevin Stagg. New York: Routledge, 2006.

States, Bert O. *Great Reckonings in Little Rooms: On the Phenomenology of Theater*. Berkeley: University of California Press, 1985.

Torrey, Michael. "'The Plain Devil and Dissembling Looks': Ambivalent Physiognomy and Shakespeare's *Richard III*." *English Literary Renaissance* 30, no. 2 (2000): 123–53.

The True Tragedie of Richard III. London, 1594.

Turner, David M. "Introduction: Approaching Anomalous Bodies." In *Social Histories of Disability and Deformity*, edited by David M. Turner and Kevin Stagg. New York: Routledge, 2006.

Vaughan, William. *The Spirit of Detraction Conjured and Convicted in Seven Circles*. London, 1611.

Weimann, Robert. *Author's Pen and Actor's Voice*. Edited by Helen Higbee and William West. Cambridge: Cambridge University Press, 2000.

West, William. "What's the Matter with Shakespeare? Physics, Identity, Playing." *South Central Review* 26, nos. 1–2 (2009): 103–26.

Weimann, Robert and Douglas Bruster. *Shakespeare and the Power of Performance: Stage and Page in the Elizabethan Theatre*. Cambridge: Cambridge University Press, 2010.

Wilks, John S. *The Idea of Conscience in Renaissance Tragedy*. London: Routledge, 1990.

Williams, Katherine Schaap. "Enabling Richard: The Rhetoric of Disability in *Richard III*." *Disability Studies Quarterly* 29, no. 4 (2009): unpaginated. Available from http://dsq-sds.org/article/view/997/1181

Wood, Alice I. Perry. *The Stage History of Shakespeare's King Richard the Third*. New York: AMS Press, 1965.

Ship of Fools: Foucault and the Shakespeareans

Richard Wilson

Half a century after Michel Foucault's career was launched in the Anglo-Saxon world, with the English translation of Folie et Déraison: Histoire de la Folie à l'âge classique *as* Madness and Civilization, *his reputation within Shakespeare studies appears to have sunk without trace. In particular, his claim that "in Shakespeare madness occupies an extreme position" that "opens into a tear in the fabric of the world", because there is "no going back to reason" from Lear's lunacy or the delirium of Lady Macbeth, has never recovered from Jacques Derrida's crushing deconstruction of its illusory premise that it is possible to let "madness speak for itself". However, the fact that this work is now discredited as history, for relying on literary and artistic sources such as Bosch's* Ship of Fools, *makes it all the more vital to reconsider what Foucault might yet contribute as a reader of Shakespeare. What can be salvaged for literary criticism from the great wreck of this Ship of Fools? The answer, Foucault's late lectures suggested, is a critique that identifies the dark affinity between the sovereign and the beast in Shakespeare's Ubu-esque king: a monster who reveals not madness "outside", but "within the hollow crown".*

> O, I have suffered
> With those I saw suffer! A brave vessel,
> Who had, no doubt, some noble creature in her,
> Dashed all to pieces! (*The Tempest*, 1.2.5–8)[1]

Half a century after Michel Foucault's career as the foremost philosopher of transgression was launched in the Anglo-Saxon world, with the first English translation of his founding work *Folie et Déraison: Histoire de la Folie à l'âge classique* as *Madness and Civilization*, his reputation amongst Shakespeare scholars appears to have sunk without trace. In particular, his claim at the start of the book that in "Shakespeare

---

[1] All quotations from Shakespeare are from the Norton edition with quotations from *King Lear* taken from the conflated version.

madness occupies an extreme position" which "opens onto a tear in the fabric of the world", because "There is no going back to truth or reason" from Lear's lunacy or the delirium of Lady Macbeth, has been fatally discredited by its association with the image that illustrated it of the Ship of Fools, "a strange drunken boat that wound its way down the wide, slow-moving rivers of the Rhineland and round the canals of Flanders".[2] Nothing Foucault ever wrote has done more to wreck his reputation in Shakespeare studies than his categorical assertion that among all the legendary ships of the classical and Renaissance literary imagination, the vessels of madmen piloted by madmen immortalized in *Narrenschiff*, Sebastian Brandt's anti-Papal satire of 1494, "alone had a genuine existence … these boats that drifted from one town to another with their senseless cargo".[3] However, in the 1965 translation of Foucault's book, this was only the most flagrant of innumerable statements of fact that had to be taken on trust, since the French pocket edition on which it was based had been printed without scholarly apparatus, and with only a handful of the thousands of footnotes that had supposedly supported the original publication. *Madness and Civilization* did, however, benefit from the talent of an illustrious American translator, and it was Richard Howard's prose that fuelled the fantasies of a generation of campus professors and their hallucinating students:

> Something new appears in the imaginary landscape of the Renaissance, soon it will occupy a privileged place there: the Ship of Fools, a strange "drunken boat" that glides along the calm rivers of the Rhineland and the Flemish canals. The *Narrenschiff*, of course, is a literary composition, probably borrowed from the old Argonaut cycle, one of the great themes recently revived and rejuvenated, acquiring an institutional aspect in the Burgundian estates. Fashion favoured the composition of these Ships, whose crew of imaginary heroes, ethical models, or social types embarked on a great symbolic voyage which would bring them the figure of their destiny or their truth … Bosch's painting, of course, belongs to this dream fleet. But of all these romantic or satiric vessels, the *Narrenschiff* is the only one that had a real existence—for they did exist, these boats that carried their insane cargo from town to town. Madmen then led an easy wandering life.[4]

Recommended to its London publisher as not only "brilliantly written" but also "intellectually rigorous" by R. D. Laing, the anti-psychiatry guru who considered schizophrenics to be super sane, with its valorization of the madman's meandering voyage as "an absolute Passage" towards "strange paths of knowledge", *Madness and Civilization* seemed to be offering the spaced-out 1960s counter-culture a carnivalesque Renaissance precedent for its own Fool's Paradise of "an easy wandering life", and Foucault's lunatic hulk would inspire scores of postmodern fictions and psychedelic artworks.[5] For the ship has been not just a means of transport, the theorist would

---

[2]Foucault, *History of Madness*, 8, 38.
[3]Ibid., 9.
[4]Foucault, *Madness and Civilization*, 7–8.
[5]Ibid., 11, 25.

insist, but "from the sixteenth century up to our time the greatest reservoir" of the imagination. A sailing vessel is a "heterotopia par excellence", he explained; meaning "a piece of floating space" that is both inside and outside culture, a type of "actually realized utopia in which all the other real emplacements that can be found within the culture are represented, contested, and reversed". Self-enclosed yet "delivered over to the boundless expanse of the ocean", the Ship of Fools was therefore a prime instance of those placeless places that are "reserved for individuals who are in a state of crisis with respect to society".[6] Therefore, the voyage of the "strange drunken boat" that heralded Foucault's entry into English was not only an apt figure for the idea Shakespeare critics took from his work, that as Stephen Greenblatt concluded in *Renaissance Self-Fashioning*, apropos his own account of "the noble ship of Venice" (*Othello*, 2.1.22) that carries Desdemona, Othello and Iago to Cyprus, transgression is "engendered by the very process of punishment, surveillance, discipline, and constraint" to which it is subjected.[7] The philosopher also needed the wandering bark of madmen to launch his Nietzschean theory of the "limit experience", or "going beyond" this impasse, which linked him with earlier thinkers of transgression such as Georges Bataille, the paradox that it is constraint that makes resistance, and thereby freedom, possible:[8]

> Water and navigation certainly play this role. Confined on the ship, from which there is no escape, the madman is delivered to the river with its thousand arms, the sea with its thousand roads, to that great uncertainty external to everything. He is a prisoner in the midst of what is the freest, the openest of routes: bound fast at the infinite crossroads. He is the Passenger *par excellence*: that is, the prisoner of the passage.[9]

"Yes, I'm very fond of boats myself. I like the way they're—contained": one writer who seems to have read *Madness and Civilization*, and instantly applied it to Shakespeare, was Tom Stoppard, whose Guildenstern made Foucault's point about the mad-ship as a perfect image for the dialectic of fate and free will: "You don't have to worry about which way to go, or whether to go at all—the question doesn't arise, because you're on a boat, aren't you? ... I think I'll spend most of my life on boats."[10] In Stoppard's 1965 play the ship taking the two spies to England is, of course, carrying them to certain death, as "Rosencrantz and Guildenstern are dead" at the end of *Hamlet* (5.2.315), and they only enter "real" time when they get caught up in Shakespeare's tragedy. The dramatist never lets us forget that the "divinity that shapes" their ends (*Hamlet*, 5.2.10) is literature, that there is nothing outside the text. By contrast, in Foucault's book "the sweet joy of Ophelia" and "the bitter sweet dementia of *King Lear*" are

---

[6]Foucault, "Different Spaces," 179, 184–5.
[7]Greenblatt, *Renaissance Self-Fashioning*, 80.
[8]For Foucault's debt to Bataille, see Pearce.
[9]Foucault, *Madness and Civilization*, 11.
[10]Stoppard, 3, 55.

said to "bear witness" to the actual existential "experience of madness", when the insane "were allowed to wander in the open countryside", or float upon the current "mermaid-like" (*Hamlet*, 5.1.147), in a "wild state", like Ophelia in the painting by Millais, that "can never be reconstituted". These hyperbolic words about the "torn presence" of "madness itself, in all its vivacity, before it is captured by knowledge", were cut from the revised edition of 1972.[11] Moreover, after he was subjected to scathing critiques by the historian Roy Porter and others, Foucault's defenders argued that he had only ever meant the Ship of Fools "as a striking (and rich) *symbol*" of what he called "that inaccessible primitive purity".[12] Yet when a complete text at last appeared in English in 2006, as the *History of Madness*, although his translators had curbed Foucault's giveaway verbal tic of "sans doute", its veridical claims about the luxury cruises of transgression were revealed to be both literal and unambiguous:

> for they really did exist, these boats that drifted from one town to another with their senseless cargo. An itinerant existence was often the lot of the mad. It was common practice … The arrival in the great cities of Europe of these ships of fools must have been quite a common sight … And it may be that these ships of fools, which haunted the imagination of the Early Renaissance, were in fact ships of pilgrimage, highly symbolic ships filled with the senseless in search of their reason.[13]

For fifty years Foucault's mighty tome had enjoyed a spectral existence in the minds of American and British academics, as a sort of Flying Dutchman of philosophy, the substance of which could only be guessed. His admirers always claimed he footnoted so lightly because he wished to read the past through the thinnest possible "grid".[14] However, when the *History of Madness* finally docked on Anglo-Saxon shores, its skeletal documentation caused genuine shock, not least because its crucial assertion that the Ships of Fools "really did exist" proved utterly unsubstantiated; and the leading article of *The Times Literary Supplement* (*TLS*) on 23 March 2007 spoke for even erstwhile Foucauldians, with the deadly headline, "Foucault's Fictions: Scholarship of Fools". The "frail foundations of Foucault's monument" were attributable to its having been researched in exile in Sweden, the spookily named Andrew Scull speculated in this devastating piece of *schadenfreude*. However, "its central image of 'the ship of fools' laden with its cargo of mad souls searching for their reason, floating down the liminal spaces of feudal Europe", had been "careless and inventive", at best, and at worst, a deliberate fabrication: "The ship of fools was real. They existed, these boats that carried their crazed cargo from one town to another. But it wasn't; and they didn't." *Madness and Civilization* had cast a malign spell over the psychiatric

---

[11]Foucault, *History of Madness*, xxxii–iii, 37–8.
[12]"torn presence": ibid., 164; "a striking (and rich) symbol": Gutting, 72, n.21. For the refutation of Foucault's history of madness, see, in particular, Porter and Stone. For other important interventions, see Midelfort; Sedgwick; Merquior, Chap. 2; Gordon, "*Histoire de la folie*"; Scull, "Michel Foucault's History of Madness"; Gordon, "History, Madness and Other Errors"; and Roudinesco et al. For a recent overview, see Beaulieu and Fillion.
[13]Foucault, *History of Madness*, 9–10.
[14]Marchetti and Salomoni, 348.

enterprise during the neo-liberal assault on public services, when it became expedient to dismiss psychiatrists as "nothing more than prison guards", Scull alleged; so the consequences of these falsifications were real for patients discharged to go their wandering ways in the great decommissioning of Western public health. Thus the real lesson of Foucault's Shakespearean foolery "might be amusing", the review concluded, if it had "had no effect on people's lives: the ease with which history can be distorted, facts ignored, and the claims of human reason disparaged and dismissed, by someone sufficiently cynical and shameless, and willing to trust in the ignorance and credulity of his customers".[15]

By reviving the insinuation that the chronicler of the Ship of Fools was responsible for the bag ladies of New York, the *TLS* was stirring controversy; and Scull's polemic duly scandalized the Foucauldians, who likened its "extreme prejudice" to the Sokal hoax that purported to explode post-structuralism, and protested that the philosopher had driven his Jaguar "often and fast from Uppsala" to toil in the Paris archives.[16] However, if the unabridged version has destroyed any lingering faith among Shakespeare critics in Foucault's volume as a serious work of Renaissance history, it merely confirms what had been made obvious decades before, when, in a famous act of parricide, Jacques Derrida punctured the hubris of the grand attempt "to write a history of madness *itself. Itself.* Of madness itself. That is by letting madness speak for itself", as yet another totalitarian "internment. A Cartesian gesture for the twentieth century."[17] Foucault had highlighted Descartes' disavowal of madmen who fantasize that "they are kings when they are paupers, or say they are dressed in purple when they are naked", as the instant of "the Great Confinement", when reason excludes unreason, Erasmus' praise of folly and Montaigne's doubt are overcome, and "A great forgetting falls on the world that was criss-crossed by the free slavery of the ship of fools", which is henceforth "berthed at the quay. No longer a boat at all, but a hospital."[18] However, with a cruel dig at his teacher's own record of mental illness, Derrida dashed the rationality of the Cartesian subject as a mere repression of the fear of madness, when "the reassurance given against the anguish of the fear of being mad" is "the point of greatest proximity to madness". Thus the pathos attending Foucault's deluded mission "to try to capture, in history, this degree zero of madness, when it was undifferentiated experience", was that of an emperor without clothes, the irreverent pupil hinted, since the *folie de grandeur* of such a megalomaniac historicism was symptomatic of "this crisis in which reason is madder than madness".[19] Foucault had performed his own thesis, it was wickedly insinuated, for this colossal construct of His Majesty the Ego was *itself* a gigantic fool's errand:

---

[15]Scull, "Scholarship of Fools," 3–4. For Foucault's alleged culpability in the release of mental patients onto the streets of New York, see Weissmann.

[16]Gordon, "Extreme Prejudice." See also *The Times Literary Supplement*, "Letters," 6 and 20 April 2007.

[17]Derrida, 33, 55, 57.

[18]Foucault, *History of Madness*, 41, 44–5.

[19]"to try to capture, in history": Foucault, "Preface to the 1961 Edition," ibid., xxvi–xxxvi (xvii); Derrida, 61.

> It is only by virtue of this oppression of madness that finite-thought, that is to say, history, can reign … one could say that the reign of finite thought can be established only on the basis of the more or less disguised internment, humiliation, fettering and mockery of the madman within us, of the madman who can only be the fool of a logos which is father, master, and king.[20]

Derrida's iconoclastic deconstruction of *The History of Madness*, as a certifiable specimen of a historicism haunted by the "terror of going mad", accounts for the ferocity of Foucault's notorious response, when the book was reissued in 1972, that such textualization was itself "a historically well-determined little pedagogy … which teaches the student that there is nothing outside the text … a pedagogy that gives to the voice of the master that unlimited sovereignty that allows it to indefinitely re-say the text".[21] The ensuing schism in French theory would resemble nothing so much as the lunatic scene aboard the Ship of Fools in *The Tempest*, when, as the vessel founders, Shakespeare's voyagers fight over who and where is the master (1.1). However, Foucault grasped well enough that what was at stake in this graceless altercation was whether it was "possible that there might be something anterior or exterior to philosophical discourse. Could it have its condition in an exclusion, a refusal?"[22] The answer to his question seemed to have been, no, for after Derrida's sabotage Foucault systematically abandoned the concept of unmediated "experience".[23] As Ian Hacking points out in the Foreword, successive rewritings of *The History of Madness* therefore reveal its author turning himself inside out, as the Foucault who valorized the "romantic fantasy" of "the dream of madness in the wild", and "the purity of the possessed, those who speak the truth in paradox, like the fools in Shakespeare", disappears, until nothing remains of this archaeologist of "unreason" but the grin, like that of Alice's Cheshire Cat, of the genealogist who in *The History of Sexuality* argues, contra his own earlier "repressive hypothesis", that power is productive and inclusive, rather than deductive and exclusive, and thereby does indeed embrace the "madman within":[24]

> We pass from a technology of power that drives out, excludes, banishes, marginalizes, and represses, to a fundamentally positive power that fashions, observes, knows, and multiplies itself on the basis of its own effects.[25]

The translation *The History of Madness* has been relished by Foucault's Anglo-Saxon detractors as an embarrassment comparable to that of Althusser's *The Future Lasts a Long Time*, the memoir in which the Marxist theoretician claimed to have read

---

[20]Ibid.

[21]"terror of going mad": ibid., 62; Foucault, "My Body, this Paper, this Fire: Appendix to the 1972 Edition," in Foucault, *History of Madness*, 550–74 (573).

[22]Ibid., 552.

[23]See Paras, 121–2, 142–4.

[24]"romantic fantasy": Hacking, ix–xi.

[25]Foucault, *Abnormal*, 48.

barely a word of Marx.[26] However, the fact that this work is now discredited as history, for relying on literary and artistic sources such as Bosch's *Ship of Fools* or Cervantes' *Don Quixote*, makes it all the more vital to reconsider what Foucault might yet contribute as a reader of Shakespeare. What can be salvaged for literary criticism from the great wreck of this Ship of Fools? For whatever the evidence for "the ritual embarkation" of the insane, Foucault had asserted, "one thing is certain: the link between water and madness is deeply rooted in the dream of Western man".[27] More specifically, in his study "Staying Afloat", Bernhard Klein has commented that "only a cultural imagination that still encoded the sea as the morally transgressive and inherently repulsive realm of formless and unfinished matter was amenable to such a literary conceit" as this ghostly galleon that sails the seas without destination, given that "No greater conceptual difference from the spirit of Columbus's enterprise can be imagined than the lack of purpose that defines Brandt's mad voyage."[28] So, that Foucault was on to something, with his reverence for Shakespeare as the poet of the unfathomable "dark backward and abyss" (1.2.50) of death and madness, dreams and night, is a powerful undercurrent of Steve Mentz's *At the Bottom of Shakespeare's Ocean*, which riffs upon the *topos* of the capsizing "ship boring the moon with her main mast" (*The Winter's Tale*, 3.3.92) to float the thesis of a new "blue cultural studies": that "Shakespeare asks us to read for salt … as if certain narratives can help us embrace and endure ocean-driven disorder".[29] In our latest fanciful Shakespeare phenomenology, therefore, it seems that Foucault returns, but as himself a poet and fabulist rather than historian, whose importance was indeed to have recognized in these liminal dramas the rites of passage that define the threshold of the modern:

> The madness to be found in the works of Shakespeare leads to death and murder …
> [Thus] they in all probability still bear witness to the tragic experience of madness
> born in the fifteenth century more than they reflect the critical or moral experience
> of unreason that is nonetheless a product of their era. Through time, they connect
> with a kind of madness that is in the process of disappearing, and which will live on
> only under the cover of darkness.[30]

In his very first publication, his 1954 essay *Dream and Existence*, Foucault saluted Shakespeare as a laureate of the "dark space" of night, whose texts were among the last to figure the irrational not as a reflection of reality, but as "something of great constancy", truer than the waking world (*A Midsummer Night's Dream*, 5.1.26).[31] As I pointed out in *Shakespeare and French Theory*, by enthroning the Bard as a "king of shadows" (3.2.348) in this rapturous way, the philosopher was interpreting the plays within a French Romantic tradition that valorized them as "the Gothic ruins of the

---

[26]Althusser.

[27]Foucault, *History of Madness*, 11.

[28]Klein, 94.

[29]Mentz, 99.

[30]Foucault, *History of Madness*, 37.

[31]Foucault, *Dream and Existence*, 54–5.

Dark Ages".[32] Hence, after Shakespeare, *The History of Madness* related, the "dark power" of resistance to the therapeutic society "begins to lose its violence", as "that darkness into which man stared and made out impossible forms slowly begins to retreat". The surprise turn Derrida's acid critique of this "romantic illusion" of exclusion prompted, however, was to reread Shakespeare not as a staging of the triumphant "cortège of reason", but a commemoration of the incorrigible "madman within" the disciplinary order.[33] Thus, throughout his courses at the Collège de France in the 1970s and 1980s, Foucault kept raiding the plays for traces of the insidious irrationality at the heart of the modern regime of "biopolitics" that was his theme. And tellingly, the madman who came back in these Shakespeare citations was no longer an ostracized scapegoat on the margins of modernity, one of those "outsiders-who-make-the-insiders-insiders", but a psychopathic maniac in the seat of power, with the grotesque body yet exalted office of the king.[34] For long before Alan Bennett wove *The Madness of King George III* around scenes from *King Lear*, what was Shakespearean theatre, Foucault asked repeatedly in these talks, but "a sort of ceremony, or rememorialization of public right", in the face of the mad arbitrariness, indeed criminal illegitimacy, of sovereign power?[35] Thus, Shakespeare appealed to the late Foucault as a precursor of Absurdism, who had installed the grinning "antic" on the throne, "within the hollow crown / That rounds the mortal temple of a king" (*Richard II*, 3.2.156–9), and thereby exposed the *grotesque* unworthiness of rule:

> I am calling "grotesque" the fact that … a discourse or an individual can have effects of power that their intrinsic qualities should disqualify them from having. The grotesque or, if your prefer, the "Ubu-esque", is not just a term of abuse … I think there is a precise category of historico-political analysis, that would be the category of Ubu-esque terror, grotesque sovereignty, or, in starker terms, the maximization of effects of power on the basis of the disqualification of the one who produces them … The problem of the infamy of sovereignty, of the discredited sovereign, is, after all, Shakespeare's problem.[36]

In a recent article, Zita Turi demonstrates how, despite the popularity of Alexander Barclay's 1509 translation of Brandt's *Narrenschiff*, in Tudor England "the critical aim of *The Ship of Fools*" was steadily focused upon the licensed role of the court jester.[37] Critics have, of course, long identified in the cap and bauble of Shakespeare's Fool the signifiers of phallic privilege that Foucault also understood when he told a conference in Japan that in a tragedy such as *King Lear* the lunatic spoke the truth to power, "for he saw what the other characters did not see, and he revealed the ending of the plot … the madman is a character who expresses with his body the truth that the other actors and

---

[32]Wilson, *Shakespeare in French Theory*, 75. See also Wilson, *Will Power*.
[33]Foucault, *History of Madness*, 41.
[34]"Outsiders-who-make-the-insiders": Stallybrass and White, 22.
[35]Foucault, *Society Must be Defended*, 174–5.
[36]Foucault, *Abnormal*, 11–13.
[37]Turi, unpaginated.

spectators are not aware of".[38] The idiot rides alongside Caesar, and strikes him, from time to time, to remind the victor of mortality. As Shakespeare's Countess says, "There is no slander" in such "an allowed fool" (*Twelfth Night*, 1.5.80). However, what Foucault noticed in the monstrous Richard III, or even the charmer Henry V, was something darker about the grotesque Ubu-like buffoonery of power, which was the cunning with which sovereignty intrudes itself as "odious, despicable, or ridiculous". No wonder Alfred Jarry based his preposterous tyrant on the infantile Macbeth. For Shakespeare was a genius, on this view, in the representation of "vile sovereignty": the aberration whereby its self-portrayal as "abject, despicable, Ubu-esque", far from curtailing its effects, instantiates "the unavoidability, the inevitability of power, which can function in its full rigor and at the extreme point of its rationality even when in the hands of someone who is effectively discredited". Thus, all the "mediocre, useless, imbecilic, superficial, worn-out", reviled and sordid functionaries of the modern bureaucratic machine, as depicted by Dostoyevsky or Kafka, are prefigured, according to the later Foucault, when Shakespeare's madcap prince presents himself to us, warts and all, as the wisest fool, who has "sounded the very base-string of humility", to make himself as much beloved by "all the good lads in Eastcheap" (*1 Henry IV*, 5–13), who he will betray, as he is despised by us for his own callous and casual criminality.[39]

"Theatre is not set over against power, but is one of power's essential modes": the lesson Greenblatt and New Historicism learned from Foucault was the old one that power uses circuses, that the king will "play bo-peep" with clowns, "And go the fools among" (*King Lear*, 1.4.154–5), so that "in the perfectness of time" he can "Cast off his followers … Turning past evils to advantages" (*2 Henry IV*, 4.3.75–8).[40] Much of the debate in Shakespeare studies during the Foucault years was therefore about the degree to which this immunological trick to "imitate the sun, / Who doth permit the base contagious clouds / To smother up his beauty from the world" (*1 Henry IV*, 1.2.175–7), operated as *containment*, or whether the plays demonstrated how these "filthy rites" of abjection were vulnerable to more radical *subversion*.[41] If transgression was a strategic ruse, a "bourgeois bohemia", was Shakespearean theatre itself a mimetic *staging* of repressed desire, as Mikhail Bakhtin had shown Carnival to be a periodic fit of madness, the "temporary liberation from the prevailing truth of the established order"; or did it, as Peter Stallybrass and Allon White countered in *The Politics and Poetics of Transgression*, effectuate "a strange carnivalesque diaspora" that carried the heresy of a world turned upside down beyond the mere interrogation of boundaries and towards a transformational politics?[42] Greenblatt's Kafkaesque answer, that there is "subversion, no end of subversion, but not for

---

[38]Foucault, "Madness and Society," 340.
[39]Foucault, *Abnormal*, 11–13.
[40]Greenblatt, "Invisible Bullets," 46.
[41]Greenblatt, "Filthy Rites."
[42]Bakhtin, 109; Stallybrass and White, 190–201.

us", took its cue from Foucault's dispiriting pronouncement, in his "Preface to Transgression", his homage to Bataille, that if transgression is "for our culture" what dialectic was for Sartre's, its meaning lies "almost entirely in the future".[43] However, the critique of Shakespeare outlined in the lectures at the Collège de France was altogether more engaged, indeed enraged, about the idiocy of power and the madman in the palace:

> Ubu the "pen-pusher" is a functional component of modern administration ... just as in the grotesque character of someone like Mussolini power provided itself with an image in which power derived from someone who was theatrically got up and depicted as a clown or a buffoon ... This is precisely the problem posed by Shakespeare in the royal tragedies, without, it seems to me, the sovereign's infamy ever having been theorized. But from Nero down to the little man with trembling hands crowned with forty million deaths who, from deep in his bunker, asks only for two things, that everything about him be destroyed and that he be given chocolate cakes until he bursts, you have the whole outrageous functioning of the despicable sovereign.[44]

Grimacing "man, proud man, / Dressed in a little brief authority ... Plays such fantastic tricks before high heaven / As makes the angels weep" (*Measure for Measure*, 2.2.120–5): the Chaplinesque Shakespeare Foucault quoted in his lectures stood out among the lickspittles by his refusal to sing "power's ode to itself". At a time when historicists like Thomas Hobbes were struggling to "get around the terrible problem of the Conquest", the ineffaceable aporia that the English state had been founded by violent usurpation, Shakespeare, according to this account, instead revelled in the bastardy and madness of the monarchy.[45] Foucault's grasp of English history was shaky, and he seems to have thought Monmouth's Rebellion of 1685 was a Saxon rising against the Normans, led by the medieval chronicler Geoffrey of Monmouth, a howler that remained uncorrected in 2003![46] However, in his reading of these dramas as "one of the great ritual forms in which public right was displayed and its problems discussed" by ceaselessly revisiting the primal scene of founding violence, he unerringly foretold current thinking about Shakespeare as a witness to "the uncanny proximity" of the sovereign and the beast.[47]

Despite disastrously hailing the return of the Ayatollah as the return of a "political spirituality" that had been forgotten in the West since the Renaissance, Foucault never used the term "political theology", and had presumably never heard of Carl Schmitt.[48] However, he organized his most political work, *Discipline and Punish*, around the theological nostrum he derived from Ernst Kantorowicz and *The King's Two Bodies*, that "In the darkest region of the political field" the condemned criminal "represents the

---

[43]"Subversion, no end of subversion": Greenblatt, "Invisible Bullets," 65; Foucault, "Preface to Transgression," 33.
[44]Foucault, *Abnormal*, 13.
[45]Foucault, *Society Must be Defended*, 110, 174.
[46]Ibid., 101.
[47]Santner, 47.
[48]Foucault, "A Quoi rêvent les Iraniens?"

symmetrical, inverted figure of the king".[49] Moreover, in Richard III's anachronizing self-realization as "Deformed, unfinished, sent before my time" (*Richard III*, 1.1.20), he identified a Shakespearean premonition of the theme of "the link between the sovereign above the law and the criminal beneath" which he developed in these lectures: the homology that "the first moral monster is the political monster ... The first monster is the king ... Kings are nothing else but tigers."[50] Like Ubu, Shakespeare's "king of shreds and patches" is "A cutpurse of the empire and the rule" (*Hamlet*, 3.4.89–92); and what that means for Foucault is that this sovereign lawbreaker "is who decides on the exception":[51]

> Shakespeare's "historical" tragedies are tragedies about right centered on the problem of the usurper and dethronement, of the murder of kings and the birth of the new being who is constituted by the coronation of a king. How can an individual use violence, intrigue, murder, and war to acquire a public might that can bring about the reign of order? How can illegitimacy produce law? At a time when the theory and history of right are trying to weave the unbroken continuity of public might, Shakespearean tragedy, in contrast, dwells on the wound, on the repeated injury that is inflicted on the body of the kingdom when kings die violent deaths and illegitimate sovereigns come to the throne.[52]

"We touch here on an apparently marginal problem that I think is important", Foucault explained to bemused listeners at the Collège, when he swerved from his subject of "governmentality" to Shakespeare, "and this is the problem of theatrical practice in politics, or the theatrical practice of *raison d'état*".[53] For unlike recent American critics who present the plays as propagandist fanfares for the political theology of divine right, and follow Greenblatt in viewing Shakespearean theatre as one of sacred kingship's "essential modes", an idealization of "high Christian royalism" and the mysterious ways of the executive decision, in these lectures the French theorist never lost sight of drama as performance.[54] Such dramatization might well be "a mode of manifestation of the sovereign as holder of state power", he conceded. However, he had grasped Kantorowicz's point about the difference between the fiction and the man enough to insist on the "contrast and opposition" between the "traditional ceremonies in which royalty wanted to be shown", those displays which, "from anointment to coronation up to the entry into towns or the funerals of sovereigns, marked the religious character" of monarchy, and "this modern kind of theatre" in which the scenario was always the exception, the emergency of the "*coup d'Etat* carried out by the sovereign himself".[55] Theatre, on this view, was indeed set over against power, which it depicted

---

[49]Foucault, *Discipline and Punish*, 29; Kantorowicz.
[50]Foucault, *Abnormal*, 92, 94, 97.
[51]"Sovereign is he who decides": Schmitt, 5, 33.
[52]Foucault, *Society Must be Defended*, 174.
[53]Foucault, *Security, Territory, Population*, 265.
[54]"high Christian royalism": Shuger, 56 passim.
[55]Foucault, *Security, Territory, Population*, 265.

as operating in "a wilderness of tigers" (*Titus Andronicus*, 3.1.54), for Shakespeare's significance was to have demonstrated how *raison d'État* was not *rational* at all. Thus, just as the Kantorowicz of *The King's Two Bodies* crowned Dante over his erstwhile *Fuhrer*-type Frederick II, on the grounds that while the emperor stood for "the manipulation of myth, the *Commedia* (like *Richard II*) stands for the fiction that knows itself as such", so the Foucault of these lectures advanced Shakespeare above the maniacal monarchs he served, in awed appreciation of how the plays stage the clownish irrationality of power, and over and again confront the Pascalian catch-22 that prefaces *The History of Madness*, that "Men are so necessarily mad, that not being mad would be being mad through another trick that madness played":[56]

> Shakespeare's historical drama really is the drama of the *coup d'État* ... Just as in politics *raison d'État* manifests itself in theatricality, so this theater is organized around the representation of this *raison d'Etat* in its dramatic, intense, and violent form of the *coup d'État* ... State, necessity, and risky *coups d'État* will form the new tragic horizon of history. At the same time as the birth of *raison d'État*, I think a certain tragic sense of history is born ... in this theatrical and violent form ... something that quite remarkably makes one think of Hitlerian nights, of the night of the long knives.[57]

"Why was he sent into England? Why, because he was mad. A shall recover his wits there; or if a do not, 'tis no great matter ... 'Twill not be seen in him there. There the men are as mad as he" (*Hamlet*, 5.1.138–42): with his Ship of Fools bound for England, Foucault's Shakespeare is the undeceived servant, in these lectures, of the Ubu-esque "Wisest Fool in Christendom", a writer who through the performances he plots for a mad and murderous monarchy "represents the state to itself".[58] Thus his Prince of Denmark is truly "mad north-north-west" (*Hamlet*, 2.2.361), if we follow this logic, in aspiring to the kind of foolish sovereignty that was personified by the King of Scots, or his brother-in-law Christian, the actual Danish prince, who before his coronation in 1596 was carted by actors from London on a ship of fools dressed up as the pope and on his return from the ceremony robed as a whore.[59] Nothing more is heard about the "author function", as a means to insure "the possibility of transgression attached to the act of writing", in Foucault's praise of the playwright as the author whose function was to "hold as 'twere the mirror up" (3.2.20) to such moral and juridical monstrosity, and reveal how "The grotesque is one of the essential processes of arbitrary sovereignty." Instead, the philosopher whose history of madness had been

---

[56]"the manipulation of myth": Kahn, 95–6; cf. Boureau, 106: "Kantorowicz inverted Schmitt's understanding of political theology. Political theology did not furnish an authoritarian arm to secular sovereigns because they possessed it already. Political theology used the moment of the Incarnation as the model ... to create fictions that remove man from the direct pressures of nature, power, and the group." Blaise Pascal, *Pensées*, 414, quoted by Foucault, "Preface to the 1961 Edition", in *History of Madness*, xxvii.
[57]Foucault, *Security, Territory, Population*, 265–6.
[58]Ibid., 266.
[59]See Wade.

trashed for confusing fact and fiction, Renaissance experience and Shakespearean literature, rejoices in the uninhibited transgressiveness of dramas that represent "the person who possesses power" as, "in his costume, his gestures, his body, his sexuality, and his way of life, a despicable grotesque, and ridiculous individual".[60] "The limit and transgression depend on each other",[61] Foucault had written in his "Preface to Transgression"; but in Shakespeare, where the Ship of Fools became the ship of state, it seems he found at last a form of symbolic transgression that was itself "as mad as the vexed sea, singing aloud" (*King Lear*, 4.3.2).

References

Althusser, Louis. *The Future Lasts a Long Time*. Translated by Richard Veasey. London: Chatto & Windus, 1993.

Bakhtin, Mikhail. *Rabelais and his World*. Translated by H. Iswolsky. Cambridge, MA: MIT Press, 1968.

Beaulieu, Alain, and Réal Fillion. "Review Essay: Michel Foucault, *History of Madness*." *Foucault Studies* 5 (2008): 74–89.

Boureau, Alain. *Kantorowicz: Stories of a Historian*. Translated by Stephen Nichols and Gabrielle Spiegel. Baltimore: Johns Hopkins University Press, 2001.

Derrida, Jacques. "Cogito and the History of Madness." In *Writing and Difference*, translated by Alan Bass. London: Routledge & Kegan Paul, 1978.

Foucault, Michel. "A Quoi rêvent les Iraniens?" *Le Nouvel Observateur*, 16 October 1978, 48–9.

———. *Abnormal: Lectures at the Collège de France, 1974–1975*. Edited by Valerio Marchetti and Antonella Salomoni, translated by Graham Burchill. New York: Picador, 2003.

———. "Different Spaces." Translated by Robert Hurley. In *Essential Works of Foucault: 1954–1984, III: Aesthetics, Method, and Epistemology*, edited by James D. Faubion. London: Allen Lane, 1998. Originally published as "Des Espace Autres." *Architecture, Mouvement, Continueté* 5 (October 1984): 46–9.

———. *Discipline and Punish: The Birth of the Prison*. Translated by Alan Sheridan. Harmondsworth: Penguin, 1977.

———. *Dream and Existence: Michel Foucault and Ludwig Binswanger*. Edited by Keith Hoeller and translated by Forrest Williams. Atlantic Highlands, NJ: Humanities Press, 1993.

———. *History of Madness*. Translated by Jonathan Murphy and Jean Khalfa. London: Routledge, 2006.

———. *Madness and Civilization: A History of Insanity in the Age of Reason*. Translated by Richard Howard. New York: Pantheon, 1965; London: Tavistock, 1967.

———. "Madness and Society." Translated by Robert Hurley. In *Essential Works of Foucault: 1954–1984, III: Aesthetics, Method, and Epistemology*, edited by James D. Faubion. London: Allen Lane, 1998.

———. "Preface to Transgression." In *Language/Counter-Memory/Practice*, translated by D. Bouchard and S. Simon. Ithaca, NY: Cornell University Press, 1977.

---

[60]"the possibility of transgression": Foucault, "What is an Author?," 205; "The grotesque": Foucault, *Abnormal*, 12.

[61]Foucault, "Preface to Transgression," 34.

————. *Security, Territory, Population: Lectures at the Collège de France, 1977–1978.* Translated by Graham Burchell. Basingstoke: Palgrave, 2007.

————. *Society Must be Defended: Lectures at the Collège de France, 1975–1976.* Translated by David Macey. London: Allen Lane, 2003.

————. "What is an Author?" In *Essential Works of Foucault: 1954–1984, III: Aesthetics, Method, and Epistemology*, edited by James D. Faubion. London: Allen Lane, 1998.

Gordon, Colin. "Extreme Prejudice: Notes on Andrew Scull's *TLS* Review of Foucault's *The History of Madness*." *Foucault Blog*, 20 May 2007 [cited 1 September 2012]. Available from http://foucaultblog.wordpress.com/2007/05/20/extreme-prejudice/

————. "*Histoire de la folie*: An Unknown Book by Michel Foucault." *History of the Human Sciences* 3, no. 1 (1990): 3–26.

————. "History, Madness and Other Errors. A Response." *History of the Human Sciences* 3, no. 3 (1990): 381–96.

Greenblatt, Stephen. "Filthy Rites." In *Learning to Curse: Essays in Early Modern Culture*. London: Routledge, 1990.

————. "Invisible Bullets." In *Shakespearean Negotiations: The Circulation of Social Energy in Renaissance England*. Oxford: Oxford University Press, 1988.

————. *Renaissance Self-Fashioning: From More to Shakespeare.* Chicago: Chicago University Press, 1980.

Gutting, Gary. "Foucault and the History of Madness." In *The Cambridge Companion to Foucault*, edited by Gary Gutting. Cambridge: Cambridge University Press, 2005.

Hacking, Ian. "Foreword." In Eric Paras, *Foucault 2.0*. New York: Other Press, 2006.

Kahn, Victoria. "Political Theology and Fiction in *The King's Two Bodies*." *Representations* 106 (2009): 77–101.

Kantorowicz, Ernst. *The King's Two Bodies: A Study in Medieval Political Theology.* Princeton, NJ: Princeton University Press, 1997.

Klein, Bernhard. "Staying Afloat: Shipboard Encounters from Columbus to Equiano." In *Sea Changes: Historicizing the Ocean*, edited by Bernhard Klein and Gesa Mackenthun. London: Routledge, 2004.

Marchetti, Valerio, and Antonella Salomoni. "Course Context." In Michel Foucault, *Abnormal: Lectures at the Collège de France, 1974–1975*, edited by Valerio Marchetti and Antonella Salomoni, translated by Graham Burchill. New York: Picador, 2003.

Mentz, Steve. *At the Bottom of Shakespeare's Ocean.* London: Continuum, 2009.

Merquior, José. *Foucault.* London: Fontana, 1985.

Midelfort, H. C. Erik. "Madness and Civilisation in Early Modern Europe: A Reappraisal of Michel Foucault." In *After the Reformation*, edited by Barbara C. Malament. Philadelphia: University of Pennsylvania Press, 1980.

Paras, Eric. *Foucault 2.0.* New York: Other Press, 2006.

Pearce, Frank. "Foucault and the 'Hydra-Headed Monster': The *Collège de Sociologie* and the two *Acéphales*." In *Michel Foucault and Power Today*, edited by Alain Beaulieu and David Gabbard. Lanham, MD: Lexington Books, 2006.

Porter, Roy. "Foucault's Great Confinement." In *Rewriting the History of Madness: Studies in Foucault's "Histoire de la folie"*, edited by Arthur Still and Irving Velodie. London: Routledge, 1992.

Roudinesco, Elisabeth, et al. *Penser la folie.* Paris: Galilée, 1992.

Santner, Eric. *The Royal Remains: The People's Two Bodies and the Endgames of Sovereignty.* Chicago: Chicago University Press, 2011.

Schmitt, Carl. *Political Theology: Four Chapters on the Concept of Sovereignty.* Translated by George Schwab. Chicago: University of Chicago Press, 2005.

Scull, Andrew. "Michel Foucault's History of Madness." *History of the Human Sciences* 3, no. 1 (1990): 57–67.

———. "Scholarship of Fools: The Frail Foundations of Foucault's Monument." *Times Literary Supplement*, 23 March 2007, 3–4.

Sedgwick, Peter. *Psycho Politics*. London: Pluto Press, 1982.

Shakespeare, William. *The Norton Shakespeare: Based on the Oxford Edition*. Edited by Stephen Greenblatt, Walter Cohen, Jean E. Howard and Katherine Eisaman Maus. New York: Norton, 1997.

Shuger, Debora. *Political Theologies in Shakespeare's England: The Sacred and the State in "Measure for Measure"*. Basingstoke: Palgrave, 2001.

Stallybrass, Peter, and Allon White. *The Politics and Poetics of Transgression*. London: Methuen, 1986.

Stone, Lawrence. "Madness." *The New York Review of Books*, 16 December 1982, 28–36.

Stoppard, Tom. *Rosencrantz and Guildenstern are Dead*. London: Methuen, 1965.

Turi, Zita. "'Border Liners': The Ship of Fools Tradition in Sixteenth-Century England." *Trans: Revue de littérature générale et comparée* 10 (2010): unpaginated.

Wade, Mara. "The Coronation of Christian IV." In *Europa Triumphans: Court and Civic Festivals in Early Modern Europe, Volume 2*, edited by James Ronald Mulryne, Helen Watanabe-O'Kelly and Margaret Shewring. Aldershot: Ashgate, 2004.

Weissmann, Gerald. "Foucault and the Bag Lady." *Hospital Practice* (August 1982): 28–39.

Wilson, Richard. *Shakespeare in French Theory: King of Shadows*. London: Routledge, 2007.

———. *Will Power: Essays in Shakespearean Authority*. Hemel Hempstead: Harvester Wheatsheaf, 1993.

"Untimely Ripp'd": On Natality, Sovereignty and Unbearable Life

Arthur Bradley

This essay is a set of notes towards a new history of political theology that seeks to focus on the concept of "unbearable life". To begin with a hypothesis that I will cash out in more detail in the essay, unbearable life is not life that can be killed with impunity because it is not deemed worthy of life—such as Agamben's Homo Sacer—*but rather life that does not need to be killed because it is not permitted to "live" in the first place. For a certain tradition of political theology—which can be traced from Augustine to Schmitt—the challenge of rule becomes to foreclose the birth of species of life which, by the bare fact of their coming into the world, would constitute a challenge to the sovereign biopolitical command over what constitutes life and death. By abjecting certain forms of life of the very possibility of existence—by rendering them unbearable life—I further want to contend that political theology does not thereby find it possible to exclude them altogether but rather only to consign them to other ontological domains (myth, poetry, eschatology) and to other forms of species-existence: the beast, the spectre, the monster, the demonic, the machinic. If political theology seeks to repress the promise and the threat of unbearable life, however, we will see that the repressed returns to haunt it in its very interiority—and even in the increasingly unbearable figure of the sovereign himself. In the essay, I will try to exemplify this larger argument via a reading of Shakespeare's* Macbeth.

In her classic work *The Human Condition* (1958), Hannah Arendt offers a famous analysis of the bare condition of being born: "natality". To recall her well-rehearsed argument, Arendt insists that the three fundamental categories of the *vita activa* are labour, work and action. As she goes on to show, all three human activities are in some sense related to the phenomenon of natality. Both labour and work, for example, are necessary to create and preserve a world into which new human beings are constantly being born. However, it is what Arendt calls the political activity par excellence—action—which is most closely connected to the phenomenon of natality. For Arendt, natality is the condition of possibility of all action because the new begin-ning which is the act of being born reveals that the human being inherently "possesses the capacity of beginning something anew, that is, of acting".[1] If natality is the original new beginning—a beginning which happens anew with every new birth—it is also the guarantee of the novelty, singularity and unpredictability of all human action: "this again is possible only because each man is unique, so that with each birth something uniquely new comes into the world".[2] Such is why Arendt is famously able to conclude that natality is the "central category" of political thought.[3]

It is no coincidence, of course, that Arendt only begins to explicitly formulate her politics of natality in the aftermath of the publication of the first edition of her *Origins of Totalitarianism* (1951). As Miguel Vatter has recently shown via a reading of her letters to Karl Jaspers, Arendt defined totalitarianism biopolitically as the elimination of everything that was deemed superfluous to the realisation of the general species "man".[4] Not only did natality become the name for everything totalitarianism sought to eradicate—novelty, individuality, singularity—but Arendt even elevated it into the founding principle of her own anti-totalitarian biopolitics. To put it in Julia Reinhard Lupton's words, the totalitarian dream is the violent "foreclosure"[5] of this foundational natality in the name of a (literally preconceived) idea of the body politic: "Totalitarianism", Arendt famously writes, "knows neither birth nor death."[6] By seeking to obtain total sovereignty over natality via the elimination of that which is deemed surplus to the requirements of the general species of human life, totalitarianism effectively becomes a thanatopolitics: a politics of death. In the modern biopolitical imaginary, which has been most eloquently and influentially mapped by Giorgio Agamben, this politics finds its paradigmatic site in the Nazi concentration camp: the wretched figure of *der Muselmänn* becomes the defining figure of a bare life that can be killed with impunity because its life was deemed unworthy of being lived.[7]

Yet, in this essay, I want to advance the modest proposal that there may still be something missing from Arendt's classic diagnosis of totalitarianism as a form of thanatopolitics—and that "something" is what I want to call un-born or, better, unbearable life.[8] It is not quite enough to say that totalitarianism's foreclosure of natality consists in the right

---

[1] Arendt, *The Human Condition*, 9.

[2] Ibid., 177–8.

[3] Ibid., 9.

[4] Vatter, 137–59.

[5] Lupton, "Hannah Arendt's Renaissance," 9.

[6] Arendt, *The Origins of Totalitarianism*, 473.

[7] Agamben, 185. In *Homo Sacer*, Agamben famously invokes Primo Levi's discussion of the figure who—in the jargon of the camp—was ironically named "'The Muslim' [*Der Muselmänn*]: a being from whom humiliation, horror, and fear had so taken away all consciousness and all personality as to make him absolutely apathetic" (185).

[8] To be sure, Arendt's biopolitics of natality can be criticised in a number of ways that I do not have time to explore here. Firstly, it is possible to suspect a residual—and even residually theological—vitalism at work in any philosophy of life (from Arendt to Deleuze) as an endlessly giving or creative plenitude which precedes and exceeds all formation. If we are prepared to grant that such a principle of life does indeed exist, the claim that it intrinsically resists or evades political capture also seems to be something of a self-fulfilling prophecy: it is only necessary to look at the "pro-life" anti-abortion movement in the USA to see a particularly reductive politicisation of something like natality. To what extent might Melinda Cooper also be correct when she argues that capital is nothing

to kill with impunity, I wish to argue, because the totalitarian gesture also consists in the sovereign right to decide what forms of life are permitted to be born *as* life or not. After all, Nazi biopolitics did not simply consist in the mass extermination of life in the camps or even the euthanasia of which Agamben speaks but in the eradication of *birth*.[9] Think, for example, of its policy of compulsory sterilisation for people suffering from hereditary diseases or genetic disorders.[10] For the Nazi regime, the *Untermensch* were not simply life unworthy of life (*Lebensunwertes Leben*), life that could be killed without committing murder or sacrilege (as Arendt, Agamben and Roberto Esposito all variously argue), but rather an entire species of virtual or potential life that must be prevented from ever being born. In other words, I want to hypothesise that totalitarianism's war against natality is waged at a more virtual (in a quasi-Deleuzean sense of the term) level than the now common charge of thanatopolitics allows: it is not a war against actual living beings but a preventative, quite literally pre-natal, besieging of the pre-individuated, metastable field out of which the actual is formed.[11]

This essay is part of a larger history of political theology from Augustine to Schmitt that seeks to focus on the (to my view) critically underdeveloped biopolitical category of the un-born. To quickly outline the premise of this project, what I call "un-born" or "unbearable" life is not life that can be killed with impunity because it is not deemed worthy of life —such as Agamben's *Homo Sacer* or, differently, Judith Butler's precarious life and Eric Santner's creaturely life—but rather "life" that does not need to be killed because it is not permitted to live in the first place. It is "life" that is metaphysically, theologically and politically forbidden to be born because the bare fact of its birth would represent a challenge to the sovereign biopolitical command over what constitutes life and death. For a certain tradition of political theology, I want to propose that the sovereign challenge of governance becomes to foreclose the absolute singularity of natality which, by the bare fact of its coming into the world, challenges any pre-determined monopoly over the value of the human species. Such a gesture variously involves a re-writing of the past (Augustine's revisionary reading of Greek mythology from the perspective of the City of God); of the present (Hobbes' attempt to exclude the possibility of Christian martyrdom from the Commonwealth); and even of the future (Schmitt's philosophy of history as the

---

other than the political mobilisation of a neo-vitalist philosophy of life itself as endless surplus or becoming? See Cooper.

[9]It is now commonplace to criticise Agamben's (otherwise compelling) account of sovereignty for its unswerving conviction that biopolitics finds its logical conclusion in killing, in mass death, in necro-politics. As a consequence, his own reading of Nazi biopolitics in *Homo Sacer* is notably more interested in the politicisation of death (whether it be the extermination of the Jews or the euthanasia programme) than of birth (the sterilisation programme). See Agamben, 119–80.

[10]As is now well documented, the Law for the Prevention of Genetically Diseased Offspring (*Gesetz zur Verhütung erbkranken Nachwuchses*) was passed in 1933 and permitted the compulsory sterilisation of any citizen who, in the opinion of a "Genetic Health Court", suffered from a list of alleged genetic disorders.

[11]See Deleuze, 207–8. In Deleuze's famous words, "the virtual is opposed not to the real but to the actual. *The virtual is fully real in so far as it is virtual ...* Indeed, the virtual must be described as part of the real object—as though the object had one part of itself in the virtual into which it plunged as though into an objective dimension" (208).

endless restraining of the arrival of the Anti-Christ) by the simple act of saying: "this cannot be". Yet, all this is still only one side of the story of unbearable life because I also want to argue that there is a certain paradoxical symmetry between the subject and the object of sovereign power, between the misery of the unborn subject and the majesty of the figure of the sovereign, between the one who is placed beneath all life and the one who is positioned above all life. By abjecting certain forms of life of the very possibility of existence—by rendering them unbearable life—sovereignty does not thereby find it possible to exclude them altogether but rather only to consign them to other ontological domains (myth, poetry, eschatology) and to other forms of species-existence: the beast, the spectre, the monster, the demonic, the machinic. Just as sovereignty seeks to foreclose the promise and the threat of unbearable life, so I want to suggest that the repressed returns to haunt it in the interiority of its field of formation —and even to reveal something unbearable within the figure of the sovereign himself. Perhaps we might even go so far as to re-write Carl Schmitt's famous claim about sovereignty in his classic *Political Theology* (1922)—"Sovereign is he who decides upon the exception"—in the following way: *Sovereign is he who is un-born*.[12] In what follows, I want to briefly put some of these larger hypotheses to the test via a reading of William Shakespeare's *Macbeth*.

To be sure, *Macbeth* is—all too literally—a play about natality.[13] It teems with tropes of child birth—naked new-born babes, birth-strangled babes, a bloody child, a child crowned with a tree in his hand and a child untimely ripped from his mother's womb. As many critics have observed, though, natality is never merely a natural condition in the play: the body of the "naked new-born babe" (1.7.23) is continually connected (whether as a direct link in the Great Chain of Being or a more general medieval cosmological hierarchy) to the body politic of the people, the nation and the sovereign.[14] However, as a tragedy of regicide, *Macbeth* chooses to dramatise the rule of this Early Modern biopolitical order negatively, via what Georges Canguilhem calls the mechanism of the monstrous or demonic exception to natality.[15] Who or what are the signs and wonders of this monstrous birth? Firstly, of course, the Weird Sisters: they possess what Chris Laoutaris has recently observed to be a kind of demonic sovereignty over the whole process of physical and metaphysical reproduction.[16] They have the power, as Banquo puts it, "to look into the seeds of time / And say which grain will grow, and which will not" (1.3.58-9). By the same token, Macbeth's own usurpation of Duncan is both an act of regicide against his sovereign lord and master and an act of matricide against the political "mother" who nurtures

---

[12]Schmitt, *Political Theology*, 5. In Schmitt's famous phrase, "Sovereign is he who decides on the exception."

[13]See also the following discussions of childbirth in the play, all of which have influenced my own reading in what follows: Adelman, *Suffocating Mothers* and "Born of Woman"; Krier; and, particularly, Laoutaris, 176–211.

[14]References to *Macbeth* are to the Arden edition.

[15]Canguilhem, 172. In Canguilhem's account, the monster remains "the living example of negative value" whose purpose is to produce and reinforce the regime of the normal.

[16]Laoutaris, 176–211.

him: "I have begun to plant thee", Duncan tells his protégé in Act One, "and will labour / To make thee full of growing" (1.4.29–30). If Macbeth's arrogation of power is political matricide, we might equally argue that Lady Macbeth's complicity in their crime is an act of symbolic infanticide performed by a woman who has stripped herself of any maternal instinct: "I would, while it was smiling in my face, / Have plucked my nipple from his boneless gums / And dashed the brains out, had I so sworn" (1.7.55–7). Just as the murder of Duncan is a revolt against natality—of the son against the mother and the mother against the son—so this inversion of natural law is replicated throughout the universe of *Macbeth*: a falcon "towering in her pride of place, / Was by a mousing owl hawk'd at, and kill'd" and Duncan's horses, the "minions of their race", turn "wild in nature" as if they "would make / War with mankind" (2.4.10–17). Perhaps most dramatically of all, this revolution against nature returns to haunt Macbeth and his wife in a loss of sovereignty over their own bodies: the guilty couple suffer visions, insomnia, sleepwalking and so on. In his demonically inspired overthrow of the natural order of natality, it seems that Macbeth presides over the birth of a new and monstrously unnatural order that, in the words of Lennox, is "New hatched to th' woeful time" (2.3.59–60).

Yet all this is common knowledge to scholars of Shakespeare's play. It might be more original to observe that Macbeth's usurpation is not just a monstrous birth which inverts the natal order, but also the beginning of a larger war against natality itself. As we have already begun to see, totalitarianism consists in the attempt to foreclose natality's constitutive excess over any pre-existent concept of the body politic and we can witness exactly this violent preventative gesture at work in Shakespeare's play. Not only is the play a meditation on sovereign power over life and death, in other words, but on the power over what is allowed to *become* life in the first place. To secure his own regime, for instance, Macbeth institutes a bloody policy of state-sponsored "birth control": the tyrant seeks to extinguish not just his living rivals (Duncan, Banquo, Macduff), nor even their sons (Malcolm, Fleance, Macduff's son) but ultimately their *unborn* children as well. For Macbeth, the murder of Banquo—who the Witches prophesise will beget kings without becoming king himself—is less an attempt to dispense with a living rival (for he will never personally displace Macbeth) than to render permanently unbearable the future line of kings that will issue from him:

> If't be so,
> For Banquo's issue have I fil'd my mind;
> For them the gracious Duncan have I murther'd;
> Put rancours in the vessel of my peace,
> Only for them; and mine eternal jewel
> Given to the common Enemy of man,
> To make them kings, the seed of Banquo kings! (3.1.63–9)

In Act Four, this unbearable future is powerfully dramatised in the ghostly procession of kings conjured up by the Weird Sisters that stretches onwards seemingly to "th'crack of doom": Macbeth is horrified to see that the final king "bears a glass, / Which shows me many more" and "the blood-bolter'd Banquo ... points at them for his" (4.1.119–24). By killing "the father to a line of kings" (3.1.59) earlier in the play, Macbeth is seeking (impossibly) to prevent that virtual line of kings from ever becoming actual.

Perhaps we might speculate that Macbeth's war on unborn life increases exponentially throughout the play as he goes on to render more and more lives unbearable. It is only according to this logic that the—otherwise gratuitous—slaughter of Macduff's family after the latter has fled to England begins to make sense: "The castle of Macduff I will surprise; Seize upon Fife; give to th'edge o'th'sword / His wife, his babes, and all unfortunate souls / That trace him in his line" (4.2.150–3). To Rosse, Macbeth's logic culminates in the attempt to put natality *itself* to death: "Alas, poor country! ... It cannot / Be call'd our mother, but our grave" (4.3.164–5). By symbolically killing Mother Scotland, Macbeth also seeks to arrest the order of natality and preserve his own power in aspic. If the national mother is dead, then all her children— which is to say all human life in the body politic—are consigned to the impotent category of the orphan or, more precisely, to that of the stillborn child for whom the womb becomes the grave: "where sighs, and groans, and shrieks that rent the air / Are made, not mark'd" (4.3.168–9). Finally, of course, the tyrant's pretension to total sovereignty over natality finds its most powerful expression in the Sisters' prophecy that "none of woman born / Shall harm Macbeth" (4.1.79–81). In many ways, Macbeth's belief that his sovereignty is immune to natality—hubristically misplaced though it may be—encapsulates what Arendt calls the totalitarian dream of a power that knows neither birth nor death but only an eternal, unending present.

For Macbeth, such a dream of supreme sovereignty over natality represents both the apogee of his power and, of course, the beginning of his fall. It is the usurper, rather than his enemies, who increasingly comes to be constituted as unbearable life during the remainder of the play—life that is not permitted to be born as life. As John Drakakis has recently argued in an excellent essay, the tyrant increasingly approximates what Agamben calls bare or animal life as the circle of his power closes ever more tightly around him: Macbeth famously compares himself to a walking shadow, to an idiot "signifying nothing" (5.5.24–9) or to a bear tied to a stake (5.7.1–2).[17] Even animal life might be above Macbeth in the end because animals (recall Duncan's horses, the hawking owl or the "poor wren" (4.2.8) to which Lady Macduff refers) at least normally obey natural law. Rather, the usurper is barely life at all: Caithness goes so far as to compare Macbeth to a disease that has infected the body politic and who must be purged in order to cure it (5.2.27–8).[18] Yet it would be somewhat premature to read *Macbeth* as simply the

---

[17]Drakakis, "*Hamlet, Macbeth* and 'Sovereign Process,'" 8, 16.

[18]See Derrida, *The Beast and the Sovereign* for a study of the analogy between the animal and the sovereign. In Derrida's account, the animal and the sovereign "share a space of some exteriority with respect to 'law' and

story of the emergence of a demonic exception to a natural sovereign order and the restoration of the normal biopolitical order of rule with the coronation of Malcolm because, as Schmitt famously observes in *Political Theology*, "the exception is more interesting than the rule. The rule proves nothing; the exception proves every-thing."[19] To put it simply, I want to speculate that Macbeth's exceptional attempt to obtain sovereignty over birth by outlawing the unborn also reveals something about the unbearable condition of *all* sovereignty. Such is the paradoxical symmetry between the subject and the sovereign I referred to at the beginning of this essay: what is placed beneath all life—the unborn body—returns to cast light on the body of what is placed above all life. If Malcolm and his supporters must render Macbeth's demonic order unborn, in other words, it is not because the latter is so utterly removed from the natural order of things *but because it is so close to it*: both are radically out with the sphere of the living. What form does this unbearable symmetry take? Firstly, I think we can observe it in what Laoutaris rightly calls the uncanny "proximity" between the demonic power of the Weird Sisters and the divine power of the King.[20] They both exercise sovereignty over the natal order. They are both able to intervene in and manipulate the process of nature from without, tumbling altogether the treasure of Nature's germens (4.1.58–9). They both inhabit the world of the living but, at the same time, are strangely removed from that world (1.3.39–43). When the natural and political order of things is restored, moreover, it is heralded by a series of portents that are (at least apparently) every bit as unnatural as those that accompanied Macbeth's usurpation: Great Birnam Wood famously "comes" to Dunsinane Hill. By the same logic, the tyrant who waged a merciless war against the natal order is overthrown by one who "was from his mother's womb / Untimely ripp'd" (5.8.15–16). Finally, the rightful heir to the throne, Malcolm, is (as Laoutaris notes) symbolically characterised by his alienation from the maternal and feminine sphere: the young King's mother "Died every day she lived" (4.3.109–11) according to Macduff and Malcolm himself confesses that he is "yet / Unknown to woman" (4.2.25–6). Perhaps such symbolic acts of matricide contain an uncanny echo of Macbeth's murder of his own political mother, Duncan, before his own process of nurturing was complete. In the case of both sovereigns—Macbeth and Malcolm—as well as in the figure who mediates between them, Macduff, we encounter the same aberrant figure of birth: untimely, violent and motherless.

Why, though, does *Macbeth* seem to imply that *all* sovereigns—Malcolm and Macbeth, natural and unnatural, divinely ordained kings, witches and bloody usur-pers—are, so to speak, "unborn"? Is it, as the feminist/psychoanalytic readings of Adelman and Laoutaris both argue, a fantasy of absolute escape from maternal

---

'right' (outside the law; above the law; origin and foundation of the law)" (14). Could we say the same about the *disease* and the sovereign?

[19]Schmitt, *Political Theology*, 15.

[20]Laoutaris, 195.

power into a paternal dream of parthenogenesis?[21] Or can we offer an alternative explanation by putting the play back into the theologico-political context of its own birth?[22] It is not possible to do more than sketch an answer here but let me begin by returning to what I see as the fundamental argument about sovereignty in Schmitt's *Political Theology*: a sovereign (like God) cannot be of the same order as the order over which he presides.[23] As a consequence, any attempt to obtain sovereignty over the order of life logically requires that the sovereign himself be in some sense excepted from that order: *all* forms of sovereignty (not just totalitarianism) aspire to the condition of knowing neither birth nor death. To quickly unpack the paradoxical logic with which I began: Sovereign is he who decides upon the exception; Sovereign is he who "is" the exception; Sovereign is he who is excepted from life and death; Sovereign is he who is neither born nor dies; Sovereign is he who is unborn. For Shakespeare, such an unbearable theory of sovereignty is still chiefly articulated through the medieval doctrine of the King's Two Bodies: Duncan, for example, possesses a *corpus mysticum* that cannot be destroyed by mere homicide—his "Most sacrilegious Murther hath broke ope / The Lord's anointed Temple" (2.3.66–7)—and that, like the royal touch of Edward the Confessor described by Malcolm later in the play, he leaves "to the succeeding royalty" (4.3.155).[24] By the same token, Kantorowicz himself cites the ghostly procession of past and future kings summoned up by the Weird Sisters (4.1.112–24) as an example of the undying perpetuity of Royal *Dignitas*.[25] Yet, if the King's Two Bodies is the pre-modern answer to the question of how to remove the sovereign from the order of life and death over which he presides, it could be argued that modernity increasingly replaces the mystical body with a mechanical one. Perhaps one might argue that Thomas Hobbes' *Leviathan*—for all its repudiation of early modern theories of the theological body politic—offers a materialist re-writing of the doctrine of the King's Two Bodies in which the mortal, perishable body of the sovereign is incorporated into an unliving, immortal body. Just as the mortal body of the Renaissance King is infused by, and participates, in the *corpus mysticum* of Christ, so Hobbes encases the mortal body of his own ideal ruler within the *corpus artificialis* of the state machine. Both sovereigns—divine and mechanical, mystical and artificial, eternally constituted by God and recently constructed by men—body forth a

---

[21]See Adelman, "Born of Woman," 53–68 and Laoutaris, 195.

[22]If there are now many studies of Shakespeare and political theology, particularly surrounding the enabling legal fiction of the King's Two Bodies, *Macbeth* does not figure as largely as texts like, say, *Richard II*. See, for example, Lupton, *Citizen Saints*.

[23]For Schmitt, modern politics is famously a secularisation of theology and the figure of the sovereign is a secularisation of God. In Schmitt's account, the sovereign decision is also a secularisation of the divine act of creation *ex nihilo*: "That constitutive, specific element of a decision is, from the perspective of the content of the underlying norm, new and alien. Looked at normatively, the decision emanates from nothingness." See Schmitt, *Political Theology*, 31–2.

[24]See Kantorowicz, *The King's Two Bodies* for the most famous discussion of this legal trope. In this work, Kantorowicz gives a famous discussion of *Richard II*.

[25]Kantorowicz, 387.

sovereignty that is removed from the nexus of life and death over which they rule.[26] Such an artificial model of sovereignty—albeit hollowed out of all authority to the point where only the bureaucratic, administrative shell remains—is, in Schmitt's view, still the dominant model of sovereignty in mid-twentieth-century liberal capitalist modernity.[27] If the historical dynamic changes radically over time, however, I want to hypothesise here that the theologico-political logic remains recognisably the same from Shakespeare to Schmitt: *sovereignty is the power to render oneself and others unbearable life.*[28] In its complex imaginings of the figure of the un-born—that virtual life which is not allowed to live because it is simultaneously absolute subject *and* absolute sovereign, impotence *and* supreme power, less than life *and* more than life—*Macbeth* discloses the biopolitical aporia of sovereignty itself: Sovereign is he who is "Untimely ripp'd".

In bringing this essay to a close, however, I want to add one final entry to the ledger of unbearable life in *Macbeth*. It was out of the thanatopolitics of the camp, remember, that Arendt's own biopolitics of natality first emerged. As she wrote in a 1951 letter to Karl Jaspers, "[w]hat radical evil is, I do not know, but it seems to me it somehow has to do with the following phenomenon: making human beings as human beings superfluous".[29] Yet, as *Macbeth* teaches us, it is not always necessary to kill human beings to make them superfluous: totalitarian biopolitics consists also in the capacity to virtually foreclose upon life before it is even allowed to be born. To witness this remorseless logic of rendering life unbearable at work one more time, we need only recall the grisly ingredients that the Sisters throw into their womb-like cauldron at the beginning of Act Four:

> Liver of blaspheming Jew;
> Gall of goat, and slips of yew,
> Sliver'd in the moon's eclipse;
> Nose of Turk, and Tartar's lips;
> Finger of birth-strangled babe,
> Ditch-deliver'd by a drab. (4.1.26–31)

For the Sisters, of course, what connects the "birth-strangled babe" with the dismembered body parts of the Jew, the Turk and the Tartar is that they are all forms of life unbaptised by the Church—and so are all lives unsaved, unredeemed, even damned. They are each consigned by the Christian imaginary to a kind of spiritual

---

[26]See Attie for an excellent discussion of Hobbes' revitalisation of the old trope of the body politic.

[27]Schmitt, *The Leviathan*, 65–86. In Schmitt's view, liberalism empties the Leviathan of all political authority until it merely becomes a bureaucratic husk to administer for private men.

[28]This formulation is intended to both recall and re-write Agamben's own claim in *Homo Sacer* that sovereignty is the power to render oneself and others *bare* life. See Agamben, 101: "for the sovereign, death reveals the excess that seems to be as such inherent in supreme power, as if supreme power were, in the last analysis, nothing other than *the capacity to constitute oneself and others as life that may be killed but not sacrificed*" [Agamben's emphasis].

[29]Arendt and Jaspers, 166.

bare life—or even unbearable life—because they have not been theologically re-born into the Kingdom of God. If I do not have the time and space to say more here, I think the Sisters' incantation returns us once more to the promise and threat of what I have called unbearable life. What, then, is the political and theological fate of unbearable life today? How does the primal biopolitical scene around the witches' cauldron relate to that defining biopolitical scene of modernity, namely, the camp? What if Shakespeare's Jew, Turk and Tartar (whose bodies, recall, are indiscriminately consigned to an infernal furnace) are the distant ancestors of that other wretched Jewish Turk or Turkish Jew—the *Muselmänn*?[30]

Acknowledgements

I am very grateful to Simon Bainbridge, François-Xavier Gleyzon, Yvonne Sherwood and audiences at Lancaster University, UK, the American University of Beirut, Lebanon and the University of Notre Dame in London for offering valuable feedback and criticism of earlier versions of this essay. In the process of researching, writing and re-writing it, the intellectual and personal friendship of Michael Dillon has been indispensable and I would hereby like to dedicate the essay to Mick.

References

Adelman, Janet. "'Born of Woman': Fantasies of Maternal Power in *Macbeth*." In *Shakespearean Tragedy and Gender*, edited by Shirley Nelson Garner and Madelon Sprengnether, 105–31. Bloomington: Indiana University Press, 1996.

——— . *Suffocating Mothers: Fantasies of Maternal Origin in Shakespeare's Plays*, Hamlet to The Tempest. New York: Routledge, 1992.

Agamben, Giorgio. *Homo Sacer: Sovereign Power and Bare Life*. Translated by Daniel Heller-Roazen. Stanford, CA: Stanford University Press, 1998.

Arendt, Hannah. *The Human Condition*. Chicago: University of Chicago Press, 1958.

——— . *The Origins of Totalitarianism*. 3rd ed. New York: Harcourt, Brace and World, 1973.

Arendt, Hannah, and Karl Jaspers. *Hannah Arendt and Karl Jaspers: Correspondence 1929–1969*. New York: Harcourt Brace, 1992.

Attie, Katherine Bootle. "Re-membering the Body Politic: Hobbes and Construction of Civic Immortality." *ELH* 75, no. 3 (2008): 497–530.

Butler, Judith. *Precarious Life: The Power of Mourning and Violence*. London: Verso, 2004.

Canguilhem, Georges. *La Connaissance de la vie*. Paris: Vrin, 1992.

Cooper, Melinda. *Life as Surplus: Biotechnology and Capitalism in the Neoliberal Era*. Washington, DC: University of Washington Press, 2008.

Deleuze, Gilles. *Difference and Repetition*. Translated by Paul Patton. London: Athlone, 1994.

Derrida, Jacques. *The Beast and the Sovereign, Volume 1*. Translated by Geoffrey Bennington. Chicago: University of Chicago Press, 2009.

---

[30]In Levi's account, *der Muselmänn* (the Muslim) was the ironic name of "the anonymous mass, continually renewed and always identical, of non-men who march and labour in silence, the divine spark dead within them, already too empty to really suffer. One hesitates to call them living: one hesitates to call their death death" (90).

Drakakis, John. "*Hamlet, Macbeth* and 'Sovereign Process.'" In *Taboo and Transgression in British Literature from the Renaissance to the Present*, edited by Stefan Horlacher, Stefan Glomb and Lars Heiler. New York: Palgrave, 2010.

Esposito, Roberto. *Bios: Biopolitics and Philosophy*. Minneapolis: Minnesota University Press, 2008.

Hobbes, Thomas. *Leviathan*. Edited by Richard Tuck. Cambridge: Cambridge University Press, 1991.

Kantorowicz, Ernst. *The King's Two Bodies: A Study in Medieval Political Theology*. Princeton, NJ: Princeton University Press, 1957.

Krier, Theresa M. *Birth Passages: Maternity and Nostalgia, Antiquity to Shakespeare*. Ithaca, NY: Cornell University Press, 2001.

Laoutaris, Chris. *Shakespearean Maternities: Crises of Conception in Early Modern England*. Edinburgh: Edinburgh University Press, 2008.

Levi, Primo. *Survival in Auschwitz: The Nazi Assault on Humanity*. New York: Simon and Schuster, 1996.

Lupton, Julia Reinhard. *Citizen Saints: Shakespeare and Political Theology*. Chicago: University of Chicago Press, 2005.

——— . "Hannah Arendt's Renaissance: Remarks on Natality." *Journal of Religion and Cultural Theory* 7, no. 2 (2006): 1–18.

Santner, Eric L. *On Creaturely Life: Rilke/Benjamin/Sebald*. Chicago: University of Chicago Press, 2006.

Schmitt, Carl. *The Leviathan in the State Theory of Thomas Hobbes: Meaning and Form of a Political Symbol*. Chicago: University of Chicago Press, 2006.

——— . *Political Theology: Four Chapters on the Concept of Sovereignty*. Translated by George Schwab. Cambridge, MA: MIT Press, 1985.

Shakespeare, William. *Macbeth: Arden Shakespeare*. Edited by Kenneth Muir. London: Methuen, 1951.

Vatter, Miguel. "Natality and Biopolitics in Hannah Arendt." *Revista de Ciencia Política* 26, no. 2 (2006): 137–59.

Syllogisms and Tears in *Timon of Athens*

Drew Daniel

This essay focuses upon a single dramatic scene in order to address a general problem: what is the relationship between theoretical abstraction and emotional display? William Shakespeare and Thomas Middleton's collaborative play Timon of Athens *seemingly insists upon the isometric correlation between affective service and the capacity to pay. Against this backdrop, there stands the ethical counterexample of Flavius, the "one good man" who, with tears in his eyes, remains loyal to his destitute master. Flavius' affect prompts Timon to deploy a peculiar and symptomatic form: the logical syllogism. In what sense do Timon's syllogisms constitute a response to Flavius' tears? In pursuit of answers to this question, this essay contextualizes the ambient tension between rhetoric and logic within early modern England, and considers the intersection of this dramatic scene with Hegel's account of the dynamic interdependence of lord and bondsman, and with Hegel's account of the relationship between logic and sexual difference. If weeping is shown to be a gendered act that sunders the capacity of logic to denote a singular human "all", what does that suggest about the limited purchase of philosophical generality?*

Anticipating both Hegel's account of the dialectical reciprocity of lord and bondsman and Hardt's concept of affective labour, William Shakespeare and Thomas Middleton's collaborative play *Timon of Athens* depicts Athens as an economically precarious society in which servants and masters mutually define and determine each other through bonds which are at once financially determined and emotionally expressive.[1]

---

[1] I am, of course, not the first critic to notice the tangled interdependence of love and service within early modern drama. The topic has attracted substantial critical attention of late, most decisively in David Schalkwyk's foundational declaration in *Shakespeare, Love and Service* (2008) that: "Shakespeare's mimetic art depends in the deepest sense of the word on the conjunctive play of love and service" (1). Unsurprisingly given its roots in the stock character types of classical drama, the topic of masters and servants has been a perennial critical subject, modulated by shifts in critical vocabulary. Schalkwyk's recent intervention was preceded by several other authors, including notably Mark Thornton Burnett and David Evett. In this essay I hope to further pursue the messy work of establishing precisely how the "conjunctive play" of love and service functions in *Timon of Athens*, and how that illuminates the contradictory embrace of economic, political and affective registers. For reasons of space I am also bracketing the substantial critical literature on scenes of *anagnorisis* in drama.

Pressurizing the Greek past with a proximity to the stratified reality of early modern London in which they lived and worked, Shakespeare and Middleton subtract slavery from the classical world, re-imagining the polis as a curiously modern sort of service economy in which "tendance" and payment go together from the play's first scene:

> POET: You see how all conditions, how all minds,
> As well of glib and slippery creatures as
> Of grave and austere quality, tender down
> Their services to Lord Timon? His large fortune,
> Upon his good and gracious nature hanging,
> Subdues and properties to his love and tendance
> All sorts of hearts. (1.1.54–60)[2]

Beneath the courtly crust, the poet's point seems clear enough: fortune garners service, in so far as wealth purchases labour. More magnet than touchstone, Timon's large fortune draws "all" (greater and lesser, better and worse) into a protective and productive orbit of plenitude. The poet already knows what Timon will come to learn: there is something intractably powerful—powerfully indifferent and powerfully indifferentiating—about wealth's capacity to subdue all minds, all hearts. Marx and Engels celebrated the play for its recognition that the money form has the seemingly magical ability to level down the difference between persons as it "makes contradictions embrace".[3] If the money form itself—absolutely grave in its quantifiable solidity, endlessly slippery in its transferability—functions at the level of plot as that from which both masters and servants are suspended, the poet's hymn to the flow of loving affects between and across subjects hails "generous nature" as that which precedes and ratifies economic bonds, a claim that both confirms and parodies Antonio Negri's assertion that "the value of labor resides in affect".[4] However, one might well ask: what's love got to do with it?

Within the world of the play, the master is only master in so far as he can pay his servants to do his bidding; as a mode of subjection, servitude is therefore conditional, consensual and temporary. Accordingly, it would be easy to read the poet's speech as simply a tissue of courtly affectation, of a piece with the bootlicking boilerplate of dedicatory letters, and in performance, the speech can be variously delivered as unctuous, credulous or sinister in its familiarity with the workings of "slippery creatures". In so far as these supposedly besotted devotees abandon Timon as soon as his debts catch up with him, *Timon of Athens* demonstrates the constitutive power of money to form or dissolve affective bonds by uprooting or transforming the very natures from which generosity flows. Timon's progress from a wealthy patron surrounded by (seemingly)

---

[2] All references to the playtext are from Shakespeare, *Timon of Athens: The Arden Shakespeare*.
[3] Marx, 43.
[4] Negri, 79.

loving friends and devoted servants to a howling, hateful, impoverished hermit punctures the poet's canting allegation that good natures inspire corresponding devotion. However, against this legible backdrop of structured exchange and economic determination in which the end of fortune is the end of service and the end of love, Shakespeare and Middleton lodge a haunting counterexample: the loyal, loving steward Flavius who visits Timon in his misanthropic isolation in Act Four, Scene Three and attempts unsuccessfully to serve his former master even after the money has run out.

Faced with this emotional display of fidelity from his former steward, Timon responds first with denial, then incredulity, and steadily ramps up to mockery and abuse. If this reaction merely exemplifies Timon's witheringly indifferentiating stance of misanthropy, the pressure of Flavius' affect ultimately prompts Timon to deploy a peculiar and, I shall argue, symptomatic form: the logical syllogism. Redoubling the declarations about "the all" of Athens as an economic totality, the "all" coiled within Timon's syllogistic logic constitutes a means of theoretical resistance to affective display, a way of refusing exceptions. What does this failed encounter tell us about the connection between the "all" of the social totality mediated by the money form and the scandalous exception of Flavius' tears? Can affective investment transcend economic determination? If the initial terms of exchange framed by the poet (in which "tendance" is offered for "fortune") prove inadequate to the emotional force of these bonds, what is disclosed by the play's revised terms of exchange within this scene? Specifically, in what sense do Timon's syllogisms constitute a response to, if not a repayment for, Flavius' tears?

In the context of a collection of essays upon "Shakespeare and Theory", it may not come as much of a surprise that my reading of this scene shall invoke some of the organizing figures within Hegel's account of lordship and bondage in the *Phenomenology of Spirit*, in which "recognition" (*anerkennung*) functions as a crucial term of mediation and co-creation across these social and psychic divides. Indeed, this scene between Timon and Flavius is particularly conducive to such a schematic translation, in so far as it minimally stages the dynamic possibility of a mutually constitutive acknowledging across the void defined by those highly over-determined subject positions. However, it must be said that Hegel is a slippery creature of his own, and in order to force even a tenuous overlap with early modern drama, one must grant the possibility of a basic historical impertinence.[5] Placing a pre-emptive warning sign in the path of my intended reading, in *Shakespeare, Love and Service* (2008), David Schalkwyk asserts that:

> Shakespeare differs from Hegel (and this is the mark of their historical distance) insofar as he does not entertain the promise of the "real and true independence" of the servant that the dialectic contains. Although he recognizes the logical interdependence of master and servant, he is primarily concerned with the ethics of human

---

[5]However, not total impertinence, as one notes with pleasure that the archive of Hegel's juvenilia commences with "A Conversation of Three: A Scene from *Julius Caesar*" in which a young Hegel reconceives a snippet from this Roman play; this forced grafting of Shakespeare into the Hegelian corpus constitutes the very first entry in *The Miscellaneous Writings of G. W. F. Hegel* (Stewart 3–8).

relationships—of what goes on between people rather than their relationship within a system of metaphysical speculation. It might be going too far to say that the possibility of independence lies beyond the reach of Shakespeare's imagination; it certainly plays no part in either his representations of reality or the creations of his dreams.[6]

Schalkwyk's local point is that Shakespeare's servants do not long for independence from any and all masters as such, but rather seek "equality of affection and mutual acknowledgement" within the bounds set by the power differentials of their distinct status, and his book's sensitive and persuasive exposition of this dynamic across numerous Shakespeare plays attests to this.[7] Hence, Shakespeare's servants, so read, fail to instantiate the possibility held out for them by Hegel's analysis—a failure that may index simply a horizon for the political imagination set by Shakespeare's historical positioning, or that may index a yet more basic tension between Shakespeare and theory as such.

Though I will return to the play shortly, Schalkwyk's formulation is worth tarrying over, for its allegation that Shakespeare does not consider "the possibility of independence" for servants from masters only draws into further relief Shakespeare's curious predilection for staging a scenario which is logically obverse yet reciprocally implied by that very dynamic: the solitary figure of the master without a servant. If, according to Schalkwyk, a politically radical moment in which a servant truly thinks their own categorical independence does not stand within the imagination of Shakespeare, we need only turn to the second half of *Timon of Athens* to see the opposite: a master who refuses to be master and rejects his servant's attempts to serve, a master who suicidally undoes the very terms of relationality that tie him to the human world and its contracts, obligations and rights. If, that is, Shakespeare lacks the positive and anticipatory rhetoric of a proto-democratic call for manumission, together Shakespeare and Middleton are capable of articulating a negative, anti-relational space in which the project of mastery chokes itself upon a misanthropic rejection of all forms of human sociality, including those of love and service. It seems to me that Shakespeare and Middleton are interested in these figures because they offer up tense moments of recognition approached and then deferred, whereby the condition of lordship is worked through and sounded for its limits.

Permit me to briefly indicate the plot arc of this rarely performed play: driving himself into debt by spending "all" in a wasteful display of philanthropic largesse, Timon exposes his former associates as a pack of flatterers and false friends in a shaming banquet of stones and water, and is left at the eclipse of his fortune with "nothing", stripping himself bare and howling furious curses to an empty room: "Burn house, sink, Athens, henceforth hated be / Of Timon man and all humanity!" (3.7.103–4). Yet in the wake of seeing "all" reduced to "nothing", in the second half of the play Timon transforms this subjective destitution into a new kind of "all" by

---

[6]Schalkwyk, 40.
[7]Ibid.

entering the totality of a material and natural world radically stripped of value. Choosing a life of solitude and self-imposed exile from his home, his city and his species, Timon fashions a cave/shelter only to discover, in an ironic anti-miracle, a hoard of gold within the earth. This transvaluation—from "all" to "nothing" to "all" again— triggers an increasingly irritating sequence of Athenian visitors who alternately fawn upon and critique Timon while grasping for this gold. Tightening the rhythm of this stroboscopic alternation between the "all" and the "nothing" while heading towards a watery grave offstage, Timon repulses his final clutch of visitors with the deathbound declaration that "Nothing brings me all things" (5.1.188).

Sound familiar? In his account of lordship and bondage in the *Phenomenology of Spirit*, Hegel describes this negative pursuit of the "all" as a moment necessary to the incomplete task of autarkic self-constitution. There, Hegel's phrase for the process which removes all that is not-self as it aspires towards a total self-identity of pure negativity is "*die Bewegung der absoluten Abstraktion, alles unmittelbare Sein zu vertilgen*", which A. V. Miller translates as "the movement of absolute abstraction, of rooting out all immediate being".[8] Hegel's "alles" and Timon's "all" arguably occupy similar, high-altitude positions. That is, the process of reduction and cancellation in the leap inwards towards a pure negativity offers us a possible model by which to comprehend the misanthropy of Timon as precisely an arrested moment—both philosophical and political in its vicissitudes—which is staked upon the wielding, and critical emptying, of the "all". Abstraction, in order to be abstraction, must abide within the generalized space of the all, an unbroken expanse of totality defined simply as the "not-self". In a phenomenological conundrum familiar at least from Descartes onwards, subjective self-constitution stands thus at once within and outside the all of an ontological surround, which implicitly precedes it but from which the self abstracts and extricates itself in a moment of self-conscious negativity.

Timon's isolation after the collapse of his estate and before his sequence of visitations thus constitutes a delicate temporal interim of a misanthropy only partially realized. Before the relationship of self-consciousness to the totality of what stands outside can be gathered up into the distinctly unequal relational dynamic in which lord and bondsman constitute self and other, Timon abides within a moment in which the self experiences itself as pure negativity. This attainment of a pure self-consciousness through a repudiation, clearing or rejection of the totality of being that is not-self thus abides before the entry into relationality and recognition, and frames the master-and-servant dynamic as one which has encrypted within it a lost moment of purity, an idealized void or null point inseparable from a radical cancellation of the plurality of all others in so far as they are others. It is their violation of this purity which Timon cannot forgive as, exasperated, he is cursed with visitors: Alcibiades, Phrynia, Timandra, Apemantus, Flavius, the Poet, the Painter, the Thieves and Senators swarm upon his isolation with vibrant demands for attention, recognition and gold.

---

[8]Hegel, *Phenomenology*, (186) 113.

The intrusions of Timon's visitors—Flavius chief among them—enforce an encounter with what stubbornly remains outside the boundary of the individual, spoiling the dream of self-constitution with the fact of a juxta-political adjacency to all that had supposedly been left behind. Jean Luc Nancy might as well be glossing Timon when he articulates this bitter twist in *The Inoperative Community*:

> To be absolutely alone, it is not enough that I be so; I must also be alone being alone —and this of course is contradictory. The logic of the absolute violates the absolute. It implicates it in a relation that it refuses and precludes by its essence. This relation tears and forces open, from within and from without at the same time, and from an outside that is nothing other than the rejection of an impossible interiority, the "without relation" from which the absolute would constitute itself. Excluded by the logic of the absolute-subject of metaphysics (Self, Will, Life, Spirit, etc.), community comes perforce to cut into this subject by virtue of this same logic. ... The relation (the community) is, if it is, nothing other than what undoes, in its very principle—and at its closure or on its limit—the autarky of absolute immanence.[9]

Though his subject here is Hegel, I want to suggest that Nancy's remarks inadvertently capture what is so irritating about the temporary, forced experiences of being-in-common imposed upon Timon by his steady flow of emissaries from the community of Athens. In their insistent particularity, these figures not only shatter the silence of the "nothing" into which Timon hopes to deliver himself—they also pose a distinct threat to the integrity of Timon's bitter conceptual judgments against "the all" he has tried to leave behind.

Among this sequence of intrusions and feints, the tense, failed scene of "recognition" between Flavius and Timon is particularly crucial, for within that scene *Timon of Athens* stages the master/servant bond as an unravelling quilting point between affective and economic registers. Yet it should go without saying that the simple designation of masters and servants as a mutually interdependent binary will not be critically sufficient. Hoping to pre-empt the risk of over-familiarity implicit in wielding the much distorted stock figures of master and bondsman from the *Phenomenology*, I also want to wager that the specificity of Timon's deployment of the syllogism as a means of resistance to his recognition of Flavius might be more beneficially read if the *Phenomenology*'s dynamic of negativity and recognition is placed in conjunction with an entirely distinct component of the Hegelian corpus: the account of the syllogism within the *Encyclopaedia Logic*.[10] Timon deploys logic as both a means of divesting himself from his former status as master, and as a way to model a kind of higher

---

[9]Nancy, 4.

[10]In "Hegel in France", Alain Badiou has mapped the dissemination of Hegel within French philosophy in terms of a prioritization of the *Phenomenology* over the rest of Hegel's work as a result of the pre-eminence of Kojeve; Badiou concludes with typical polemic energy that this over-emphasis requires a salutary redress: "this requires that we give back a voice to the Hegel who has been gagged—the essential Hegel, the one so feverishly annotated by Lenin, the one whose knowledge was required, Marx declared, for understanding *Capital*: the Hegel of the *Science of Logic*" (25). With distinctly more modest aims in mind, I simply hope to read *Timon* by bringing excerpts from both of these two distinct Hegels into temporary alignment.

order theoretical mastery over the passions threateningly embodied in Flavius' tears, which he scornfully regards as feminine. I shall argue that Hegel's enigmatic remarks upon the relationship between sexual difference and the syllogism can provocatively illuminate the gendered scene in which Timon syllogistically shames Flavius' emotional display.[11] However, before further theoretical encounters between Shakespeare and Middleton and Hegel can take root, I must first prepare the soil by examining the particular scene in which Timon's syllogism erupts, and Flavius' tears flow.

Flavius' encounter with his former master Timon begins and ends with compromised acts of disavowed, partial recognition: when Flavius first sees Timon, he asks: "O you gods! / Is yon despised and ruinous man my lord, / Full of decay and failing?" (4.3.453–5). At the end of their interaction, Flavius is bitterly dismissed by that lord with the final kiss off—"let me n'er see thee" (4.3.531). What falls between these mirroring moments of disavowed perception is a testing of the strength of Timon's misanthropy against the counterexample of Flavius' steadfast love. The conceptual totality of the "all" of a despised humanity stands poised to erode in the face of the possibility of an exception, and, sensing this, Timon coyly refuses to grant Flavius that status, choosing instead to indulge in a self-consciously didactic exercise in theoretical nicety:

FLAVIUS: My dearest master!
TIMON: Away! What art thou?
FLAVIUS: Have you forgot me, sir?
TIMON: Why dost thou ask that? I have forgot all men.
              Then, if thou grant'st thou'rt a man, I have forgot thee.
FLAVIUS: An honest poor servant of yours—
TIMON: Then I know thee not.
              I never had honest men about me, I; all
              I kept were knaves to serve in meat to villains. (4.3.466–73)

It is here that Timon first deploys the assertive language and nesting structure of the syllogism, defined by Aristotle in the *Prior Analytics* as "discourse in which, certain things being stated, something other than what is stated follows of necessity from their being so".[12] Clicking Flavius into a contained place within a universal category, Timon's response to his servant's greeting serves up a universal major premise, a particular minor premise and a conclusion that necessarily follows from them:

Major Premise: I have forgotten all men.
Minor Premise: You are a man.
Conclusion: I have forgotten you.[13]

---

[11] Hegel, "Life," 293.
[12] Aristotle, "Analytica Priora," Vol. 1, Book I, 2, 24 b.
[13] Aristotle describes this particular formulation in "Analytica Priora," Vol. 1, Book I, 9, 30 a.

Approximating but falling off from the absolute generality of the syllogistic form known as "Barbara", the singularity of Timon's particular minor premise prevents this utterance from constituting what Aristotle termed a "perfect" syllogism, in that it "needs nothing other than what has been stated to make plain what necessarily follows", but if we transpose the initial assertion from "I have forgotten all men" to the properly universal form "All men have been forgotten by me", then Timon's response can be said to exhibit the customary sequence of moves made in the classic example of the quasi-syllogism:

> Major Premise: All men are mortal.
> Minor Premise: Socrates is a man.
> Conclusion: Socrates is mortal.[14]

With a proceduralism that mirrors the legal indifference of the senators to Alcibiades' impassioned special pleading earlier in the play's trial scene, Timon here deploys the apparatus of the syllogism to deny the possibility that there might be differences between and among men, reducing Flavius to one local instance of a universal. However contingent and accidental we might find the claim "I have forgotten all men", dependent as it is upon a first person epistemological report, and a prima facie implausible one at that, nonetheless Timon's first demonstrative premise necessarily applies to this particular man if it applies to all men. The structure is blind to the validity of the axioms it assumes, and since the conclusion follows from its axioms, the effect of this quasi-syllogism is one of instantaneous self-validation, with no possibility of appeal except to contest the premises themselves. If, as Sarah Beckwith has claimed, "the Shakespearean grammar of forgiveness is up to humans", then Timon constitutes a judge for whom the state of being human is already a crime, and Flavius—whoever he is—is thus already guilty.[15]

We cannot ascertain with any security the extent of Shakespeare and Middleton's familiarity with primary texts in logic, nor does space permit more than a cursory explanation of the broader context of logic's dissemination in early modern England. Wilbur Samuel Howell's *Logic and Rhetoric in England, 1500–1700* transmits the essential story of the waning of Aristotelian hegemony as medieval scholastic logic within the universities gradually gave way in the sixteenth and early seventeenth centuries to the works of Ramus and, later, the Port Royal logic. Thomas Wilson published the first book in English on logic, *The Rule of Reason*, in 1551, and while there can be no definitive proof of Shakespeare or Middleton's familiarity with his logical text (though Shakespeare would have known Wilson's *Art of Rhetoric* [1560]), the dissemination of syllogistic logic as a wearily familiar, even fetishized, component of university education would have been broadly familiar by the late sixteenth century. Logic

---

[14]Aristotle, 24 b.
[15]Beckwith, 116.

chopping was the often satirized tendency of pedantic, learned persons, and the syllogism was the most visible and portable example of logical structure.

Against this backdrop, Timon's choice is legible and typical, and brings with it an
inkhorn, academic connotation. Scholastic logicians distinguished between analysis
and debate about the validity of propositions, termed *inventio* (invention), and the
arrangement of propositions into syllogisms and discourses, which was known as *iudi-
cium* (judgment).[16] Timon's response to Flavius places him in the latter category,
suggesting that the implicit ethical judgment passed within the content of his major
premise is itself formally reduplicated at the structural level in the very practice of
logical construction as, itself, a stance of judgment distinguished from both the
pathos of rhetoric and the open-endedness of debate. In his *Dialectique*, Ramus rendered the link between the syllogism and legal judgments more explicit in a panegyric
to the form:

> Finally let us remember that the syllogism is a law of reason, truer and more just than
> all the laws which Lycurgus and Solon once fashioned, through which the judgment
> of the doubtful proposition is established by a necessary and immutable verdict—I
> say, a law of reason, proper to man, not being in any sense shared with the other
> animals, as the preliminary judgment can in some sense be shared, but solely in
> things pertaining to sense and belonging to the body and the physical life.[17]

In so doing, Ramus locates the syllogism at once beside and beyond the legal sphere;
the syllogism achieves the ideals of truth and justice to which human laws aspire, but
transcends their ontic limitations through its absolute immutability.

In wielding the syllogistic form against his weeping interlocutor, Timon tries on precisely this unanswerably autocratic stance. However, for all his conspicuous rage for
order, Timon's totalizing theory of misanthropy founders upon the practice of dialogue in so far as the dialogic interaction offers an implicitly rule-governed behavioural
back and forth between co-participants whose success at the level of comprehension
implies an infra-thin fellowship that chips away at the hatred which lurks behind his
syllogism's initial major premise. In speaking and answering at all Timon already
imputes to Flavius the capacity to hear, understand and respond, and together the
two thus instantiate a minimal form of human community whose fragile endurance
compromises Timon's announced withdrawal. Humanity may be fundamentally
untrustworthy in some ultimate sense, but the ensuing volley of conversation
cramps Timon's absolute posture against all mankind by enforcing a kind of
tenuous return to reciprocal practices of exchange.

In the sweeping premises of Timon's syllogism, the social "all" initially invoked by
the poet's speech to designate Athens in its generality returns with a difference. Where
the poet in the play's opening speech invited us to see that "all kinds of hearts" were
drawn in service to Timon, and in the process drew our attention to the width of

---

[16]Howell, 15.
[17]Ibid., 161.

variety that separated the "glib and slippery" flatterers from the "grave and austere" character of the truly devoted, Timon retrospectively narrows the "all" in scope, collapsing differences of character and kind. Confirming Marx's reading of the play, payment defines this capacity: since the people who greedily accepted his prodigal gift-giving and the servants who oversaw the process of this ruinous dispersal were all paid with the same currency, the universality of the money form has now rendered them retrospectively all alike.

Against this swift and categorical elision of his service with the flattery of Timon's "friends", Flavius insists upon particularity and difference with a showstopping emotional performance. Faced with Timon's paranoid hostility to the social "all", Flavius offers a direct and ostensibly self-verifying, physical demonstration of his inward authenticity: tears.

> FLAVIUS: The gods are witness,
>   Ne'er did poor steward wear a truer grief
>   For his undone lord than mine eyes for you.
> TIMON: What, dost thou weep? Come nearer then. I love thee
>   Because thou art a woman and disclaim'st
>   Flinty mankind, whose eyes do never give
>   But thorough lust and laughter. (4.3.474–80)

Timon stands on the threshold of "recognizing" Flavius in both the literal, referential sense—seeing this individual, unknown person as Flavius his former steward—and in a possibly deeper, ethical sense. To recognize Flavius in this secondary sense would be to acknowledge that Flavius' act of weeping at the sight of Timon troubles the integrity and sweep of Timon's misanthropic judgments upon mankind as pitiless, false and predatory. From the perspective of classical theories of communication, Flavius' appeal to emotion aligns him with rhetoric and implicitly sets him against Timon's deployment of logic; taken together, these contrary strategies suggest Zeno's oft-cited gesture as rendered by Thomas Wilson in *The Rule of Reason* (1551): "beying asked the difference between Logique and Rehtorique, made answere by Demonstration of his Hande, declaring that when his hande was closed, it resembled Logique, when it was open and stretched out, it was like Rehtorique".[18] Where Flavius opens his tear ducts and lets emotion flow out of the body and towards his spectator, Timon performs a logical act of closure, forcing Flavius into a set and closing off the possibility of exceptions.

Ducking back into a laboriously "witty" twisting of his would-be interlocutor's words, logic protects Timon from the forceful claim embodied by Flavius' tears. Refusing empathy in favour of a shaming response, Timon takes a coldly comedic stance instead, and mocks Flavius' tears by suggesting that Flavius must not be a man after all via a sarcastic rephrasing of the same quasi-syllogism:

---

[18]Ibid., 15.

Major Premise: Men don't weep (because they are flinty, stone-like)
Minor Premise: You are weeping.
Conclusion: Therefore, you are not a man but a woman.

Timon's joke relies upon an essential indeterminacy in the designation of the word "man", a historical disjunction in referential coverage now apologized for by the *OED* editors in a notably fretful codicil to the term's definition: "*Man* was considered until the early twentieth century to include women by implication, though referring primarily to males ... it is difficult or impossible to tell whether 'man' is intended to mean 'person' or 'male human being'."[19] Pre-dating more full-throated feminist arguments such as Carole Pateman's claim that universal terms such as "man" and "individual" are implicitly patriarchal and exclude women, the failed inclusivity of the term was already noticeable enough in early modernity to prompt self-conscious clarifications such as Hamlet's remark to Rosencrantz and Guildenstern that "Man delights not me—no, nor woman neither, though by your smiling you seem to say so" (2.2.307–9).[20] Against a patriarchal backdrop in which the production of the generic signifier "man" founders upon the fact of sexual difference, the philosophical wielding of syllogistic claims about "all men" are themselves set up for comic puncture from both sides of this constitutive divide: Hamlet's answer at once flags that "man" fails to successfully designate absolute humanity, and declares that at least some men are not "delighted" by women either, thus sundering the implicit self-similarity of males by forcing the issue of differences between men with respect to their own desires, pleasures and directives.

This doubled split within Hamlet's remark, in which humanity is divided into two sexes, and sexes are themselves divided internally, also structures Timon's comedic response to Flavius' tears. Timon's gag is obvious: not all of humanity are "men", and this ripple in Timon's thinking suggests the possibility of sexual difference as a way of acknowledging differences within humanity itself that might have complications for his attempts to philosophically reduce humanity to a single kind, a single essence. In so far as Flavius feels emotions of pity and is capable of acts of generosity and love, he is associated with femininity, with an alternate gender and, perhaps, an alternate way of being. Flavius' putative effeminacy instantiates what I have termed "gender recusancy": the anxious phenomenon of an interior deviation from maleness imagined to somehow obtain within early modern masculinity as a regressive or atavistic possibility endemic to Galenic developmental physiology.[21] If in early modernity women were regarded under the so-called "one sex model" as embryonically stalled en route to their developmental destination as males, then the project of masculinity was itself occasioned by the haunting fear that men might somehow defect and reveal themselves to be tainted by an inner femininity.

---

[19]*OED*, "Man."
[20]Pateman, 171; Shakespeare, *Hamlet* (taken from the 1623 publication).
[21]Daniel, 251–90.

In an assertive casting decision, Nicholas Hytner's recent stage production of *Timon of Athens* at London's National Theatre turned Timon's punning joke upon Flavius' gender into a statement of fact by casting Deborah Findlay as "Flavia, Timon's steward."[22] Hytner's choice redresses a traditional critical complaint about the claustrophobically homosocial environment of the play's (nearly) all male environment with a diversifying supplement. However, without the spectacle of a clearly male Flavius sobbing in despair at his master's situation, the scene loses its capacity to provide a living counterexample to Timon's own universalizing assumptions about the pitiless nature of "men", "man" and "mankind". In effect, Hytner's staging thus seems to accede to the implicitly gendered frame of Timon's own structuring views; by sexually re-assigning Flavius as Flavia, we are spared a certain encounter with the troubling spectacle of gender recusancy implicit in witnessing the protestations and tears of an (overly) emotional male. In the place of Timon's shaming of effeminacy —which cannot help but prompt memories of his own tears earlier in the play during his toast to his friends at the banquet—the presentation of a female Flavia increases the gender diversity but at the cost of a certain critical edge of audience discomfort, re-assigning the emotional role to a gender more normatively associated with emotional display.

However, whether the figure proposed as a counterexample to an imagined masculine norm is a woman or a recusant male, in Timon's response the generality of the "all" as an inclusive set for humanity is riven by the fact of sexual difference. In wielding the feminine as that which disrupts the smoother operation of the universal, Timon here strikingly anticipates Alain Badiou's theorization of the logic of sexuation (itself an adaptation of Lacan), in which "Woman is 'not all' (*pas toute*); woman is what punctures this totality."[23] Badiou and Lacan's formulations are themselves modern variants of a claim which Hegel makes in the *Encyclopaedia Logic* regarding the function of sexual difference within substantial categories of universality:

> The particularizing of this universality is the relation of the subject to another subject of the same genus, and the judgment is the relationship of the species to these individuals which are determined vis-à-vis one another in this oppositional way—*the difference of the sexes.*[24]

The context of this remarkable passage is Hegel's development of the implications of the even more startling declaration which precedes it, the statement that "The living being is the syllogism whose very moments are inwardly systems and syllogisms. But they are active syllogisms, or processes."[25] Moving first "inside" through its particular corporeity and then "outside" in a confrontation with the surround of an inorganic

---

[22]William Shakespeare, *Timon of Athens*. Director Nicholas Hytner. Olivier Theatre/National Theatre, London, Summer Season, 5 August 2012.
[23]Hallward, 185–93, 187.
[24]Hegel, "Life," (220), 293.
[25]Ibid., (217), 292.

nature which it attempts to master, the vital syllogism of a living being undergoes a sequence of three processes as it attempts to attain a status that Hegel terms "substantial universality". In its second process, that substantial universality encounters a disruptive force when, in the midst of determining the relationship across and between subjects of the same genus, sexual difference erupts as the manifestation of an inescapable divergence of non-self-similarity within the genus. For the vital syllogisms that are living beings, sexual difference particularizes the project of universality itself, sowing opposition at its core. As I read the satirical thrust of their collaboratively written scene's encounter with the syllogism, Shakespeare and Middleton do not seem to me to share Hegel's sanguine estimation that living beings are always already emergent, processual vital syllogisms. However, they do not need to do so in order for this intersection of Shakespeare and "theory" to stick. For Act Four, Scene Three of *Timon of Athens* does articulate the way in which the fact of sexual difference confounds the syllogism's attempt to nest particularly sexed human individuals within the broad conceptual category of a humanity-wide genus. In both Hegel's philosophical text and in Shakespeare and Middleton's satirically syllogizing scene, sexual difference is rendered at once aberrant to, and yet centrally involved within, the project of mediation by which the syllogism achieves its vital, harmonious interlocking of the particular and the universal.

As that scene grinds on, the repetitive production of the syllogistic form as a structuring series of moves becomes ironized by its insistent return in the wake of Flavius' now heavily gendered tears. Timon is trying not to recognize Flavius, and in doubling down upon the syllogism as a means of response to Flavius' emotional plea, the return of the syllogism is thus itself increasingly pressurized by Timon's brick wall of rationality. The automatism of the syllogistic framework as a free-standing and repeatable series of moves performed upon a set of terms generates the "witty" effect (and here one might well note that Ralph Lever's 1573 textbook on logic translated this Greek term as "witcraft"), yet the very speedy execution of the movement also risks appearing strangely vapid in its moment of triumphant closure. The robotic effect of a system that goes to work upon variables instantaneously and thus in a sense thoughtlessly confirms Hegel's insight in his *Logic* that "*Formal syllogizing* is indeed 'rational' in a way that is so devoid of reason that it has nothing to do with the rationality of its basic import."[26] Notoriously, logical validity is a quality of arguments, but logical validity is no guarantee of truth; logically valid arguments can birth scandalously counterintuitive conclusions. Such is the case with Timon's argument: as a derivation from its premises, the conclusion is valid, but its very implausibility solicits sceptical and ironic responses that corrode our faith in the premises itself.

Smarting from the insult but soldiering on, Flavius tries again to cut through the banter and raillery to something more direct: "I beg you to know me, good my lord" (4.3.483), a line that strongly recalls Alcibiades' plea to the senators in the trial

---

[26]Hegel, "The Syllogism," (181), 257.

scene "My lords I do beseech you, know me" (3.6.90). Flavius' demand to be known flags "recognition" as itself a site of contention between the deictic claims of particularity (it is *I* who ask this) and the impassive mask of theoretical generality before a "blind" and indifferent figure of justice. Recognition thus names at once an inter-subjective dynamic between persons and a de-subjectivized structural process fraught with political implications. In so far as Hegel's account of the co-constitutive dialectic of lordship and bondage in *The Phenomenology of Spirit* has birthed a complex theoretical inheritance surrounding "recognition" (*Anerkennen*) as a mutually constitutive force field of tensions between these interdependent figures locked in their struggle-unto-death, the term cannot be invoked in proximity to a dramatic scene of contest between a master and servant without a certain effect of déjà vu. Which makes Katrin Pahl's spirited argument in *Tropes of Transport: Hegel and Emotion* that Hegelian "anerkennen" ought to be rendered as "acknowledging" rather than "recognition" particularly apt. As Pahl observes, in the *Phenomenology* "the movement of mutual acknowledging is necessarily shared, but—because of its incompleteness—it does not produce recognition as a good to be exchanged in reciprocity".[27] In resonant sympathy with work in affect theory by Rei Terada and others, Pahl's own reading would de-emphasize understandings of emotions as the expressive properties of subjects, stressing instead the processual and trans-personal flights of affect at the level of Hegel's text rather than inside the persona-like "shades of consciousness" afoot within it (and Shakespeare's own text does afford such moments of affective transfer, as when Flaminius declares "I feel my master's passion" [3.1.54]). However, what is useful in Pahl's account for my more modest purposes here is her resolute insistence upon the incompleteness that haunts the process of mutual acknowledgment, her sense of its trembling fragility.

Flavius seeks to return to Timon's service and, in a gesture at once touching in its delicate humility and yet also disastrous, Flavius offers Timon what little money he has left. This pressure almost works, and it occasions a swerve of emotional orientation as, again, the possibility of emotional recognition dawns for Timon:

> TIMON: Had I a steward
> So true, so just and now so comfortable?
> It almost turns my dangerous nature mild.
> Let me behold thy face. Surely this man
> Was born of woman. (3.6.485–9)

Gender inflects this bend in Timon's thinking. As Julia Lupton and others have noticed, the intrusion of the language of the Book of Job ("born of woman") into the playtext triggers an essential turn in the dialogue, as Timon breaks misanthropic character for an instant of self-lacerating disclosure.[28]

---

[27]Pahl, 121.
[28]Lupton, 154.

Timon's tenuous, momentary ability to see Flavius as Flavius, as "his" steward, interrupts the affective feedback loop of hatred recounting its sufferings in order to trigger more hatred. This intrusion of the other into his self-regard precipitates a crisis in the self-maintenance of misanthropy itself:

> TIMON: Forgive my general and exceptless rashness,
> You perpetual sober gods! I do proclaim
> One honest man. Mistake me not: but one,
> No more I pray, and he's a steward. (4.3.490–3)

If Timon's speech inserts a gender difference, it also marks a theological and historical scission between the pagan world of classical Athens and the Anglican world of early modern London. The phrase "one just man" introduces a pronounced scriptural resonance familiar to early modern playgoers: the image of a fallen world of sin and selfishness which might be saved or redeemed by the exceptional difference of one just man offers a narratological pattern that connects Flavius with the story of Noah's exceptional difference from the sinful world destroyed by the flood and its later echo in the rescue of Lot and his family before the destruction of Sodom in the Old Testament. These Old Testament figures would have been re-read within early modern sermons as typological forecasts of the coming of Christ as the ultimate messianic redeemer of an entire world fallen into sin. If Shakespeare and Middleton choose not to weigh Flavius in the heavy chains of expectation generated by this archive, Timon's wielding of the "one just man" momentarily brings the pressure of messianic possibility to bear upon him all the same. Yet such a reminder might be used precisely to cordon off Athens at a pre-Christian remove.

However, despite these theological resonances implicit in his language, the scene as a whole resists transcendence in favour of a characteristically deflationary effect. Timon demurs from the opportunity to look steadily and think deeply about the implications of Flavius' goodness that his steward's visit affords. Instead, Timon seems to see the counterexample in fits and starts, instrumentalizing Flavius as a spur to a self-criticism whose virulence seems to perpetuate the very excesses of passion it purports to critique. The gods are "perpetual-sober", that is, they embody a kind of absolute mastery over the passions and emotions, the forces that inevitably compromise human reasoning. Timon would like to be like them, and to suppress any distracting emotional displays such as those exhibited by Flavius' tears, so that he might perceive things impartially, soberly and, implicitly, from a position finally cleared of the affective registers in which his previous transactions of patronage were saturated.

However, Timon remains so attached to his image of mankind as deceptive (so attached, that is, to the premises which underwrite his "general and exceptless rashness") that his lukewarm act of demi-recognition ultimately articulates what we might now recognize as a familiar cliché: "the exception proves the rule". Flavius may be one good man, but humanity in general remains subject to destruction regardless of this exceptional case.

If I may risk a moment of critical mimesis by assuming the critical posture of the quibbler myself, there is a malingering ambiguity in the phrase "general and exceptless rashness" itself: does the problem lie with the "rashness" or the "generality"? That is, is Timon guilty of being too emotional, too passionate, too "rash" and therefore insufficiently philosophical? Or is he guilty of being too philosophical, too attached to his theory at the expense of other persons, too "general" and therefore insufficiently attuned to the emotions of others around him? In the grip of an apparently disciplinary conflict of the faculties between logic and psychology, members of the audience watching this scene are faced with a kind of disappearing middle in which they must make a false choice between emotion and philosophy: either the rashness clouds his judgment, or the generality falsifies the world.

Since Shakespeare and Middleton are dramatists and not philosophers, participants in an older critical moment might well regard such a question as rigged from the start: of course playwrights are going to affirm emotion and critique philosophy, or, at the very least, demonstrate the human dramatic and emotional outcome of a philosophical commitment as a way of leveraging the dramatic encounter against a philosophical framework that can always be made to seem overly rigorous, insufficiently calibrated to the particularities of personhood because of its investment in the power of categories. From an Aristotelian perspective, one could avoid turning this into a debate between philosophy and emotion by insisting, with the scold Apemantus, upon the "too much ness" itself as precisely an ethical problem of its own; as Apemantus puts it: "The middle of humanity thou never knewst, but the extremity of both ends" (4.3.300–1). Timon's problem is not passion as such, but an affective excess, a surplus amount of passionate intensity, which one might variously describe as "choler", "furor", *ira*, rashness, hostility or hatred. This excess is both a philosophical failing and a passionate character flaw: in rashly rejecting all humanity simply because some human beings are untrustworthy, Timon has gone beyond the mean, and the consequences are both a distorted emotional perspective and a correspondingly distorted philosophical stance that confirms and ratifies that perspective by projecting its premises onto everything Timon sees, leaving him incapable of recognizing counterevidence.

However, we cannot do justice to this interaction with Flavius and Timon if we regard it as such a conflict in the first place. It is not that, in refusing at first to recognize Flavius and insisting upon a facile display of syllogistic logic, Timon has simply chosen philosophical distance over affective engagement. One cannot refuse affect, only choose between affects, for even so-called "flat affect" itself constitutes a legible mode of emotional display (for a phenomenologically first-hand example, we can distinguish easily enough between the withdrawn blankness of catatonia and the sly blankness of Buster Keaton).[29] Brandishing syllogisms instead of a smile, a nod, or

---

[29]Nor does the supposed suppression of feeling arise without its own attendant feelings, as Rei Terada notes in citing a lyric from the indie band Modest Mouse: "I don't feel and it feels great" (87).

some other mode of hospitality constitutes a complex but legible form of display all by itself: Timon registers hostility, distress and enervation beneath the surface of a showy "coldness" that works to mask these "hot" emotions through the logical performance of closure implicit in the successful presentation of syllogistic self-verification. Timon has not refused to display emotion, but has simply made a particular choice to manifest the feeling of aggressive self-mastery associated with displaying distance. It might be so categorical as to not need stating, but living systems are always located at some position upon the map of affective participation (however subject to debate the precise desig-nation of culturally specific or species-wide the coordinates of such a map may be). There is no "neutral" setting for the human face, no neutral tone to the human voice and no neutral position for the human body: every choice has affective conse-quence and resonance.

More locally, the initial premises that launch Timon's syllogisms are themselves saturated with a certain affective investment. Timon's showy claim that "I have forgot-ten all mankind" is designed to register the pain of his betrayal by his former friends. Taken literally, the assertion is so prima facie implausible as to immediately double back upon itself, functioning as an indirect but effective solicitation of his interlocu-tors' interpretive energy, sympathy and care. The entrance of Flavius phenomenologi-cally implies a being-together-with-others, and since that dynamic has been soiled by association, Flavius' return re-triggers a cascade of mixed affects: Timon's immanent anger is mixed with a surreptitious longing for redress, and that compound feeling is routed through the theatrical presentation of a supposedly hardened indifference to the other's presence. The presentation of that indifference punishes Flavius, but also has the added auto-immunitary benefit of self-verification: if Timon can only suc-cessfully enjoy hurting Flavius with the refusal to acknowledge his difference, then he will himself have justified his own critique of humanity from the ground up. Timon will finally know and practise the "direct villainy" he ascribes to others, and will have one-upped his persecutors by having exceeded them in that practice of directness. Yet this attempt at purity fails and, in failing, redoubles itself:

> TIMON: How fain would I have hated all mankind,
> And thou redeem'st thyself. But all save thee
> I fell with curses. (4.3.494–6)

Here we see the conceptual tenacity of "the all" as a fetishized rhetorical gesture whose invocatory power grows in response to Timon's own failure of nerve. The impotence of the term to truly subsume and contain its own cases induces a kind of run on the bank of Timon's emotional reserves, spurring him to magnify his hatred into a fantasy of mass killing, imagining his curse to have the power of "felling" some imaginary out-lying all of the generalized social surround.

Timon almost turns the corner on his misanthropy, but by the end of the scene his choices reveal that he is, for all his self-critique, fundamentally unwilling to permit counterevidence to erode the negative certitude of misanthropic generality.

Temporarily, Flavius' own capacity to stand in as the singular exception falters as Timon speculates that, in so far as tales of Timon's discovery of gold must have reached Flavius' ears, suggesting an altogether less savoury explanation for his reappearance: "Is not thy kindness subtle, covetous, / A usuring kindness and, as rich men deal gifts / Expecting in return twenty for one?" (4.3.502–4). Once unleashed, it's a suspicion that the play can neither ratify nor fully dispel. Flavius is not granted another moment of soliloquy that could cash out to the extent to which this allegation hits home (though his return later with the senators can be staged as a kind of complicity with the ravenous Athenian patrician class), but his denial of this interpretation induces at least grudging assent.

However, if Flavius' loyal and forthright response seems to turn the page, Timon's parting benediction reveals that Timon's fundamental misanthropic agenda—the dissolution of Flavius' difference from humanity as such—remains unalterably dominant in his mind regardless. The smooth indifference of "the all" to personal difference must be upheld. Pursuing this goal by seeking to incorporate Flavius into himself, Timon enforces a strange mimetic duty onto his disappointed steward:

> TIMON: Thou singly honest man,
> Here, take. [He offers gold.] The gods out of my misery
> Has sent thee treasure. Go, live rich and happy,
> But thus conditioned: thou shalt build from men.
> Hate all, curse all, show charity to none,
> But let the famished flesh slide from the bone
> Ere thou relieve the beggar. Give to dogs
> What thou deniest to men. Let prisons swallow 'em,
> Debts wither 'em to nothing. Be men like blasted woods,
> And may diseases lick up their false bloods!
> And so farewell and thrive. (4.3.528–38)

The pressure of sustaining a belief in the conceptual integrity of "the all" folds Timon's advice into a double knot of noticeably paternalistic hypocrisy. Timon simultaneously orders Flavius to be "like" him (take this money, go and be a misanthrope) and to not be like him (don't give anyone else any money). Timon's imperative mandates not a positive duty towards others but a negative space, a duty to the void left behind by the foreclosure of charity: don't help others, don't give, ignore beggars and starving people. In this passage the intensity of Timon's white-hot hatred of others is conveyed most directly in what is perhaps the play's darkest image: the flesh sliding off the bones of a beggar. Eliding plague, leprosy and venereal infection, this image triggers deep-seated cultural reflexes of disgust and aversion. Moreover, it is here that Timon reaches the crescendo of his reach towards "the all": "Hate all, curse all" (4.3.522). This urge towards completeness, and the conceptual cleanliness of a final narrowing of the scope of justice to exclude everyone, without exception, seems related to the violent intensity of Timon's emotional delivery. To take up a suitably extreme point of comparison, one might compare it with the insistence upon completeness within the Radio Television Libre Mille Collines radio broadcasts immediately preceding the genocidal massacres in Rwanda:

> It was difficult to credit that normal people could broadcast such things as "You have missed some of the enemies in this or that place. Some are still alive. You must go back there and finish them off." Or, "The graves are not yet quite full. Who is going to do the good work and help us fill them completely?"[30]

Above and beyond the brutality of the tragic—because politically avoidable—effects that this speech engendered, we can see within the utterance itself an already violent marriage of the language of completeness, efficiency and totality with unlimited fantasies of human destructiveness. If I run the risk of an obscene disjunction of scale in even offering such a comparison, I do so because these overlapping voices seek to suppress human sympathy precisely by making a fetish of the fantasy of a total human clearing. From this perspective, the persistence of the exceptional cases comes to function as the last obstacle standing in the path of the ideal; their very existence is felt to solicit a violent response. Ordering one human being to "live rich and happy" while simultaneously shivering with delight at the thought of beggars dying from starvation, Timon's sermonette to Flavius enacts a recursive feedback loop whereby the rational articulation of a calculus of completeness becomes coextensive with the channelling and focusing of overwhelming hatred. Timon's hypocrisy in violating his own creed through his act of valedictory charitable giving triggers an escalating overcompensation in this rhetoric.

Yet this outburst of loathing utterly fails to convert Flavius, and instead seems only to trigger Flavius' protective and consolatory instincts. Timon's very excess, and the distress it evokes, makes Flavius want to do precisely the things that Timon has told Flavius he must not do:

FLAVIUS: Oh, let me stay
      And comfort you, my master.
TIMON: If thou hat'st curses,
      Stay not; fly, whilst thou art blessed and free.
      Ne'er see thou man, and let me ne'er see thee. (4.3.528–531)

Whether he cannot or simply chooses not to recognize his servant, by the end of the scene Shakespeare and Middleton pose the threat of emotion to certitude only to come to rest in a deflationary moment of philosophically inflected willing in which Timon does not let himself know the meaning of Flavius, and instead seeks to refashion Flavius in his own image. The possibility of redemption, forgiveness and atonement,

---

[30]Prunier, 224. For a reading of the Rwandan genocide and the phenomenon of "moral exclusion", see Opotow, 137.

in short, the possibility of an experiential learning that would transform the self, is offered in this scene only to be snatched away. The closed fist of Logic remains closed.

The bitter lesson of this scene is the failure of lessons as such. Even as each party solicits and releases affective intensity in each other's presence, for all their passionate display Timon and Flavius do not acknowledge each other's hatred and love, cannot experience it as justified and hence do not truly yield to each other: rather, each holds fast to an emotional script that precedes and structures the failure of their encounter to revise either party's self-understanding. Accordingly, their valedictory economic gestures of financial transaction as a means of articulating their feelings towards each other conclude and seal that mis-recognition, effectively folding both seemingly exceptional figures back into the Athenian civic world of bond, debt and payment from which Timon has fled and Flavius has followed.

Affects flow between these men, but the possibility of a deeper acknowledging (to use Katrin Pahl's word) of the implications of these characters' mutual dependence and difference is upstaged by the workings of "fortune" as it generates a cascade of elisions that separate, stereotype and flatten down each party, pulling them apart after their momentary near collision. By the end of the scene, for all his nakedness and savagery, Timon is not really different from other patrician Athenians, in so far as his interaction with Flavius partakes of the same fundamental asymmetry that we witness throughout the play, as when Lucullus attempts to buy off Timon's servant Flaminius with a paltry three solidares (3.1.44). Like other members of his class, Timon instrumentalizes his own wealth into bargaining power, and leverages his newfound gold in order to produce obedience in someone he perceives as his inferior. From his side, Flavius is not really different from other servants. At the end of all the handwringing and tears, Flavius takes the money and departs. In dutifully doing so rather than insisting upon remaining, Flavius follows at least the minimal conditions of Timon's dictates. Which makes him, for all his exceptional goodness, just like any other servant. Later, Timon will render his imagined capacity to weep as a dismissive joke, telling his final vistors: "Lend me a fool's heart and a woman's eyes / And I'll beweep these comforts, worthy senators" (5.2.42–3). The gendered deadlock of his repudiation of tears remains steadfastly in place.

Timon cannot bear to see and know Flavius' goodness, and cannot let himself be loved and served by Flavius, and so he banishes the only person who might force him to rethink his philosophical commitments. His own commandment "let me never see thee" is only too apt, because in a sense his final will to force Flavius into alignment with his own misanthropic politics designates that he has not permitted himself to see Flavius in the first place. This final scene stages the failure of instruction, the failure of philosophy to transmit commitments to other people that they can use to alter or transform their character, in both directions. At the level of affective charge in performance, this moment constitutes the most overtly pathetic scene of the play, upstaging Timon's tearful toast to his flatterers; in performance Flavius' tears of sorrow and pity at his master's self-exile can bring audience members close to tears of their own. However, because of the very failure of recognition and transmission, this scene also becomes, paradoxically, the bitterest scene in the play, in so far as the financialization of both philosophical master and emotional servant bleakly reinforces the constitutive power of money across the spectrum from philanthropy to misanthropy, flattening the force of the plot's progression from the former to the latter. Money does its levelling work, even in the radical moment of the supposedly exceptional ethical miracle. Flavius offers money to Timon, then Timon gives some money to Flavius and sends him on his way; in the world of this play an affective exchange separate from an isometric correlation via capital is not permitted. Neither Flavius nor Timon can truly extract themselves from a monetary system of exchange that regulates how both express care and concern for each other, and even within the radically critical outside zone of misanthropic separation from Athens and humanity, all sorts of hearts pump life into bodies that dutifully reach into purses and pockets for gold. If, to quote Hegel, "the truth is the whole", then the economic constitutes a sphere of mediation that absolutely saturates even this marginal space. The exchange of tears and syllogisms between Flavius and Timon offers a failed moment of transcendence in which the shattering possibility of the exception is manifested, considered and ultimately refused.

References

Aristotle. "Analytica Priora." In *The Works of Aristotle*, translated by J. A. Smith and W. D. Ross. Oxford: Oxford University Press, 1955.

Badiou, Alain. "Hegel in France." In *The Adventure of French Philosophy*, translated by Bruno Bosteels. London: Verso, 2012.

Beckwith, Sarah. "Acknowledgment and Confession in *Cymbeline*." In *Shakespeare and the Grammar of Forgiveness*. Ithaca, NY: Cornell University Press, 2011.

Burnett, Mark Thornton. *Masters and Servants in English Renaissance Drama and Culture: Authority and Obedience*. London: Macmillan, 1997.

Daniel, Drew. "My Self, My Sepulcher: Assembling Melancholy Masculinity in *Samson Agonistes*." In *The Melancholy Assemblage*. New York: Fordham University Press, 2013.

Evett, David. *The Discourses of Service in Early Modern England*. London: Palgrave, 2005.

Hallward, Peter. "Love and Sexual Difference." In *Badiou: A Subject to Truth*. Minneapolis: University of Minnesota Press, 2003.

Hegel, Georg Wilhelm Friedrich. "Life." In *The Encyclopaedia Logic*, translated by T. F. Geraets, W. A. Suchting and H. S. Harris. Cambridge: Hackett, 1991.

———. *The Phenomenology of Spirit*. Trans., A.V. Miller. Oxford: Oxford University Press, 2004.

———. "The Syllogism." In *The Encyclopaedia Logic*, translated by T. F. Geraets, W. A. Suchting and H. S. Harris. Cambridge: Hackett, 1991.

Howell, Wilbur Samuel. *Logic and Rhetoric in England, 1500–1700*. New York: Russell & Russell, 1961.

Lupton, Julia Reinhard. "Job of Athens, Timon of Uz." In *Thinking with Shakespeare: Essays on Politics and Life*. Chicago: University of Chicago Press, 2011.

Marx, Karl. *The Economic and Philosophic Manuscripts of 1844*, Third Section (XLIII). Translated by Martin Mulligan. Moscow: Progress, 1959.

Nancy, Jean Luc. "The Inoperative Community." In *The Inoperative Community*, translated by Peter Connor, Lisa Garbus, Michael Holland and Simona Sawney. Minneapolis: University of Minnesota Press, 1991.

Negri, Antonio. "Value and Affect." Translated by Michael Hardt. *Boundary 2* 26, no. 2 (1999): 77–88.

Opotow, Susan. "Hate, Conflict, and Moral Exclusion." In *The Psychology of Hate*, edited by Robert J. Sternberg. Washington, DC: American Psychological Association, 2005.

Pahl, Katrin. "Acknowledging." In *Tropes of Transport: Hegel and Emotion*. Evanston, IL: Northwestern University Press, 2012.

Pateman, Carole. "Feminism and the Marriage Contract." In *The Sexual Contract*. Stanford, CA: Stanford University Press, 1988.

Prunier, G. *The Rwanda Crisis: 1959–94: History of a Genocide*. Kampala: Uganda Foundation, 1995.

Schalkwyk, David. *Shakespeare, Love and Service*. Cambridge: Cambridge University Press, 2008.

Shakespeare, William. *Hamlet: The Texts of 1603 and 1623: The Arden Shakespeare*. Edited by Ann Thompson and Neil Taylor. London: Thomson, 2006.

———. *Timon of Athens: The Arden Shakespeare*. Edited by Anthony B. Dawson and Gretchen E. Minton. London: Cengage, 2008.

Stewart, Jon, ed. *The Miscellaneous Writings of G. W. F. Hegel*. Evanston, IL: Northwestern University Press, 2000.

Terada, Rei. "Pathos (Allegories of Emotion)." In *Feeling in Theory: Emotion after the "Death of the Subject"*. Cambridge, MA: Harvard University Press, 2001.

Opening the Sacred Body or the Profaned Host in *The Merchant of Venice*

François-Xavier Gleyzon

This text was conceived and begun in the Orient, the Middle East (American University of Beirut) and was completed in the Occident (University of Central Florida). Between the beginning of an end, the birth of a death, the end of a beginning and the death of a birth, in that painful intersection, this text aims at tracing the phenomena and events of opening and cutting that leave their imprints upon the textual landscape of The Merchant of Venice. *It will not be a question here of repeating or returning to the paradigm of the circumcision, but of highlighting that Shylock's attempt to open the body, to make an incision into the Christian body of Antonio represents and reproduces a willingness to attack and to profane the Eucharist.*

There is in the corpus of Erasmus a text about the body—quite a distinctive and particular body—that of the Silenus. Reading "closely" *Sileni Alcibiadis*, as Erasmus recommends, the body of the Silenus reveals at its heart a soul or a divine and spiritual internal substance, which, once open, and consequently bruised and sacrificed, is reminiscent of the body of Christ itself:

> Silenuses were little figurines split down the middle *(imagunculas … sectiles)* and manufactured in this way so that they could be opened to display their richness, whereas, when they were closed, they showed the ridiculous and grotesque outline *(ridiculam ac monstruosam … speciem)* of a flute-player. Open *(apertae)*, they suddenly revealed the figure of a god *(numen)* […], a great soul, a sublime and truly philosophical soul *(animum … sublimem ac vere philosophicum)*, despising everything for which other mortals rush around, go to sea, perspire, have arguments, make war. […] Was not Christ a marvellous Silenus? […] If we observe the external appearance of the Silenus, what could we see that is lower or more contemptible in popular estimation? […] But if we have the good fortune to examine this Silenus *more closely*, once open *(apertum hunc Silenum)*, that is to say when he consents to show himself to the purified eyes of the soul *(ipse se purgatis animi luminibus ostendere)*, then, Immortal God, what an ineffable treasure *(ineffabilem … thesaurum)* we will discover![1]

---

[1]Erasmus, 3–8.

Opening the Body

The lines that Erasmus offers us to read uncover simultaneously an invitation and a profound desire to "*open*", to split the body of the Silenus, the body of Christ, in order to discover there a treasure embodying nothing other than a living and fertile metaphor for internal spirituality. In the folds of its body, so ordinary nevertheless (even *grotesque* according to Erasmus), the Silenus may be said to incorporate a "hidden God",[2] offering himself/opening himself and closing himself again so as to suck in his subject-onlookers into a mystical space that we could easily term, in an expression so dear to Georges Bataille, an "inner experience" ["*expérience intérieure*"].[3] The Silenus seems, in fact, at first glance, to exhibit that correspondence/symmetry between external and internal that the latter (the *visual* Silenic object-subject) seems subsequently to annul in an operation-movement which may be said to consist precisely—according to the formula that will be entirely devoted to it: *aperire imagines et corpus*—*of opening the image, opening the body* so as to gain access to "the mystical thought inside". It will be noted, however, that what Erasmus does not describe is surprisingly the whole process, the gesture itself, which consists in opening this body. This celebrated humanist adage thus radically omits the necessary and essential violence undergone on the sensitive surface of the body, which nevertheless presides over its opening and *sui generis* its examination with a view to penetrating the soul. What about that slot (*imagunculas … sectiles*) that little "apestra" as Alberti would call it, or "door" according to Bataille, in the middle of the body of the Silenus, and in addition, the penetrating and incisive, even *transgressive*, gesture that calls for the opening and crossing of the body? It is also in this same kinetic relationship, this face to face with the image-body that comes to open up, offer itself to our gaze and suffer from it, that Bataille was able to feel and formulate the idea of a door which would just fly to pieces: "If I place the image in front of me it opens the door or rather it pulls it off its hinges" ["*Si je replace l'image devant moi elle ouvre la porte, ou plutôt elle l'arrache*"].[4]

What Bataille, a posteriori, complements and fulfils here, is that sort of "meaning" ["*vouloir-dire*"] that Erasmus's text seems to hold back. In other words, it is that logic of cruelty, seemingly repressed and *inter*-dicted in Erasmus, which manifests and deploys itself in Bataille in the act of opening, and gives way to the anatomical exhibition of the image-body of the Silenus, or of Christ, while creating a tension for the *double-bind* of the *sacer* in all its states, if not its *pieces*, both *sacr*-ed and *sacr*-eligious. If this "Immortal God" agrees to open himself, to show himself at one and the same time accessible and visible, it is only through the trenchant gesture to which is linked a whole logic of cruelty, violence and suffering. There will therefore take place the whole of a long work, a travail, *travel*,—from Erasmus onwards, through the arts and literature of the Renaissance down to modern thought—a

---

[2]Wind, 223.
[3]Bataille, "L'Expérience Intérieure," 25.
[4]Bataille, "Note pour *Le Coupable*," 514.

phenomenological journey, which will discover what was dormant in the language and what was waiting to be awoken. This travail and journey, as we know, will generate a whole style of writing based on exegesis and a new artistic method focusing on a certain *folly of seeing*, as Christine Buci-Glucksman terms it, of seeing and searching—always —*inwardly*.[5] In point of fact the Latin Vulgate version of Saint John's Gospel (19:37): *videbunt in quem transfixerunt* [*They shall look on him whom they pierced*] reveals all of the mission and the motto for a Renaissance writing and painting that will pour out in a poetics and a dramatization of opening in the body, and in the body of Christ more especially. Therefore, it is known that the devotional writings of Camilla Battista Varano or Catherine of Siena, with all their deep compassion and ecstatic dimension, will concentrate on the gaping wounds of the crucified body of Christ that the devout subject must lick and afterwards kiss as a mouth in order to gain entrance to the truth of Salvation through Christ.[6] The wounds, the stigmata, *open* then, even become wider so as to welcome devotees in their entirety ("I will snuggle up to the wounds of Christ").[7] If, in the annals of mystical and devotional thought, the "fabric of the text" incisively *incorporates* the opening up to the body of Christ on the level of his wounds, the opening up is also magnified in Renaissance iconography, more especially, and in a way as radical as it is sublime, in the work of Carlo Crivelli. The opening up of/ to the body in Crivelli offers itself to our gaze in all its pity and its piety. In his famous *Lamentation over the Dead Christ* (1473) (Figure 1(a)), everything indicates suffering in the opening up of the flesh—all the gaping wounds of the crucified body are visible (as the Virgin Mary's right hand seems to point out, which seems to hold Christ's perizonium so as to show her son's wound much more than to cover it). The wound on the right, rimmed and horizontal next to the heart, as well as the oblong wound on Christ's left hand give themselves up to be read one after the other in a polycentric and polyorganic sequence like a lip and a mouth out of which gush shouts of suffering and mourning; and in the same way, like a veritable point of entry for the passing of a gaze—from a point both of emission and of intromission—to which the apostles will dive so as to welcome the Divine Word (Figure 1(b), (c)).[8] There is then in Christianity this pressure as *puzzling* as it is enigmatic—"this pressure of a necessity", as Jean-Louis Schefer writes", "is that of the inwardness of the body, which is nothing other than "*an anatomy*, only resolved through both the opening up-destruction of the body and the very symptom that the body represents far more than it can figure".[9]

The gaze is therefore haunted by a cruel dramatization of openings, by those oblong stigmata incising the tortured flesh of the body of Christ to the point of signifying it and dis-*figuring* it in a sort of sordid, even *formless*, ignobility. It is understood therefore here that to open the body, to which may be added this desire to look, *to see inside*,

---

[5] Buci-Glucksman, *La Folie du Voir, De l'Esthétique Baroque*, 28.
[6] See Varano. Also quoted by Wirth, 322.
[7] Catherine of Siena, 143.
[8] See Gleyzon, *Shakespeare's Spiral*, especially "The Passio of Lear," 81–6.
[9] Schefer, "On the Object of Figuration," 28.

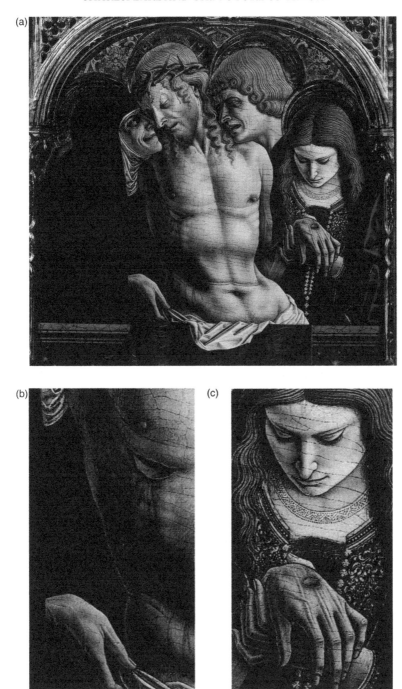

Figure 1 (a) Carlo Crivelli, *Lamentation over the Dead Christ*, 1473, Ascoli Piceno, S. Emidio Cathedral, Capella del Sacramento. Courtesy of the Web Gallery of Art, www. wga.hu. (b) Detail 1. (c) Detail 2.

signifies *to harass, to injure, to break*, even *to destroy*. In other words, opening up is not conceivable other than through the act itself of an event-transgression that comes to penetrate and invade the body. Here is the whole of the logic behind a cruelty as disconcerting and disturbing as it is *puzzling* that will make its way and reaches its acme in the modernist thought of Baudelaire.[10] Baudelaire's famous text entitled "La Morale du Joujou" ["A Philosophy of Toys"] (1853) will question and anatomize better than anyone else all the poetics–problematics involved in opening up with the unavoidable desire to wound and to destroy:

> Most children [*marmots*] want above all to see the soul, some after a certain amount of time spent in playing, others right away. Depending on how quickly this desire manifests itself, the toy will have a short or a long life. I do not feel brave enough to blame this childish mania: it is a first metaphysical tendency. Once this desire has taken root in the child's brain marrow, it fills his fingers and his nails with a singular nimbleness and strength. The child turns and turns his toy over again, he scratches it, he shakes it, bangs it against the walls, throws it down. From time to time he has it start its mechanical movements again, sometimes in reverse. The marvellous life stops. [...] Finally, he half opens it. *But where is the soul?* It is at that moment that stupor and sadness start. There are others who break the toy immediately, almost as soon as it has been placed in their hands, virtually unexamined and, where they are concerned, I plead ignorance of the mysterious feeling which causes them to act this way. Do they fall prey to a superstitious rage against these tiny objects that imitate humanity or do they subject them to a sort of *masonic initiation* before introducing them into nursery life?—*puzzling question!*[11]

This admirable page of Baudelaire radically and directly addresses here this *puzzling* mystery of the opening by targeting the image of the body-toy in order to describe to us the successive ceremonial stages of torture which are performed as part of this rite without forgetting to mention all their quasi-religious dimensions (*But where is the soul? ... a sort of masonic initiation*). In this way Baudelaire bears witness to the martyrdom and the calvary of the opening up of the body with which childhood both plays and enjoys itself, to perform (and celebrate) a whole mass of the *sacred (sacer)* within a veritable theatre of cruelty. It is therefore not by chance if, in the same vein as Baudelaire, Victor Hugo, who, a few years later in his fragmentary text "Dieu" ["God"] (1856), finding himself haunted by the desire to penetrate with his gaze the soul of Christ, will have recourse to the trenchant gesture of opening and thereby of incision: "sacrifice Christ to see what is concealed in God; make a crucial incision in the mystery" ["*immole Christ pour voir ce que contient un Dieu; fais une incision cruciale au mystère*"].[12]

---

[10]For a study linking Shakespeare to modern thought (Baudelaire, Aby Warburg and Christine Buci-Glucksman in particular), see Gleyzon, "Christine Buci-Glucksman."

[11]Baudelaire, 587.

[12]Hugo, "Dieu (fragment)," 540.

From the Casket to the Body: (De-)Construction of the Christian Body—*The Merchant of Venice*

Opening the body, making a violent incision through the flesh: thus is the method to pierce all the mystery that the body conceals. It is also in the works of Shakespeare that Victor Hugo, an incisive and magisterial commentator of Shakespeare, will find this *living tension* of the opening into the flesh. In 1864, when he was in exile on the Channel Island of Guernsey, in a work devoted entirely to the bard of Stratford-upon-Avon—quite overlooked, in my opinion, by Anglo-American Shakespeare criticism—Victor Hugo writes: "In Shakespeare, [...] there is the possible, *that window of the dream open* on the real. As for the real, we must insist that Shakespeare overflows with it; *live flesh* everywhere."[13] Nowhere else in the works of Shakespeare does the flesh of the body of the Christian seem to be at once as targeted and exposed, given up to sacrifice in all its vulnerability, as in *The Merchant of Venice*.

Everything has to do with opening in *The Merchant of Venice*, starting at the very beginning with the plot of the caskets of which one of the three will open for the "princely suitors" (1.2.30), who must *dis-entangle* the enigma ("whereof who chooses his meaning chooses you", 1.2.27) so as to ravish Portia's heart just as much as her body. We see here how the resolution of the enigma moves us from the casket to the opening up of the body and places us in an internal space: "a space-intimate moment", according to Gaston Bachelard, "that does not open to just anybody".[14] The opening of the casket is not less illustrative of a sacrificial gesture as Portia will emphasize before Bassanio when the latter comes close to the caskets so as to make his choice: "I stand for sacrifice" (3.2.57).

> PORTIA: With no less presence, but with much more love
> Than young Alcides [Hercules] when he did redeem
> The virgin tribute paid by howling Troy
> To the sea-monster: *I stand for sacrifice*. (3.2.54–7; emphasis added)

The *topos* of the sacrifice is here confirmed by the figure of Hercules that Portia, as is underlined in the article by Harry Berger Jr.,[15] applies directly to Bassanio—"Go my Hercules", she will say—saving the Trojan virgin (Hesione) while the latter sees herself intended and offered by her father (Laomedon) for divine sacrifice to the sea monster. Portia's phrase "I stand for sacrifice" reveals and deploys in the same way the whole of a sexual metaphor linked to the penetrative and invasive gesture of opening up which is reminiscent of the stratagem of Iachimo's chest in the tragedy of *Cymbeline*. Shut inside a chest that Imogen is keeping safe in her bedroom, Iachimo at nightfall will climb out of it (2.2.10–45) and hurry to contemplate the sleeping naked body of the princess, to look for visual indications of her virginity.

---

[13]Hugo, *William Shakespeare*, 349.
[14]Bachelard, 106.
[15]Berger, 156.

The virginal place in which Imogen exposes her body in all its intimacy away from all intrusion will be thus the place of penetration, the place of rape by gaze wherein the eye penetrates intimacy and steals virginity.[16] Besides, does Iachimo not compare himself, without going as far as the act of rape itself, to Tarquin whose son, Sextus, violated the chastity of the virgin Lucretia:

> IACHIMO: Our Tarquin thus
> Did softly press the rushes, ere he waken'd
> The chastity he wounded. (2.2.12–14)

If in *Cymbeline* the vicious stratagem of the chest has as its outlet a detailed and erotic representation of the body of Imogen, the casket of lead chosen by Bassanio in *The Merchant of Venice*, however, conceals and contains an image, a portrait of Portia, in other words an *imago* as if the capture and access to the desired object and the object of desire (Portia) could not be negotiated other than, as Lacan would argue, by the medium and the aggressive rhetorical function of the sacrifice of opening.[17]

   In a well-calculated trajectory which seems to interweave one plot with the other (from the trial of the caskets in the comedy of love to the dramatic episode of the contract agreed by the merchant Antonio and the Jewish moneylender), the motif of the casket will reappear during Portia's speech in the court case. During this episode, Portia is disguised as a lawyer bearing the name of Balthazar, a character reminiscent of one of the three wise men arriving from the Orient at the time of the Epiphany. While Shylock reminds Portia vehemently of the *oath* and therefore the duty of debt that Antonio himself constitutes, since part of his body ("a pound of flesh" cut next to his heart) is engaged as a pledge, Portia, in lieu of the pound of flesh, invites the Jew to contemplate a chest that contains three times the sum of money that is due to him (4.1.229). We can see here how Portia's speech brings to the fore a whole economy of translation/conversion which aims to substitute the *physical corpus*, namely, the body, Antonio's pound of flesh, for a *monetary corpus/sign*. However, if the Jew refuses Portia's codicil by invoking the very letter of the contract: "An oath, an oath, I have an oath in heaven / Shall I lay perjury upon my soul? / No, not for Venice" and "I stand here for law" or even "I crave the law" (4.1.142 & 144), it is because the Jewish moneylender aims at the body of the Christian—he therefore aims in point of fact at the flesh of the Christian body that submits itself to be the redemption of a pledge. In other words, the *corpus verum* is a currency of both substitution and liberation against a debt contracted by the Christian to the Jew. In fact, when Shylock comes out on stage pointing with his knife to what is due to him, it is, undoubtedly, this integral and dramatic attempt to cut into and open the *corpus verum* of the Christian Antonio that animates the whole of the episode of the trial

---

[16]For a detailed semiotic analysis of the study of the trunk in *Cymbeline*, see Gleyzon, *Shakespeare's Spiral*, 81–6.
[17]Lacan, 101–24.

scene. Everything in this scene is grasped and understood through the trenchant paradigm of cutting—through "the abrahamic cut"[18] [*la coupure abrahamique*], as Derrida writes in *Glas*—which organizes and coordinates the scene dividing it up so as to bring into conflict two narratives, two distinct regimes/orders originally sharing a common ancestry: the Old Testament (Shylock) and the New Testament (Antonio). "Why [then] have a knife inserted between two texts? Why, at least, write two texts at once? What scene is being played out here? What is here desired?" And why is there this cut, this caesura, in a scene in which the law is being played out, thwarted and performed?[19]

The Body, *Non Sanz Droict*

First of all, let us make answer to these questions by pointing this out: if Shakespeare implements a lawsuit between the Jew Shylock, "the mere enemy" (3.2.260)—the absolute theological enemy—and the Christian, he seems, at the very least, in a poetic licence peculiar to himself, to leave out a major difficulty and to disregard the Roman principles of Canon Law. In fact, we know from clauses 67 to 70 of the famous *Lateran Council IV* that contracts agreed between Jews and Christians are not legally binding and therefore void. As *Lateran Council IV* reminds us forcefully and severely, a Christian citizen can never be the debtor of a Jew:

> *Jews and excessive Usury*:
> The more the Christian religion is restrained from usurious practices, so much the more does the perfidy of the Jews grow in these matters, so that within a short time they are exhausting the resources of Christians. Wishing therefore to see that Christians are not savagely oppressed by Jews in this matter, we ordain by this synodal decree that if Jews in future, on any pretext, extort oppressive and excessive interest from Christians, then they are to be removed from contact with Christians.[20]

Apart from this juridical impossibility confirmed by *Lateran IV* which Shakespeare chooses to ignore, *The Merchant of Venice* seems to make a specific reference to the *XII Tables* (the ancient Roman penal code) according the right to the lender, in an expression as famous as it is ambiguous, to "amputate his debtor" when the latter is insolvent. Hegel in his *Philosophy of Right* (1821) and subsequently Jules Michelet in *Les Origines du Droit Français: la France devant l'Europe* (1893–99) will allude, each in turn, precisely to this cruel legal text, both of them invoking the tragedy of *The Merchant of Venice*:

> Take the horrible law, which permitted a creditor, after the lapse of a fixed term of respite, [...] *to cut pieces off the debtor* [...] with the proviso that if the creditor

---

[18]Cited in Anidjar, Introduction to *Acts of Religion*, 7.
[19]Derrida, *Glas*, 76.
[20]Tanner, 286.

should cut off too much or too little, no action should be taken against him. It was this clause, it may be noticed, which stood Shakespeare's *The Merchant of Venice* in such a good stead.[21]

Faced with the "insolvent debtor" and stimulated by a reading both partial and romantic of *The Merchant of Venice*, Michelet proceeds to explain fragments 4 and 5 of Tabula III of the *XII Tables*:

> The debt acknowledged, the case duly judged, let the law be put on him (the insolvent debtor), let him be brought before the judge. The tribunal closes with the going down of the sun. If he does not satisfy the judgement [...] the creditor will lead him away and tie him up with belts or chains. [...] Let the creditor live on what he has. [...] On the third day [...] let (the creditor) cut up the debtor into several parts (*in partes secanto*).[22]

The Latin legal expression *in partes secanto*, which should "be understood as referring to a person and not to property" ["*s'entendre de la personne et non des biens*"], was also scrupulously examined some decades earlier (1855) by the same Michelet in his *Histoire de France au XVIe Siècle*. Despite the Universalist discourse that Michelet uses against the Jews, the force of the passage that I give below is of interest for the movement and the progressive development that animates the whole argument. For Michelet it will be a matter of, first, taking aim at the corpus, the monetary capital that the Jews control, in order to subsequently displace it onto the body/corpus and the Christian pound of flesh, which will find its decisive outcome through Shylock whom Michelet ultimately translates and paraphrases:

> Prolific nation that, above all others, had the strength to multiply, the strength to procreate, that could render fertile Jacob's ewes and Shylock's sequins. All through the Middle Ages persecuted, hunted, expelled, recalled, they were the indispensable intermediary between the exchequer and its victim, between the doer and the sufferer, pumping up gold from below, and pouring it out above into the king's hands with an ugly scowl. But they always had something left ... Patient, indestructible, they won through by their perseverance. They have resolved the problem of volatizing riches; and made freedmen by the inventions of bills of exchange, they are now free, they are the masters; from buffets to buffets, they are now on the throne of the world. [...]
>
> What said the Christian? "In the name of God!—The Jew killed your God!—For pity's sake!—What Christian has ever had pity on a Jew? It isn't words that are needed. A pledge is the only language understood—What has he to give, who has nothing?" The Jew will say to him quietly: "My friend, in accordance with the ordinances of the king, our sire, I do not lend on the strength of a bloody coat or a ploughshare ... No, the only pledge I require is yourself. I am not one of yours, my law is not the Christian law. I claim a more ancient right: *in partes secanto*.

---

[21]Hegel.

[22]Michelet, "Le débiteur insolvable," 433.

Your flesh shall be answerable. Blood for gold as life for life. A pound of your flesh which I shall nourish with my money, only a pound of your fair flesh."[23]

This term relating to amputation—*in partes secanto*—highlights and exposes here the live flesh, *indebted* and *held captive*, of Antonio who, substitutes his body for want of monetary means. Nothing, not even the Doge of Venice, can abrogate the law and the letter of the contract, as Antonio himself declares:

ANTONIO: The duke cannot deny the course of law.
            For the commodity that strangers have
            With us in Venice, if it be denied,
            Will much impeach the justice of his state,
            Since that the trade and profit of the city
            Consisteth of all nations. Therefore go.
            These griefs and losses have so bated me,
            That I shall hardly spare a pound of flesh
            Tomorrow to my bloody creditor. (3.3.26–34)

Moreover, Shylock adds: "If you deny it, let the danger light / Upon your charter and your city's freedom!" (4.1.38–9). Antonio's body thus *baited*, the latter takes on himself the image of the *body of the Christian martyr*—he puts on, in fact, the image, according to St Paul's expression, that consists in "always bearing about in the body [...] the dying of the Lord Jesus" (2 Corinthians 4:10). All Antonio's rhetoric of pathos in the trial scene—that of a man tortured about to be persecuted through his flesh, given over to the Jewish torturer, Shylock—seems to be catalysed in a testimony of essentially a martyr who seems to find a certain *jouissance* in a Paulinian precept: "Who now rejoice in my sufferings for you, and fill up that which is behind of the afflictions of Christ in my flesh ..." (Colossians 1:24). Here is what Antonio, believing himself to be lost, declares to Bassanio:

ANTONIO: Grieve not that I am fall'n to this for you,
            For herein Fortune shows herself more kind
            Than is her custom. It is still her use
            To let the wretched man outlive his wealth,
            To view with hollow eye and wrinkled brow
            An age of poverty—from which lingering penance
            Of such misery doth she cut me off.
            Commend me to your honorable wife.
            Tell her the process of Antonio's end.
            Say how I loved you. Speak me fair in death.
            And when the tale is told, bid her be judge

---

[23]Michelet, *Histoire de France*, 114.

Whether Bassanio had not once a love.
Repent but you that you shall lose your friend,
And he repents not that he pays your debt.
For if the Jew do cut but deep enough,
I'll pay it presently with all my heart. (4.1.278–93)

Antonio's flesh, which he thinks he is on the point of giving, will therefore constitute a work of remembrance: *a debt of remembrance* for which Bassanio will not have to *mourn* ("Grieve not") but to *bear witness* ("Speak me fair in death. / And when the tale is told …"). This is what Antonio's flesh incarnates and this is what Bassanio, according to the Eucharistic formula consecrated by Christ, giving up his body and his blood at the last supper, will do "in memory of him". This is the entire stake and the Christological gage that the trial scene *dramatizes* and offers to our gaze: *imaginem induere Christi* (*taking on the image of Christ*). In other words, when Antonio decides to *translate* his passion into the testimony of a *martyr*, he will with the same thrust bring into play, through the etymological force and embodiment of the word (*martyr*), a whole *ocular testimony* of himself as an *imago pietatis* or even an *imitatio Christi*. This entire process, however, cannot take place other than through a work of staging, which tends to "*substantialize* the sacred", in short, as Bataille argues, through a *dramatization* in a fictitious space in which law, politics and religion are intermingled:

> The point is reached through dramatization. Dramatizing is what devout people do
> [...] (but not just them). Picture the place, the dramatis personae and the drama
> itself: the torture to which Christ is led. The disciple [...] imagines a theatrical rep-
> resentation [...] It is asked of him to have the feelings he would have at Calvary. He
> is told [...] he ought to internalize these feelings.[24]

Bataille's radical thesis reminds us that when the flesh (of Antonio) appears and is summoned forth on the stage and before the court, it is only in order to both *incarnate* and *simulate*, and therefore re-enact the *image-sacrifice* of Christian *piety*. That is to say the tragic and cruel moment in which the Christian readies himself to give himself up and to suffer like an animal to the slaughter: "a tainted wether of the flock / Meetest for death" (4.1.113–4).

From the Rite to the Sacrament: From Circumcision to the Eucharist

"We have now arrived at the flesh [...], at the heart of the whole matter."[25] If the Christian martyrdom of Antonio places us before the problem of the martyr's sacrifice of the flesh, it also reminds us and bears witness in a lively manner—in a different

---

[24]Bataille, "L'Expérience Intérieure," 138–9. The expression "substantialiser le sacré" ["substantialize the sacred"] is also used by Bataille in the same work.
[25]Tertullian, *De Resurrectione Mortuorum*, 121.

ancient context but admittedly contiguous—to the writings of one of the first great theologians of the first centuries of the Latin Church, Tertullian. The latter will devote more than thirty works to Christianity with a passion overlaid with a need, even with an unremitting passion to "see" and to "go into" the subject of the flesh. In the celebrated *De Resurrectione Mortuorum*, it is once again the martyred flesh in all its states that opens up and mobilizes Tertullian's observations. One specific passage takes on a dimension as radical as it is surprising when, describing the wretched existence of a persecuted Christian, he plunges him literally into the blinding light of an amphitheatre. The flesh of the body of the Christian laid bare and exposed, he will go on to write: "There it is now [the flesh of the body of the Christian] in the full light of day, [...] torn apart by instruments of torture and, finally, destroyed by torments. But beyond this false end it is gloriously offered up to Our Lord Jesus Christ, its only debt being to no longer owe anything other than to have ceased to be His debtor."[26]

In following closely the scene that Tertullian offers us, we can see here how the instruments of torture mentioned can be set alongside the cutting blade that Shylock sharpens maliciously ("Why dost thou whet thy knife so earnestly?", 4.1.120) and with which he thinks to extract the *real* value of what is owed to him from the body of Antonio ("To cut the forfeiture from that bankrupt there", 4.1.121). In his capacity of moneylender, the Jew Shylock is looking for his Passover and readies himself in this way to acquire both a substance and a symbol. In other words, it is a matter of a true act of terror attempted and intended on the *corpus verum* or *corpus mysticum* of Antonio. It is indeed this that is signified by the act of incision and *sui generis* of opening and extraction of the fleshy Christian substance —namely, *a real Eucharistic sacrifice* whose malign intentions point to and focus on the annihilation of "the real substance" of the body (mysticum or verum). Therefore, Shylock, in one identical and double thrust, attacks the body of Christianity's founder —the body of Jesus Christ so as to destroy the juridical, political and religious foundations that this mystical body conceals and reveals at its heart—in short, the very body of the Christian state of Venice.

We know that the *corpus mysticum* and *verum* is precisely the appellation for the Eucharist in the course of which is produced and represented, as Louis Marin points out, "a sacrificial and sacramental body visible as the real presence of Jesus Christ", and this so as to define and constitute in itself the sign and the very reminder of the union and adherence of the faithful in this body ecclesial, historical and political.[27] It is therefore for purposes of *remembrance* that, at the moment of consecration, the priest will re-enact (perform) and repeat the political and historical sacrifice of Jesus Christ, and thus *pierce, incise* the liturgical bread (the host) so as to *engrave* there a cross with the help of a *lancet*.

---

[26]Ibid., 54–5.
[27]Marin, 157.

In this way according to the rite and the liturgy of Byzantium—over which the Roman Catholic Church of Venice, by reason of its location "as a liquid frontier" between East and West, will have presided at the heart of a veritable theatre of liturgical conflicts between the Roman Latinate Church and its Oriental counterpart—the paradigm of cutting–incision does not manifest itself symbolically but "truly" and "concretely" at the moment of the Eucharistic consecration.[28] The cutting and the incision materialize in the very efficaciousness of the sacrificial gesture that the priest carries out and *executes* over both kinds and particularly over the mystical body, the host. Nicholas Cabasilas, a mystical writer and a theologian, explains clearly and precisely in his celebrated *Explanation of the Divine Liturgy* (early fourteenth century) the successive stages of the Eucharistic consecration:

> The priest carves the cross on the bread and thus he signifies the way in which the sacrifice has been accomplished, that is to say by the cross. Afterwards he pierces the bread showing by that wound in the bread the wound in the Lord's side. Then he pronounces the words: "like a sheep he was led to the slaughter" […] The bread has changed from the simple bread it was into an object of sacrifice […] In this way, as for the sheep, the change from one state to another implements the sacrifice, so here, by this change, the sacrifice is truly carried out. As he digs in several times *the lancet* and divides the bread up into crumbs, the priest divides into as many sections the prophetic word, matching each part of the formula to each incision so as to show that reality is the true explanation of the divine word.[29]

The word *lancet* in this passage carries obviously a quite specific resonance in the dramatic field of the play of *The Merchant of Venice*. Following on from a seminal study by Philippa Berry—"Incising Venice"—which sets itself the task to deconstruct and "to read Shakespeare's Venice as a geographical and cultural site which, in its marking by significant rifts and fissures, can offer us new insights into the fragmented and fragmenting character of Renaissance or early modern culture",[30] Patricia Parker, in her remarkable article "Cutting Both Ways", also undertakes to trace a whole network of allusions, declensions and translations linking specifically the name of Lancelot (or Launcelot) Gobbo, the servant who leaves the home of Shylock to enter the service of the Christian Bassanio, to motifs of circumcision and castration. As Parker argues, the word *lancelet* refers obviously to the double-edged knife used either medicinally, bloodletting, or religiously, in the rite of circumcision, even in the practice of castration if one refers to the priests of Baal to be found in the First Book of Kings (18:28).[31]

---

[28]On the subject of tensions at the heart of Venice between Latin and Byzantine liturgies and rites, I would refer to two major works of reference—Hanssen, *Institutiones liturgicae de retibus orientalibus* and Salaville, *Liturgies Orientales*. The term "liquid frontier" which serves to characterize the specific situation of Venice between East and West, goes back to Buci-Glucksman, "Venise et l'oeil de l'Orient" ["Venice and the Eastern Eye"], 66.

[29]With regard to Cabasilas, I am using here the excellent translation from the Greek of *The Explanation of the Divine Liturgy*, 189.

[30]Berry, 248.

[31]Ibid., 104–7.

"(From) the knife of the trial scene [which] evokes the threat of forcible circumcision or castration [through] Morocco, from another circumcised nation, to Antonio as a castrated ram (4.1.114) along with the Jew deprived of both daughter and ducats", the play, as Parker points out, is shot through with a variety of cuts and incisions that Shakespeare writes into the very essence of the name of the character, Lancelot.[32] Among all the translations, declensions and uses of the word *lancelet*, Parker makes absolutely no comment on the fact that this same instrument, the lancelet, was used, as we have seen, in order to incise and pierce the host at the moment of Eucharistic consecration. Moreover, it may also be noted that it is this same "lancelet" or "lancelette" which will impose itself as an indispensable instrument in the field of the visual and artistic practices of medieval and Renaissance devotion to the Eucharist. Georges Didi-Huberman in his work entitled *Phasmes*, demonstrates rigorously how the disciple of Dürer, Hans Sebald Beham, performs engraving, namely, how "he gives himself over to a veritable act of painstaking cruelty", almost heretical, "by means of the lancelet". Thus, the representation of *Christ in the Chalice and the Host* (Figure 2) "is not formed from features laid down, but from hollowed-out grooves, from ridges, from inflicted wounds which, in the case of countless devotional images, are surprisingly consistent with the cruelty of the motifs themselves".[33] This infinite impulse to *engrave*, to *incise* and to pierce the body of Christ is found throughout the very construction itself of the image. The membranes of the tree are thus analogous to the membranes and the streaks in Christ's body—one of them seems to have given rise to a wound that secretes a jet of blood that is being collected in the chalice. Finally, the host that Christ is holding in his hands is distinguished by its incomparable darkness and allows one to divine the many lancelet blows so as to leave the imprint of a cross on it. As much in its liturgical dimension as in its artistic dimension, such would be the *trenchant* function of the lancelet within the framework of the institution of the Eucharist.

It will be noted, however, that if the Shakespearean criticism of these last ten years seems to have set itself to reveal the overall dynamic of traces, incisions, inscriptions and cuts that scarifies the text of *The Merchant of Venice*, it is, it seems, in order to examine in it (almost exclusively) the motif and the rite of circumcision. The erudite and masterly study of Julia Lupton's "Merchants of Venice, Circles of Citizenship" has every appearance of being its crowning point. It sees Shylock's circumcision as a "guiding motif in Shakespeare's [...] Venetian play (s), where it (circumcision) operates as the sign of an ethno-political form of religious association that excludes its bearers—Jewish and Muslim men—from participation in the Christian commonwealth".[34] With a peerless clarity of writing and thought, Julia Lupton traces the development of a conflicting theological parallelism

---

[32]Parker, 95–6.
[33]Didi-Huberman, 198.
[34]Lupton, 13.

Figure 2 Hans Sebald Beham, *Christ in the Chalice and the Host*, 1520, Engraving, Vienna, Albertina. © Georges Didi-Huberman, *Phasmes*, Editions de Minuit, Paris, p. 197, 1998.

between Jewish circumcision which, according to the Old Testament (Genesis 17), takes place in the body itself, and Christian circumcision which, according to the New Testament, takes place in the spirit, a circumcision of the heart such as Saint Paul describes it: "circumcision is that of the heart, in the spirit and not in the letter" (Romans 2:29).[35] While Shylock remains reified and fixed in his own world through the physical mark of circumcision, he will nevertheless displace and transform the Paulinian rereading and interpretation of the rite (*circumcision of the heart*) in order to *literally* convert/translate it into a weapon to be used against the Christian and *sui generis*, to take from him with the blade of his dagger a pound of flesh next to his heart.[36] It is therefore, according to Lupton, through a return to the Jewish order of things at the heart of and working against the Christian order that the trial scene is played out and divided up. However, even though the validity of this argument cannot be either deplored or reformulated, it seems to me that such a deconstruction dealing almost exclusively with the *literalization* of the rite of circumcision (of the heart) by the Jew Shylock against the Christian Antonio passes over in silence a whole dynamography which is also at work and at stake in the scene/cène (*s/cène*) of the trial,[37] namely: a murderous "eucharistic attempt" conceived by Shylock on Antonio's life.

S/cèno-graphy of the Trial or the Profaned Host: Shakespeare and Uccello

We need then to rethink in Eucharistic terms the representation of the scene/cène of the trial beginning with one of the very first scenes in which Shakespeare conjures up indeed a table and issues a dinner invitation. The response of the Jew to the invitation by Bassanio reminds us directly of Christ the Nazarene's last supper which Shylock wants no part of under any circumstances:

SHYLOCK: May I speak with Antonio?

BASSANIO: If it please you to dine with us.

SHYLOCK: Yes, to smell pork; to eat of the habitation which your prophet the Nazarite conjured the devil into. I will buy with you, sell with you, talk with you, walk with you, and so following, but I will not eat with you, drink with you, nor pray with you. What news on the Rialto? Who is he comes here? (1.3.29–36)

The invitation to table invoked in this passage uncovers here the notion of *figure* or *figura* in the sense given by the Dominican theologian Giovanni Balbi of Genoa in his *Catholicon* (thirteenth century). The notion of *figura* does not simply consist in representing a subject, an object or an event, but it implies essentially a total labour of displacement and of prefiguration (*praefigurare*), which, as Giovanni Balbi writes, "transposes or transports the meaning to another figure".[38] It is therefore in this

---

[35]Ibid., especially "Merchants of Venice, Circles of Citizenship," 89.

[36]Ibid., 92.

[37]There is a play on words here which it is not possible to render into English without comment. The French word "scène" means, of course, "scene" in English as in "scene of a play", but the French word "cène" means "communion under both kinds" and, when the letter c is capitalized, the Last Supper.

[38]Balbi.

very capacity that (the invitation to) the table in *The Merchant of Venice* translates the last supper, the Eucharist of Christ so as to *prefigure*—in a dynamic movement of pro-tension—its sacrificial imminence. This prefiguration is clearly shown when Shylock, in refusing the invitation to share the meal, hastens to ask after Antonio's merchant ships after which he will reveal his plan of hate with which he will want *to nourish himself*:

> SHYLOCK: I hate him for he is a Christian,
> But more for that in low simplicity
> He lends out money gratis and brings down
> The rate of usance here with us in Venice.
> If I can catch him once upon the hip,
> *I will feed fat the ancient grudge I bear him.* (1.3.37–42; my emphasis)

To mistreat and to feed on the body of the Christian: this is the feast and the meal to which the Jew Shylock invites himself. The hyperbole of this intention taken literally, in its *extreme literalization* in short, points to the Eucharistic act of the last supper and its ritual formula of consecration, "this is my body" (Matthew 26, 26–8), in which the body of Christ will be consumed. This perverse intention that proposes a radical reread-ing of the New Testament is ensconced in a long tradition of legends (or mysteries) and various Eucharistic theatres which set out to disseminate from the thirteenth century onwards throughout Europe crimes against the Holy Sacrament—*the profanation of hosts*—committed by the Jews. Although Shakespeare excludes the bloody *dénouement*, he nevertheless follows very closely the main strand of the story of this legend which, along with numerous avatars and analogous accounts, finds its source in the celebrated Mystery of Paris otherwise called The Miracle of Les Billettes which occurred in 1290. The most thorough documentation that can be found on this mystery of Les Billettes is down to Gilles Corrozet and his work *The Antiquities of Paris* published in 1586.

> A Jew who had lent money on pledges to a poor but evil woman dwelling in Paris, came to an agreement with this wretched woman that she would bring to him the Holy Sacrament that she would receive on Easter Sunday. She did not fail to, went to the church of St Merry, went to communion, and like a second Judas took the host to the infidel who then pierced with a knife [*s'acharna à coup de canivet*] the precious body of Our Lord, so much so that the Holy Host spurted blood in great abundance which did not stop the damned Hebrew from throwing it into the fire from whence it emerged without any lesion and began to hover around the room. The crazy Jew took it and threw it into a cauldron of boiling water and suddenly this water was changed to the colour of blood and, there and then, the Host was raised up and what was hidden under the bread, namely the form and figure of Our Crucified Saviour, became visible. This despicable crime was discovered by a son of the Jew who spoke of it to the children of Christians, not thinking that in doing so, his action would bring about the ruin of his father.[39]

---

[39]The text of Gilles Corrozet, *Les Antiquités de Paris* (1586) is reproduced in Perdrizet, 105.

Corrozet adds that the site of this new passion of Christ was converted into a church served by the Carmelites of Les Billettes. As for the profaned host and the knife, they were both exposed and carried in procession through Paris. We should point out that it is, indeed, improbable that Shakespeare was able to read this text of Corrozet, but the latter still remains, by virtue of the ideological schemes and intentions it proposes, a homologous structural point of departure that *The Merchant of Venice* delves into while offering transformations and variations. The uncanniness of these two texts laid side by side, increased twofold by a historical, linguistic and cultural time lag, would constitute scandalous conditions in the eyes of literary history unless the rapprochement of these two *corpi* presented a sort of communicability and deep articulation opening out on an *(inter)textual experience of reading*. This (inter)textual experience that consists in superimposing onto the Eucharistic legend of Les Billettes related by Corrozet the intrigue of the contract drawn up by the merchant Antonio with the Jewish moneylender Shylock demonstrates by means of this double-edged reading that *The Merchant of Venice* is, beyond all doubt, an extension of the stories dealing with the trafficking of the Holy Sacrament. The mechanism behind these two intrigues is part of the same logic—it presents us with a contract in which the regular means of a monetary transaction is lacking and is afterwards discharged maliciously out of the Christian hide by way of redemption.

We may note, however, that the dramatization of the scenario of the profanation and the Eucharistic sacrilege of Les Billettes in which the profaning Jew *injures, incises* and *pierces* the body of Christ is not a frenzied action or an aberration per se. Just as Shylock's violent intention in *The Merchant of Venice*, this action fulfils a quite specific function in the sense that it weaves, if only marginally, a whole narrative thread in which is repeated and again played out Christ's Passion. The Jew admittedly is carrying out a ritual sacrifice with the intention of committing deicide ("he pierced with a knife the precious body of Our Lord"), but he also enacts quite clearly the commemorative act/ritual that the priest carries out—host and lancelet in hand—at the moment of the Eucharistic consecration in the Byzantine liturgy to which the Roman Catholic Church, however, was opposed. The Jew is a profaner–butcher admittedly, but he is also a priest officiating in his own church and his sacrilege points at the same time (and in spite of himself) to the sacred gesture of the Oriental–Byzantine commemoration of the Eucharist. In effect, for Derrida, "what separates Christianity [as practised by the Latin Catholic Church] from Judaism, the syncope between them, the place where they cannot make contact, the area of Judeo-Christian non-contact, is exactly this attitude toward touching (for) the Jew demands to touch (physically and literally) while the Christian sublimates and loses this actual contact".[40] It would appear from an examination of the *oriental* Christian liturgy of consecration and the subversion/destruction of the Eucharist by the Jew of Les Billettes that we now know that this

---

[40]Derrida, *Le Toucher, Jean-Luc Nancy*, 302.

complexio or infinite chiasmus (as Derrida terms it) between Christianity and Judaism finds here a point of *contact* or partaking (*part-taking*) of the bloodiest type.

Let us return after this Parisian diversion of Les Billettes to Italy, not to Venice, but south of Venice or, to be more precise, to the ducal palace of the town of Urbino. We find in this town what is without doubt the most important and the most celebrated pictorial witness to the history of Eucharistic legends. The work in question is a predella by Paolo Uccello (painted towards 1467), which illustrates *The Miracle of the Host* or *The Miracle of the Profaned Host*. Jean-Louis Schefer in his admirable and erudite book, *L'Hostie Profané: histoire d'une fiction théologique*, gives a detailed semiotic analysis of Uccello's predella while tracing a liturgical, social and cultural history of the Eucharist. This picture is of interest for it reveals distinct motifs—or *intersigns*, to use a terminology dear to Louis Massignon—which seem analogically to be manifested in *The Merchant of Venice*. To be more specific Uccello's predella consists of a succession of six painted wooden panels and it was commissioned by the powerful and influential church of the Corpus Domini. The predella's efficaciousness lies in its organization into successive scenes/segments, which tend to promote a linear and cursive reading of the *istoria* that underlies it. As Pierre Francastel makes specific, the *istoria* (the narration and the composition) that the predella offers to the gaze seems to be calqued on the Parisian mystery of Les Billettes. The story is thus of the same type: in order to be able to repay a debt contracted with a Jewish usurer, a Christian woman decides to steal a host and gives it to him as they had previously agreed upon. The Jew, equipped with a knife, then cuts into the host and the latter begins to bleed.

Of the six pictures that the predella (re-)presents, the first scene seems to offer an uncanny and enigmatic tension in the reading which deserves special attention (Figure 3). A room bordered by small bright red columns frames or rather partitions the scene. In the foreground on the left, the Jewish merchant appears behind a counter and a Christian woman wrapped in a black fabric holding with her fingertips the host that she appears to elevate and show in the manner of a priest saying mass preparing to distribute the Holy Sacrament at the Eucharist. Between the window on the left and the great door on the right, both open, is delineated a floor in the form of a draughtboard in which perspective leads us to the back of the room where a chimney is situated. The latter's cover displays three distinctive signs: two crests, one bearing a scorpion impaled and the other a star, support a coat of arms in which a Moor's head is inscribed. Pierre Francastel and Jean-Louis Schefer both see in the image of the eight-branched star or "comet-star" the very sign, according to St Matthew's gospel, of the star that appeared to the wise men coming from the East to indicate the birth of Christ, the King of the Jews: "we have seen his star in the east, and are come to worship him" (Matthew 2:2).[41] As for the scorpion, it could be said to indicate a sign of infamy—it is an instrument of

---

[41]Schefer, *L'Hostie Profané*, 22. See also Francastel, 180–91.

Figure 3 Paolo Uccello, *Miracle of the Profaned Host* (Scene 1), 1465–69, Galleria Nazionale delle Marche, Urbino. Courtesy of the Web Gallery of Art, www.wga.hu

death, even a weapon of war, as Tertullian also points out in his *Scorpiace*.[42] However, what exactly is the iconic function of the Moor's head—this sign of Islam which, from where it is inscribed, placed in the top part of the picture, seems to preside over if not to coordinate the scene of the transaction? What does this "togetherness" or "fellowship" signify, this encounter between Jew and Muslim against Christianity that organizes the scene of the transaction? Uccello's first segment of the predella emphasizes and brings together in one single place the Moor and the Jew in a similar manner as Marlowe's *The Jew of Malta* portrays the religious and political enemies of Christians:

> BARABAS: Why this is something! Make account of me
> As of thy fellow; we are villains both:
> Both circumcised, we hate Christians both.
> Be true and secret, thou shalt want no gold. (2.3.215–8)

All this notwithstanding this Moor's head, which seems to be suspended and floating through the scene, brings a certain *ghostliness* to the overall composition of the work. It *haunts* the picture like an *open grave*. The Moor's head might thus be interpreted as a *spectre*, as it also seems to be reminiscent of the iconography of the myth of "the floating tomb" of the prophet Mohammed, on which writers from the Middle Ages to the Early Modern period were wont to expatiate. The myth, related by Gautier de

---

[42]Tertullian, *Scorpiace*, 2. Also cited by Schefer, *L'Hostie Profané*, 23–5.

Compiègne in the twelfth century, describes the levitation of the tomb of the prophet, followed by its suspension in the air in front of an audience of believers:

> without any support it hangs in the air,
> And without any chains holding it from above.
> And if you ask them by what artifice it does not fall,
> They erroneously repute it to be Machomus's power.[43]

If the figure of Islam springs up in the first scene to afterwards vanish completely in the rest of the predella's sequences, an analogous phenomenon appears in the structure of *The Merchant of Venice*. In other words, the figure of Islam in the predella, just like the dramatic field of Venice, is not due to simple *chance*. It is indeed by use of the word *chance* that Shakespeare, from Act Two onwards, introduces and stages pre-eminently the figure of Islam under the guise of the Prince of Morocco. Even though this scene, during which the Prince will try his fortune (2.1.44), occurs in the context of Portia's caskets, the mark of incision is perpetuated when reference is made to the Prince's offer "to make incision" (2.1.6) so as to examine his blood against his dark "complexion / the shadowed livery of the burnished sun" (2.1.1–2). He shows besides, as Jonathan Burton points out, not only his ethnic and religious membership of the Ottoman and by that token Islamic Empire, when he pulls from its sheath the scimitar with which he "slew the Sophy and a Persian prince / That won three fields of Sultan Solyman" (2.1.25–6). Basing himself on the work of Daryl Palmer, Burton also demonstrates that the emergence of the Moroccan/Islamic character in the scene of the caskets also acts as a catalyst for a specific dialectic "of contacts and contracts", namely, a cultivation and exploitation of ethnic differences for financial ends which extended out in the world of Mediterranean trafficking not just between Muslims and Christians, but between Muslims, Christians and Jews too.[44] It is because of this commercial understanding/agreement, albeit hazardous and perilous, that the Prince of Morocco, welcomed as a "fair/new comer", will choose the casket made of the most precious metal: *the golden casket*.

This argument that Burton puts forward also sheds tangential light on the function of the Moor's head in Uccello's predella and seems to be applicable to the interpretation given by Jean-Louis Schefer. Thus, the Moor's head, in the scene depicting the transaction revolving around the Eucharist, could be said to indicate financial relations with the Ottoman Empire, "where Jewish colonies carrying on the profession of moneychangers or bankers had been founded by Islam".[45] It is therefore under the eye of Islam that the transaction/conversion of the Eucharist into a monetary sign is concluded between the Jewish merchant and the Christian woman. In the exchange between the host given and the money received "everything [unfolds] as if", writes

---

[43]Gautier de Compiègne, ll.1059–63, translated and quoted by Tolan, 143.
[44]Burton, 208–9.
[45]Schefer, *L'Hostie Profané*, 22.

Derrida with regard to *The Merchant of Venice*, "the conversion [that took place], was, first and foremost, an *Abrahamic encounter* [*une affaire abrahamique*] *between the Jew, the Christian and the Muslim*. And what comes next, [*la relève*] will be precisely what happens to the flesh of the text, to the spoken body, to the translated and converted body—when the debt brings mourning to save the meaning."[46]

Avoidance and Reversal or Sacrificial Substitution

We know, to conclude, that the play of *The Merchant of Venice* will not encompass the sacrificial/bloody and profanatory fate that the predella presents counter to the Eucharist. Just when Shylock is preparing to cut a pound of flesh from the body of Antonio, Portia interrupts his action and reverses the situation by declaring:

> PORTIA:　Tarry a little; there is something else
> 　　　　　This bond doth give thee here not jot of blood;
> 　　　　　The words expressly are a pound of flesh
> 　　　　　Take then thy bond, take thou thy pound of flesh,
> 　　　　　But in the cutting it if thou dost shed
> 　　　　　One drop of Christian blood, thy lands and goods
> 　　　　　Are by the laws of Venice confiscate
> 　　　　　Unto the state of Venice. (4.1.300–7)

Christian blood will not be spilled—Venetian law imposes itself at the very last limit and turns against the Jew. Julia Lupton emphasizes that the word "jot" that Portia uses in her speech against Shylock forms directly part of a mode/climate of reflexion stemming from Christ's Sermon on the Mount—the New Covenant of Christ—thus creating a historico-theological dichotomy (Judaism/Christianity): "Think not that I am come to destroy the law, or the prophets: I am not come to destroy, but to fulfil. For verily I say unto you, Till heaven and earth pass, one jot or one tittle shall in no wise pass from the law, till all be fulfilled" (Matthew 5:17–18).[47] If, however, according to Lupton, the specific nature of that evocation "jot of blood" is deployed in order *to repeat and circle back* to the paradigm of cutting, and therefore of circumcision, it also marks, traces and returns to a figurative finality reminiscent of the sacrifice of Abraham.

If we follow closely the progression and all the build-up that leads us to the interruption and the avoidance of the sacrificial murder of Antonio by the Jew, we see that in this long movement of suspense and tension, Portia gives reason to Shylock until the very last moment. It is during this very interval that Antonio prepares himself and constitutes himself without resistance as an offering in the shape of his own flesh. ("I am armed and well prepared", 4.1.259.) In other words, Antonio pre-empts in body and in soul the sacrifice to come. In the same way, but tangentially/asymmetrically and in a sort

---

[46]Derrida, "Qu'est-ce qu'une traduction relevante?," 556.
[47]Lupton, 92–4.

of re-attribution of roles, when Abraham leads his son Isaac to the mountain that God has indicated to him and, seizing his knife, binds him to the altar above the wood so as to carry out God's order to immolate his son, it is also only through this long trail a-winding, through this total and internal accomplishment of Abraham, that divine law intervenes and interrupts the sacrifice in order to bring about, at the very last limit, a substitution (Genesis 22:1–19). Following on from the irruption of Venetian law, from a theologico-juridical providence, Antonio rises up in the place of his martyrdom, which will not take place, and *substitutes* his sacrifice for the conversion of the Jew Shylock ("He presently becomes a Christian", 4.1.382). The *corpus verum*, the Christian *corpus mysticum*, the body of Christ that Antonio takes on remains therefore in this way untouchable and intact. At this decisive moment the eye of Islam may be said to reappear and glide anew over the trial scene: Antonio is he who, just like Christ, according to the majority of Muslim exegetists, could not have suffered, nor even died on Calvary. "[…] they killed him not, / Nor crucified him … Nay, God raised him up / Unto Himself; and God / Is Exalted in Power, Wise …" (surat IV, verses 157–8).[48] Three verses further on, the Qur'an prohibits the practice of usury by Jews: "That they took usury, / Though they were forbidden … We have prepared for those / Among them who reject Faith / A grievous punishment" (verse 161).[49]

References

Ali, A. Yusuf, trans. The Holy Qur'an. Amana, 1983.

Bachelard, Gaston. "Le tiroir, les coffres et les armoires." In *La Poétique de l'espace*. 3rd ed. Paris: Les Presses Universitaires de France, 1961.

Balbi, Giovanni. *Catholicon*, 1506. Available from http://www.archive.org/details/GiovanniBalbiCatholicon1506Ed

Bataille, Georges. "L'Expérience Intérieure." In *Œuvres Complètes*. Vol. 5. Paris: Gallimard, 1970–88.

———. "Note pour *Le Coupable*." In *Œuvres Complètes*. Vol. 5. Paris: Gallimard, 1973.

Baudelaire, Charles. "Morale du Joujou." In *Œuvres Complètes*. Vol. 1. Edited by C. Pichois. Paris: Gallimard, 1975.

Berger, Harry, Jr. "Marriage and Mercifixion in *The Merchant of Venice*: The Casket Scene Revisited." *Shakespeare Quarterly* 32, no. 2 (1981): 155–62.

Berry, Philippa. "Incising Venice: The Violence of Cultural Incorporation in *The Merchant of Venice*." In *Renaissance Go-Betweens: Cultural Exchange in Early Modern Europe*, edited by Andreas Höfele and Werner von Koppenfels. Berlin: De Gruyter, 2005.

Buci-Glucksman, Christine. *La Folie du Voir, De l'Esthétique Baroque*. Paris: Galilée, 1986.

———. "Venise et l'oeil de l'Orient." In *Philosophie de l'Ornement, D'Orient en Occident*. Paris: Galilée, 2008.

Burton, Jonathan. *Traffic and Turning: Islam and English Drama, 1579–1624*. Newark: University of Delaware Press, 2005.

Cabasilas, Nicholas, trans. *The Explanation of the Divine Liturgy*. Coll. *Sources Chrétiennes*. n° 4 bis. Paris: Le Cerf, 1967.

Catherine of Siena. *The Dialogue*. Charlotte, NC: Saint Benedict Press, 2010.

---

[48]Ali, 230.
[49]Ibid., 231.

Derrida, Jacques. *Acts of Religion*, edited with an introduction by Gil Anidjar. London & New York: Routledge, 2001.

———. *Glas*. Paris: Galilée, 1974.

———. *Le Toucher, Jean-Luc Nancy*. Paris: Galilée, 2000.

———. "Qu'est-ce qu'une traduction relevante?" In *L'Herne Derrida*, edited by Marie-Louise Mallet and Ginette Michaud. Paris: Herne, 2004.

Didi-Huberman, Georges. "Dans les Plis de l'Ouvert." In *Phasmes: Essais sur l'Apparition*. Paris: Editions de Minuit, 1998.

Erasmus, Desiderius, and Johann Froben. *Sileni Alcibiadis*. Ex officinal Roberti Stephani, 1527. Original from Ghent University.

Francastel, Pierre. "Un mystère *parisien* illustré par Uccello: Le *miracle* de l'hostie d'Urbino." *Revue Archéologique* 39 (1952): 180–91.

Gleyzon, François-Xavier. "Christine Buci-Glucksman: The Archaeology of Shadows or the Aesthetics of Image-Flux." In *Modern French Visual Theory: A Critical Reader*. Manchester: Manchester University Press, 2013.

———. *Shakespeare's Spiral: Tracing the Snail in* King Lear *and Renaissance Painting*. Lanham, MD: University Press of America, 2010.

Hanssen, Johannes Michael. *Institutiones liturgicae de retibus orientalibus*. Rome: Gregorian University, 1930–32.

Hegel, Georg. *Philosophy of Right*. New York: Cosimo, 2008.

Hugo, Victor. "Dieu (fragment)." In *Œuvres Complètes Chantiers*, edited by R. Journet. Paris: Robert Laffont, 1990.

———. *William Shakespeare*. Paris: Edition Bouquins, 1930.

Lacan, Jacques. "L'Agressivité en Psychanalyse." In *Ecrits*. Paris: Le Seuil, 1966.

Lupton, Julia Reinhard. *Citizen-Saints: Shakespeare and Political Theology*. Chicago: Chicago University Press, 2005.

Marin, Louis. *Le Portrait du Roi*. Paris: Editions de Minuit, 1981.

Michelet, Jules. *Histoire de France*. Vol. 3. Paris: Hachette, 1835.

———. "Le débiteur insolvable." *Les Origines du Droit Français: la France devant l'Europe*. In *Œuvres de Jules Michelet*. Vol. 2. Bruxelles: Hachette, 1893–99.

Parker, Patricia. "Cutting Both Ways: Bloodletting, Castration/Circumcision and the 'Lancelet' of *The Merchant of Venice*." In *Alternative Shakespeares*. Vol. 3. Edited by Diana Henderson. London: Routledge, 2007.

Perdrizet, P. *Le Calendrier parisien à la fin du Moyen Age, d'après le Bréviaire et le livre des Heures*. Paris: Presses de l'Université de Strasbourg, 1933.

Salaville, S. *Liturgies Orientales: Notions générales, Elements principaux*. Bibliothèque des sciences religieuses. Paris: Bloud & Gay, 1932.

Schefer, Jean-Louis. *L'Hostie Profané: histoire d'une fiction théologique*. Paris: POL, 2007.

———. "On the Object of Figuration." In *The Enigmatic Body: Essays on the Arts*, edited and translated by Paul Smith. Cambridge: Cambridge University Press, 1995.

Tanner, Norman P., ed. *Decrees of the Ecumenical Councils*. 2 vols. London: Sheed and Ward; Washington, D.C: Georgetown University Press, 1990.

Tertullian. *De Resurrectione Mortuorum*. Translated by M. Moreau. Paris: Desclée de Brouwer, 1980.

———. *Scorpiace*. London: Kessinger, 1998.

Tolan, John. *Saracens: Islam in the Medieval European Imagination*. New York: Columbia University Press, 2002.

Varano, Camilla Battista. *Acta sanctorum maii VII*. Brussels: Société des Bollandistes, 1680–88.

Wind, Edgar. *Pagan Mysteries in the Renaissance*. London: Faber and Faber, 1958.

Wirth, Jean. *L'Image médiévale: naissance et déloppements, Vth–XVth century*. Paris: Méridiens Klincksieck, 1989.

Index

For Product Safety Concerns and Information please contact our EU
representative GPSR@taylorandfrancis.com Taylor & Francis Verlag GmbH,
Kaufingerstraße 24, 80331 München, Germany

Batch number: 08153807

Printed by Printforce, the Netherlands